The emergence of an interdisciplinary study of law and literature is one of the most exciting theoretical developments currently taking place in North America and Britain. In *Law and literature: possibilities and perspectives* Ian Ward explores the educative ambitions of the law and literature movement, and its already established critical, ethical and political potential. He reveals the law in literature, and the literature of law, in key areas from Shakespeare to Beatrix Potter to Umberto Eco, and from feminist literature to children's literature to the modern novel, rape law and *The Handmaid's Tale*, and the psychology of English property law and *The Tale of Peter Rabbit*. This original book defines the developing state of law and literature studies, and demonstrates how the theory of law and literature can illuminate the literary text.

LAW AND LITERATURE

LAW AND LITERATURE

Possibilities and perspectives

IAN WARD

University of Sussex

CAMBRIDGE
UNIVERSITY PRESS

CAMBRIDGE UNIVERSITY PRESS
Cambridge, New York, Melbourne, Madrid, Cape Town, Singapore, São Paulo

Cambridge University Press
The Edinburgh Building, Cambridge CB2 8RU, UK

Published in the United States of America by Cambridge University Press, New York

www.cambridge.org
Information on this title: www.cambridge.org/9780521474740

First published 1995
This digitally printed version 2008

A catalogue record for this publication is available from the British Library

Library of Congress Cataloguing in Publication data
Ward, Ian.
Law and literature : possibilities and perspectives / Ian Ward.
p.   cm.
Includes bibliographical references and index.
ISBN 0 521 47474 4 (hardback)
1. Law and literature.   2. Law in literature.   3. Literature – History and criticism.
I. Title.
PN56.L33W35   1995
809′.93355—dc20   94-27049   CIP

ISBN 978-0-521-47474-0 hardback
ISBN 978-0-521-05850-6 paperback

Contents

Preface

I want this book to be enjoyable to read. It certainly has been to write. All too often, as Kafka observed in his diaries and from his own experiences as a law student, learning 'the' law is like eating sawdust. The law grinds down its supplicants. That, educatively and politically, is its ambition. To lawyers like myself, in general, and certainly too often, there seems precious little fun in the law, or in learning about it. Literature, on the other hand, can be fun. It hopes to please. That is its particular ambition. One of the themes of this book is that an appreciation of literature can better educate lawyers and, indeed, non-lawyers, precisely because it is fresh and enjoyable, whilst at the same time it is capable of broadening the learning experience. I will discuss the various ambitions of law and literature, particularly the educative ambition, in chapter 1, but certainly from my experience, and from that of other law and literature teachers, the introduction of literature into the law school classroom is a positive and popular measure. Law need not be like sawdust. It need not be anything like as complex, inaccessible or downright dull as it so often seems. Its study might be enjoyable. One of the purposes of this particular book, indeed perhaps its primary purpose, is to suggest that students might better enjoy, and thus, inevitably, better understand the origins of English constitutional thought by reading *Richard II*, the inadequacies of rape law by reading *The Handmaid's Tale* and the psychology of English property law just by looking at the pictures in *The Tale of Peter Rabbit*.

Law and literature scholarship is one of the most exciting of recent interdisciplinary ventures, and its potential is enormous. Whilst embracing the possibilities which it offers, what we must not do is waste that potential by making it too intellectual and above all inaccessible for all but the most conversant in the intricacies of literary or legal theory. Intellectual pretentiousness is the pervasive evil in so much contemporary legal scholarship, and law and literature must seek to avoid falling into this particular trap. What law and literature scholarship must do is to remember that its purpose is to broaden, not merely to deepen. At the same time, importantly, it must strike out and establish its own identity, and it will only do this by returning to and concentrating upon the text. In this book, although in chapters 2 and 3 I have introduced some of the dominant themes in contemporary literary theory, I have tried to do so to the minimum extent, and only insofar as necessity dictates. What I have wanted to avoid is to write yet another book on the alleged merits and demerits of the various 'isms' which have entered the literary legal vocabulary. This is a book about literature and about text, not about theory. My discussions of the roles of the author and the reader and the text, in chapters 2 and 3, exist simply to strengthen the case for returning to the text. I have no strong opinions as to whether the author, the reader or the text is more important. For what it is worth, I don't think it matters at all. They are all important to varying degrees, but I have no idea what the extent of this variance is, and neither, I suspect, does anyone else. So in the remaining six chapters I have consciously sought to discuss literature. Thus, in chapter 4 I discuss Shakespeare as a legal historian, in chapter 5 children's literature, in chapter 6 various pieces of feminist literature and in chapter 7 some themes in modern literature. In the last two chapters I have tried to work closer still with two relatively recent novels, Ivan Klima's *Judge on Trial* and Umberto Eco's *The Name of the Rose*. If, by the end, I have convinced you that there might be a virtue in reading literature to better understand the law, I will have succeeded. Even if you have been sufficiently intrigued to go away and read some of the literature which I have used then that, too, will be a success. If, however, you decide instead that literature and law have nothing to lend to one another, educatively or otherwise, then I have failed. But I hope that it will have proved to be an enjoyable failure.

As this preface implies, one of the greatest debts that I owe is to former pupils whom I have been fortunate to teach. I also owe various debts to a number of colleagues who have made a more immediate impact on some of the chapters. Most particularly, I would like to thank Sandra French, Peter Goodrich, Michael

Lobban, Clare McGlynn and Pat Twomey. I should also like to acknowledge the editors of *Law and Critique, Legal Studies, Feminist Legal Studies, Studies in the Humanities* and the *Scottish Slavonic Review* who have been kind enough to allow me to reproduce material which has already been published.

PART I

Possibilities

CHAPTER I

Law and literature: a continuing debate

Students seek out good teaching to learn not the rules but the culture, for the rules are everywhere the same.[1]

The purpose of this introductory chapter is essentially synoptic. Indeed there is a very tangible sense in which, after more than a decade of the renewed law and literature 'debate', it seems appropriate to a number of the debaters to look back and take stock.[2] This is not to suggest any running out of ideas or cooling in the heat of debate, but rather, as both Brook Thomas and Richard Posner have recently suggested, because law and literature is becoming increasingly 'serious'.[3] It is now sixteen years since Allen Smith predicted the 'coming renaissance in law and literature', and an ancillary purpose of this first chapter is, then, not only to examine the various positions taken in the 'debate', but also to impress its enduring strength.[4] The familiar distinction taken in law and literature studies is between 'law *in* literature', and 'law *as* literature'. Essentially, 'law *in* literature' examines the possible relevance of literary texts, particularly those which present themselves as telling a legal story, as texts appropriate for study by legal scholars. In other words, can Kafka's *The Trial*, or Camus's *The Fall*, tell us anything about law? 'Law *as* literature', on the other hand, seeks to apply the techniques of literary criticism to legal texts. Although both convenient and essentially effective, it is not always possible to sharply delineate the two approaches, or indeed desirable to do so. It is very much a complementary relation; a fact which is commonly appreciated by the more prominent scholars who have produced such a wealth of material in the debate. Whenever a justification of law and literature is asserted, or indeed a limitation, considering both approaches is very much the norm – for if one is valid then it tends to suggest that the other is too. The same writers have much to say on both positions – the rules of the game might change, but the players remain the same.

LAW *IN* LITERATURE

A commonly applied distinction, in literary form, lies between the use of metaphor and the use of narrative. Richard Posner, for example, virulently denies the significance of legal narrative, but appears to be prepared to accept the validity of metaphor as a means of enhancing judicial style.[5] Just how far such a distinction can extend is, however, dubious. Although he uses it as a tool of convenience, Paul Ricoeur, for example, has stressed that substantively metaphor and narrative are simply variants of the same thing – 'storytelling'. Ricoeur posits writing as 'storytelling' in opposition to writing as 'science'. The characteristic of 'storytelling' is history; if a text seeks to present sequence and context then it is a 'story', and metaphors and narratives are defined by this attempt.[6] If legal scholarship attempts to present such context, then, in Ricoeur's analysis, legal text is, in literary terms, indistinguishable from metaphor and narrative.[7] It is, of course, the historicity of legal texts that is so hotly disputed, and as will be seen repeatedly throughout this book the whole area of historicity and hermeneutics, which lies at the very core of critical theory, is an extremely contentious one in contemporary legal writings. Another leading contemporary philosopher who clearly shares Ricoeur's position on the creation and uses of language, and who enjoys considerable influence in certain areas of legal scholarship, is Richard Rorty. According to Rorty, if we are to understand the essential problems of the twentieth century we must read the philosophy of Heidegger, Dewey and Davidson, together with the novels of Nabokov, Kafka and Orwell. The characteristic of critical scholarship, legal or otherwise, is, according to Rorty, its appreciation of the creative possibilities of metaphor as a constituent of any text, together with its willingness to supplement established theoretical texts with narrative fiction. Rorty's own metaphor, which he uses to describe the role of language in defining communities, is that of a 'conversation', and the ambition of any community can only be to 'continue the conversation', and in doing so, to strive towards an ideal of 'human solidarity'.[8] Literary forms and theories of analysis are not, of course, new, either to legal philosophy, or to philosophy in a more general sense. Ricoeur uses Aristotle and the idea of the 'fable' as the starting-point for his analysis of metaphor.[9]

More pertinent to legal theory, perhaps, is Aristotle's metaphor of the Golden Mean as the keystone of chapter 5 of the *Ethics*, whilst the column metaphor remains one of the most effective ways of describing form and substance, still used in contemporary legal formalism.[10] Aristotle consciously integrated both the analytical and the metaphorical in his writing – both were recognised as having an interpretive and descriptive value, or *phronesis*; analysis for assertion, or *telos*, and metaphor for persuasion, or *mimesis*. In Aristotle's opinion, legal scholarship, like everything else, employed this integration.[11] The extent to which widespread awareness and use of metaphor, and more especially perhaps, narrative fiction, remains somewhat alien in contemporary legal theory, is very much a consequence of the dominance of what Ricoeur describes as 'scientific' discourse, itself the legacy of the Enlightenment project.[12] Other legal traditions have continued to concentrate on metaphors, parables and fictional narratives as the primary form of legal text. Amongst the native peoples of North America parables remain the essential source of jurisprudence.[13] The same is true in Islamic and Jewish law, where both the Sharia and Talmud are constructed around a series of metaphors and parables.[14] The reason for this, of course, being that Islamic and Jewish jurisprudence, like indeed, that of the native peoples, is very much generated by a theology. To the extent that the western tradition has remained tied to the Socratic–Thomist synthesis, it has inherited not only this theological approach, but also its application of metaphor and parable. Aquinas' theory of law was very much influenced by that which he perceived in the Judaic tradition, more particularly in the writings of Maimonides.[15] Maimonides' *Guide to the Perplexed*, the essential jurisprudential text in medieval Jewish philosophy, is a patchwork of various metaphors and parables, one of which dominates, as it does in Aquinas' *Summa* – the Creation.[16] As will be seen in chapter 2, Maimonides' account of the Creation bequeathed a paradox which has haunted western jurisprudence since the thirteenth century, and which reveals an early concern with the nature of language and discourse. Only decades before Hobbes and Locke were to proclaim the ascendency of analytical jurisprudence, Bacon was using the

Creation 'story', and its determination of truth and virtue, in law and government as in everything else, as the centrepiece of his philosophy.[17]

To use metaphors or parables or narrative 'fiction' as a means of describing legal issues is not, then, new; and perhaps unsurprisingly the law and literature debate has spawned strong defences of both the need to study the nature of metaphor and the virtue of using parables as a teaching medium in law schools. According to John Bonsignore, citing Kierkegaard, 'insensitivity to the grand questions of law cannot be approached directly, no matter how well intentioned the teacher might be'.[18] However, previous usage of literary form, or indeed present usage amongst certain legal scholars, does not, of course, make it correct. And it is this question of appropriateness that has generated some of the most fierce debate in recent law and literature scholarship. At one extreme, for example, Stanley Fish suggests that:

Legal texts might be written in verse or take the form of narratives or parables ... so long as the underlying rationales of the enterprise were in place, so long as it was understood (at a level too deep to require articulation) that judges give remedies and avoid crises, those texts would be explicated so as to yield the determinate or settled result the law requires.[19]

Fish's initial position is similar to that taken by James Boyd White, one of the most committed advocates of the importance of law and literature. As we shall see in chapter 3, White's central concern is with the method of reading and understanding, and it is this concern with method which not only places White in the mainstream of critical theory, but at the same time unavoidably relates the twin projects of the law and literature movement – law *in* and law *as* literature. When we read narrative fiction, according to White, we do so with a more immediate sense of style and rhetoric, and it is rhetoric which, in many ways, is the keystone of White's thesis.[20] The texts that White has used to exemplify the power of rhetoric – such as Homer's *Iliad*, Thucydides' *History of the Peleponnesian War* and Plato's *Gorgias* – have tended to be pre-modern and not as immediately 'legal' as those used by others, such as Richard Weisberg. As narrative fiction presents itself as rhetoric, it also impresses upon us its unavoidable contingency, because it builds upon various contexts: social, historical, political, ethical and so on. In turn, narrative texts, much more obviously than legal or political texts, present to us a greater sense of community. It is the peculiar nature of language which defines our relationship with others – and indeed, our relationship with the text.[21] In emphasising this contingency and the historical nature of fiction, White presents the same kind of arguments as Rorty and Ricoeur. He is stressing the 'storytelling' function of narrative, and giving it a central role in the creation of 'community'. So, again, it is method which lies at the heart of White's thesis and which makes it so similar to those of other writers who share his concern. At the same time, this dominant interest creates a hierarchy in White's writings, so that it is 'law *as* literature' which clearly emerges as the primary interest.[22] In his recent *Justice as Translation* particular discussion of narrative texts is reduced to a minimum. Law *in* literature is then, for White, in a sense subsidiary; most useful insofar as it can illustrate the nature and style of discourse used by the author. Jane Austen's *Pride and Prejudice*, according to White,

is meant to teach the reader how to read his way into becoming a member of an audience it defines – into becoming one who understands each shift of tone, who shares the perceptions and judgments the text invites him to make, and who feels the sentiments proper to the circumstances. Both for its characters and readers, this novel is in a sense about reading and what reading means.[23]

The ability of a narrative text to reveal the tensions between alternative discourses, most immediately between the legal and the non-legal, and thus to create something of a bridge between the two, has certainly drawn support. Dunlop agrees with White that 'fiction stimulates the reader's capacity to imagine other people in other universes', adding the suggestion that '[a]fter a lawyer or law student reads Charles Dickens's *Bleak House*, he can never again be completely indifferent or "objective" towards the client across the desk'.[24]

White's wider position with regard to the relevance of literary texts has attracted support from a number of writers. Richard Weisberg, in particular, is keen to stress the complementary nature of 'law *as* literature' and 'law *in* literature'. However, he takes a much stronger position than White with regard to the immanent virtues of using literary texts for legal discourse. In contrast to White, Weisberg's texts tend to be drawn from the modern novel, particularly from Camus, Kafka, Dostoevsky and Grass.[25] Whereas for White the value of such texts lies chiefly in the

style and rhetoric which they deploy, Weisberg suggests
that such texts are justified in legal study simply for the situation
which they seek to describe and for the social and political contexts
which they imply. In *The Failure of the Word* Weisberg examines
what he perceives to be the effect of contemporary literature in the
writings of lawyer-writers in the modern period. In the much-
debated opening to his book, Weisberg commented upon a short
article written by a French lawyer during the Nazi occupation,
in which the lawyer argued on humanitarian grounds that the
state should have the burden of persuasion that a person with
only two Jewish grandparents was a Jew. Weisberg ascribes such
linguistic masking of a moral crime such as the Holocaust to the
enduring influence of Nietzschean *ressentiment,* and 'the failure of
the word'. *Ressentiment* is essentially a prolonged sense of injury
based on real or imagined insult; in Weisberg's words, 'a full-
blown intellectual malaise'. It was this *ressentiment* which, Weisberg
suggests, coloured the writings of Camus, whose hero from
The Fall, the lawyer Clamence, Weisberg suggests is a literary
companion to the French lawyer.[26] It is a powerful argument
which, it will be suggested in chapter 7, rings true in relation
to the wider critical movement of the late nineteenth and twentieth
centuries, in philosophy and psychoanalysis as well as in literature.
In an essay written two years later, Weisberg reaffirmed
the place of literature in legal studies by relating it more closely
to the wider movements in critical theory, both 'literary' and
'philosophical', as represented particularly in the writings
of Heidegger, Derrida and de Man.[27] Again, Weisberg places
the Holocaust at the centre of his work, in a sense representative
of the angst and despair which accompanies and develops from
Nietzschean *ressentiment.* In doing so, he is not only putting
into historical context the philosophical concerns of those
like Heidegger and Sartre, he is also making the same nexus as
that made by George Steiner, who suggested that the death
camps were 'the deliberate enactment of a long and precise
imagining'.[28] According to Weisberg, Dostoevsky, Kafka and
Camus were presenting a literature which at once both revealed
and complemented this 'imagining'.[29]

In more recent work, largely in response to the criticisms of
Posner and his namesake, Robert Weisberg, Richard Weisberg has
strongly reaffirmed his position, suggesting that, '[w]e must teach

and think about these texts because, here and now, they are the best medium to instruct ourselves and our students about what we do ... we need this learning in order to practice and (more importantly, at least for me) in order to understand what our assumptions are and what we do'.[30] Indeed, in contrast with White, Weisberg now suggests that, if anything, the literary text is of more value to lawyers than literary theory. From their early status in the law and literature movement as the 'fun factor', literary texts have emerged as the vital component: 'My suggestion, speaking from within, is to emphasize from now on the central place of the literary text – more than literary theory – in the debates ... Novels about law, as I have suggested, and particularly "procedural novels", are the path to human understanding.'[31] The end result, the essential accommodation of both branches of law and literature scholarship, is precisely the same as in White's work, but the dynamic is quite the opposite.[32] The divergence between Weisberg and White is most clearly drawn in Weisberg's most recent book, *Poethics*. As we shall see in chapter 3, White's retreat from literature to a theory of 'pure rhetoric' signals, according to Weisberg, a retreat from the ethics, or 'poethics', of texts. *Poethics* serves to re-emphasise Weisberg's own commitment to a Kantian ethical vision, and he analyses a number of texts, not only from modern literature, such as Barth's *The Floating Opera*, but also from previous centuries, such as Dickens's *Bleak House* and Shakespeare's *The Merchant of Venice*, in order to reassert his essentially existential Heideggerian–Kantian thesis. 'Poethics', Weisberg maintains, 'in its attention to legal communication and to the plight of those who are "other", seeks to revitalize the ethical component of law.'[33] I shall return to Weisberg's 'poethics' in chapter 8, where I will suggest a 'poethical' analysis of Ivan Klíma's recent novel, *Judge on Trial*.

Like Richard Weisberg, Robin West has emphasised the value of literary texts as a medium for jurisprudential debate, most famously by using Kafka's *The Trial* to critique Richard Posner's economic analysis of law. According to West, Kafka's characterisations revealed the practical, and above all, ethical unacceptability of a pure scientific analysis, such as that presented by Posner. In West's opinion, what Kafka was portraying was the contradictory nature of authority and submission in the modern world, and the resultant alienation of the human condition:

Obedience to legal rules to which we would have consented relieves us of the task of evaluating the morality and prudence of our actions ... The impulse to legitimate our submission to imperative authority also has within it, of course, the seeds of tragedy. That impulse is the means by which we most commonly victimize ourselves, and the means by which we allow ourselves to become tools that enable those who use us to destroy us.[34]

The susceptibility to submission and the alienation of the human condition which West perceives is precisely that which Weisberg has stressed in his 'ressentiment' thesis. Posner's world, West suggests, is quite simply too 'happy' – and too rational.[35] Many of the statements made by West betray a sympathy with the political and social expressions commonly associated with the critical legal studies movement (CLS). West's stress on the fundamental contradiction in the human condition between freedom and authority, the alienation of the individual in the modern analytical legal world and most particularly her attack on the possibility of rationalism as a foundation for legal order is very much the rhetoric of CLS.[36] This has become increasingly the case in her subsequent work, which concentrates more than ever on the role of language and literature in the political and ethical re-constitution of communities. In doing so, West quite firmly allies herself with James Boyd White against Posner. However, she also goes quite deliberately further than White, suggesting in the process that White concentrates too closely on the texts as texts, and as such presents a 'social criticism which is constrained and stunted by the texts it criticizes'. Even more damning is West's conclusion that because of this constraint, White is in danger of reproducing the same 'dehumanisation' which Posner's thesis presents.[37]

To avoid doing this West stresses the need to use literature as a means of promoting 'the interactive community', a concept remarkably reminiscent of the 'intersubjective zap' which Gabel and Kennedy advocated as the holy grail for the CLS movement back in the heady days of 1984.[38] In suggesting that '[w]hen we create, read, criticize, or participate in texts, we are indeed engaging in a form of communal reconstitution', West is using precisely the rhetoric with which innumerable CLS writers appealed for a new approach to 'lived experience' of law. We must not simply read a text, we must 'understand how it feels' to participate in the reading.[39] She concludes by urging that '[w]e need to pay attention to our literary texts about law, as White says, but we also need to produce, listen to, criticize, and participate in the production of narratives about the impact of legal norms and institutions upon the subjective lives of those whom the legal textual community excludes'.[40] West's most recent work has served to re-emphasise her commitment to a more radical political position, and, it is suggested, has contributed to her less enthusiastic subsequent critique of law and literature. In *Narrative, Authority and Law* she explicitly critiques law and literature for being a distraction from real political struggles, and implicitly critiques it by a reluctance to use literature. What is needed, she suggests, is less inter-textual debate, and more of a 'truly radical critique of power'. 'By focusing on the distinctively imperative core of adjudication, instead of its interpretive gloss', she further adds, 'we free up meaningful criticism of law.'[41] Although she concludes by suggesting that there is a place in critical legal scholarship for a literary supplement, West's recent work is clearly less sympathetic to law and literature.[42] Her ambitions are more political, less textual. However, despite West's reservations other critical legal scholars have attempted to employ metaphors and parables in their writing; in other words, to adopt the role of 'storytellers'. Amongst the most notable attempts is Patricia Williams's 'Alchemical Notes'.[43] Allan Hutchinson also has attempted to employ metaphor and narrative as a means of describing legal problems. Yet in general, despite much debate by CLS adherents on the possibilities of alternative discourse, relatively little has been done.[44] Any political or social ambitions which might be harboured in literary texts have been extracted and employed by law and literature scholars rather than by critical legal scholars.

The alternative position to that taken by those who advocate the use of literary discourse in jurisprudential debate is articulated most forcefully by Richard Posner, whose *Law and Literature: A Misunderstood Relation* represents the most substantive attack to date against the positions taken by White, Richard Weisberg and West, and represents a summation of the position which has evolved in Posner's writings since West's initial pre-emptive strike in 1985. In his reply to West's 'particularly eccentric' use of Kafka, Posner suggested that West fundamentally mistook 'the incidents and metaphors' so that the 'fiction became its meaning'. It was, he suggested, 'like reading *Animal Farm* as a tract on farm management'.[45] If West found Posner's world a little too 'happy', Posner found West's rather too serious. Kafka's texts, when 'read literally ... provide as much insight into American life in the 1980s as would *Dracula* or *The Cask of Amontillado*'.[46] Having made this assertion, however, Posner then promptly embraced the opportunity to use Kafka's fiction to deny West's vision of an ethics of free choice, thereby, as West noted in her response, rather defeating his initial suggestions that it was quite inappropriate to do so. Therefore, Kafka's literature had indeed created a 'bridge' by which West and Posner could create a constitutive dialogue or 'community'. Kafka had lured Posner into debating the nature of authority and submission, as it were despite himself.[47] The basic argument in his 'Reply to Professor West' has remained at the heart of Posner's subsequent writings on law and literature. The two, he vigorously maintains, are quite separate disciplines, enjoying their own two particular contexts. The aims of literary and legal writers, he suggests, are quite different. In an influential 1986 essay, Posner repeated his central assertion that '[a]lthough the writers we value have often put law into their writings, it does not follow that those writings are about law in any interesting way that a lawyer might be able to elucidate'.[48] Posner again concentrated his attack on the appropriateness of Kafka's *The Trial* as a jurisprudential text; he suggested that it lent very little to our understanding of 'Austro-Hungarian criminal procedure'.[49] To which the obvious counter might be that Kafka never intended it to. But it is with his attack against Richard Weisberg's 'ressentiment' thesis that Posner defines the essential difference in his position. Whereas Weisberg, like White, is occupied in presenting alternative methods of discourse, for Posner '[l]aw is subject matter rather than technique'. Of course method is important, but it is legal method that matters, not literary method – an argument which betrays a certain sympathy with the tradition of American realist writings.[50] Whilst Posner would subscribe to what Weisberg termed the 'fun' factor in literary texts, he refuses to accept the central role in legal discourse which Weisberg ascribes to them.

Posner's primary reason for this is that we cannot access or engage the context of the text, let alone the author's mind. It is this argument that he advances in his complementary criticism of 'law *as* literature'.[51] Posner's recent *Law and Literature* is very much built on the foundations of the 1986 essay, and his particular criticisms of 'law *in* literature' are the familiar ones of inappropriateness and inability to access authorial intent. A piece of literature is, he suggests, defined by its context as fiction, and therefore whatever law is to be found in a novel is purely ancillary. Novels are never chiefly about law, and so 'the concrete legal problem' must be distinguished from the inevitably wider concerns of 'the human condition' which a novel seeks to address. The various novels which have been put forward, not only by White and Weisberg, but by a number of law and literature writers, are then, at best, only incidently about law.[52] Camus's *The Outsider* is, Posner suggests, not really about criminal procedure in the civil law tradition, but more about Mersault's growth of self-awareness.[53] Of course, this not only assumes that the growth of self-awareness is not a central concern to lawyers, but also denies at least the possibility that Camus consciously chose a legal situation as a parable or 'story' because it represented a particular conception, not only of the human condition, but also of modern society. The 'lack of realism' which Posner perceives in *The Outsider* also serves to dismiss Kafka, Dickens, Shakespeare and a host of other writers whose works have been used by law and literature scholars.[54] With regard to 'law *in* literature', perhaps unsurprisingly, Posner concentrates his attack most particularly against Richard Weisberg and his idea of Nietzschean *ressentiment*. Weisberg's use of novels like *The Outsider*, together with, for example, Flaubert and Dostoevsky, is once again condemned for confusing law with psychology, or philosophy, or history, or literature and so on. The role of the examining magistrate, upon which Weisberg concentrates in a number of novels, is not primarily a description about a 'real' legal character, but instead about the human condition. Novels like *The Brothers Karamazov*, one of Weisberg's most common sources, are then 'philosophical' or even 'theological' novels, not 'realistic' novels, and are thus inappropriate for jurisprudential discourse.[55] Having dismissed Weisberg, Posner moves on to dismiss West for essentially the same reasons. He accuses them both of taking literature 'too seriously' which, given that both Weisberg and West also suspect that Posner takes a too literal approach to texts, can only lead to the conclusion that everyone thinks everyone else is far too serious.[56]

There has been tentative support for Posner's position from Robert Weisberg, who has repeated the same sort of criticisms of

White and most particularly of Richard Weisberg. However, Robert Weisberg is keen to stress that he does not favour what he perceives to be the extreme position taken by Posner. Law *in* literature presents 'fertile possibilities', and Weisberg is quick to criticise Posner's suggestion that because *The Trial* cannot instruct us with regard to the nature of Austro-Hungarian civil procedure it is of limited value to lawyers. According to Robert Weisberg, this is fundamentally to 'misunderstand ... legal realism'. At the same time, Weisberg is equally keen to reject those traces of 'foundationalism' which he perceives most strongly in White's writings, and the rigid distinctions between 'reason' and 'passion' which White and West, in particular, seem to draw from the texts.[57] He sees the same problems as Posner, most particularly the fundamental differences between the ambition of literary and legal texts, but, unlike Posner, who then simply advocates their inappropriateness and abandonment as possible jurisprudential texts, Weisberg suggests that even though these texts can tell us little or nothing about the legal situation, they can still educate lawyers about the human condition. Thus, whilst Richard Weisberg suggests that sources of *ressentiment* may be found in the writings of Camus and Dostoevsky, Robert Weisberg suggests that *ressentiment* exists outside the text, and is thus best sought outside. Most recently, Posner's position has been supported by Delgado and Stefancic in their essay directed primarily against White and his analysis of certain famous legal cases in American history, the judicial opinions in which, White has suggested, were at least in part the enunciation of the cultural philosophy to be found in contemporary narrative texts.[58] In similar vein to Posner, Delgado and Stefancic suggest that the actual impact of contemporary literature on the substance of judicial opinion-making is limited because, quite simply, judges distinguish 'legal' texts from other texts, and privilege the former. What Delgado and Stefancic say most strongly is that judges' moral positions are determined by normative social and political forces, rather than by literature, and moreover that an appreciation of 'counternarratives' on the part of judges would not necessarily help in their decision-making process. The very fact that they are 'counternarratives', counter to the pervasive social context, will tend to their dismissal by judges.[59] What they are not necessarily saying is that literary texts cannot thus be used as a means by which lawyers can understand the historicity of these normative contexts. Delgado and Stefancic are certainly not unsympathetic to the cause of developing such 'counternarratives', but the use of established narrative texts is not for them the most immediate means for development.[60]

LAW *AS* LITERATURE

Law *as* literature seeks to do two things which, at first glance, seem paradoxical. In one sense it wishes to impress the necessity of our existence in language as a living force. The keynote here is perhaps Heidegger's much-used trope: 'Language is the house of being.' Language need not be reified, although it can be. Language is something which we all use, and as such it is language which we can all design. Language is the construction of the community, and not some sort of transcendental force. It is this which makes language the essential medium for social change, and, as I shall suggest in the final part of this chapter, gives law and literature its political, as well as educative, bite. Among contemporary philosophers, perhaps the most revered exponent of this position is Richard Rorty. In Rorty's opinion the heroes of democracy are 'poets', not politicians. They will communicate with the future, because they articulate with and for the community.[61] At the same time, while it may wish to stress the 'ordinariness' of language, law *as* literature also wants to intellectualise legal study. It wishes to both widen and to deepen. In other words, law *as* literature suggests that both teachers and students must be made aware of all the various 'isms' of literary theory, structuralism, post-structuralism, deconstructionism and so on, which can then be used so that as lawyers we can better understand what a text means, both functionally and interpretively. As a complement to law and literature scholarship, law journals have increasingly presented articles about revered figures in the philosophy of language such as Derrida, Foucault, Heidegger and Wittgenstein. Law and literature scholars, on the other hand, have tended to concentrate instead on resurrecting the art of rhetoric. In doing so, they are of course reaching back more than 2,000 years to Plato and Aristotle, who both championed rhetoric as a form of logic. Perhaps the accommodation of this essential paradox in law and literature lies in this resurrection of rhetoric as a primary concern in law teaching. For the confirmed critics of the law and literature movement, most obviously Richard Posner, the recognition of rhetoric and linguistic style is the only ambition of law and literature.[62]

The essence of 'law *as* literature', then, is the suggestion that the techniques and methods of literary theory and analysis are appropriate to legal scholarship. The 'isms' already enjoy a certain familiarity in contemporary legal scholarship, quite outside the writings of recognised law and literature scholars. Scholars such as Douglas Couzens Hoy, for example, who parades no particular affinity to either CLS or law and literature, has written persuasively on the validity of applying hermeneutic techniques to constitutional interpretation. In doing so he made a scarcely veiled observation, against what he perceived to be rather primitive applications by various legal scholars, that it is time hermeneutics was used properly. Hermeneutics, he suggested, is not just a 'method' which can be applied 'a priori' to legal texts. It is a 'theory of meaning' which demands not only the external perspective of the historicist nature of understanding, but also the internal awareness of its own limitations.[63] Just as Hoy has re-investigated the philosophical substance of hermeneutics, so Jack Balkin has addressed the substantive nature of deconstructionism and semiotics.[64] In his more recent essay on semiotics, Balkin has expressed a similar enthusiasm for its application to legal studies, whilst at the same time stressing its affinity with and accommodation to theories of literary deconstruction. It is, he suggests, the historicist quality of deconstruction which reveals the essentially apolitical nature of semiotics. In making this suggestion, Balkin does not want to deny the association of semiotics, or indeed of deconstruction, with a particular brand of progressive critique, but he does want to retrieve the essentially literary origins of both.[65] In asserting that part of the semiotician's ambition is to establish 'foundations' for the interpretation of texts – foundations that are essentially defined by the dialogue – Balkin proposes an approach shared by many advocates of 'law *as* literature'.[66]

Stanley Fish, who has arrived from a particularly literary background, and brought with him the associated literary techniques, shares, as we shall see in chapter 3, a similarly sceptical approach to interpretation. For Fish, interpretation is always creation. In *Is There a Text in This Class?* he uncompromisingly suggested that '[i]nterpretation is not the art of construing but the art of constructing ... Different notions of what it is to read ... are finally different notions of what it is to be human.'[67] Again, as we shall see in chapter 3, such scepticism has provoked a response from liberal interpretivists, such as Owen Fiss and Ronald Dworkin, suggesting that such 'deconstructionism' is nothing short of literary 'nihilism'. Fish, however, appears to be more than happy to revel in this linguistic nihilism. The problem of indeterminacy of texts, of course, emerged as one of the prime dynamics of the CLS critique, and although it is quite beyond the scope of this chapter to catalogue the multifarious opinions on the nature and possible solutions to the problem, I will return to this in chapter 3.[68] Some prominent CLS scholars, such as Mark Tushnet, concentrate their essentially political critique on the linguistic problems of interpretive indeterminacy. In 1982, Tushnet denied the possibility of 'neutral application' of legal rules, both ethically and linguistically. If judges are in any way constrained in making their interpretations and judgements, the constraints are purely contingent. The critique of neutral principles, he suggested, had 'established that there are no determinate continuities derivable from history or legal principle'. Betraying the legal realist impulses behind so much of CLS thinking Tushnet concluded that it was for the judges to 'choose which conceptions to rely on'. Tushnet finally concluded that there was a need to establish a 'community of understanding' because 'we cannot assume that people who talk to each other are part of such a community merely because they seem to be speaking the same language'.[69] In 1984, the year in which he published his influential 'An Essay on Rights', Tushnet was also presenting what he termed was 'An Essay on Deconstruction'. In both these essays, with varying degrees of emphasis, Tushnet was inviting radical legal scholars to concentrate on the indeterminacy of key words such as 'rights' and, in doing so, essentially to investigate the possibilities offered by literary semiotics. At the same time, Tushnet was also embracing another interpretive theory or, as he put it, '[t]rendy label', previously more familiar in literary than in legal scholarship: deconstructionism. It was not just a matter of 'rights', it was a matter of 'rights-talk', and it is this 'language of rights [which] captures the contradictory predicament of people as at once alone and together, independent and yet necessarily in solidarity with others, individuals whose lives have meaning only in society'.[70]

The arrival of these various literary techniques confirms the increasing tendency in critical legal scholarship to concentrate its critique on the indeterminacy thesis, and to do so by an increasing engagement with literary theory. The emergence of a specific 'law *as* literature' scholarship, in a sense announced by Fish, as well as by White and Richard Weisberg, has concentrated still further on literary techniques and their application to the problems of texts and interpretation. It is 'law *as* literature' scholarship which, as the more political agenda of the CLS movement appears to have lost some of its impetus, has advanced a more precise concern with the various uses and methods of language and interpretation. Amongst the law and literature scholars, the one most heavily commited to law *as* literature is James Boyd White. As noted earlier, for White the two 'branches' of law and literature are valuable more for their convenience of distinction than for their substantive quality. The fact that literary method might be applied to legal texts means that literary texts enjoy a comparable validity to that of legal texts as relevant texts for study by lawyers. The indissoluble nexus between the two has been a consistent theme throughout White's writings. In his 1982 essay 'Law as Language' White interwove the various literary techniques of deconstruction, semiotics and hermeneutics to present perhaps the strongest case to date for 'law *as* language'.[71] Law, he suggested, like literature, is 'inherently communal', and reading legal texts is thus a 'shared process'. Once again White's rhetoric is very similar to that presented in some of the more progressive writings of the CLS movement, and, indeed, the most recent progressive writings have tended to follow the path of argument and rhetoric in legal reasoning as a means for reconstituting the legal society. Thus, Jerry Frug has suggested that 'we should abandon the traditional search for the basis of legal argument because no such basis can be found, and we should replace such a search with a focus on legal arguments, in particular, on its attempt to persuade. I suggest, in other words, that we look at legal argument as an example of rhetoric.'[72]

According to White, the familiar jurisprudential 'problem of indeterminacy' is an irrelevancy. In its stead, legal writers should focus on how they write and how they read texts, not how to access some sort of hidden answer.[73] The accessing of a writer's intent is impossible, White contends, because the action of writing is creative. 'To try to follow the intention of the writer', White suggests, 'seems an inherently unstable procedure, leading to a radical conceptual collapse.'[74] Thus reading becomes an 'interactive experience', interactive with the text, with the community and with the 'life experience'. Language use, he adds, necessitates continual retextualisation.[75] The text is in a state of continual interaction with its culture, which makes the meaning of a text wholly contingent. Despite the scepticism that such a position might seem to suggest, White is keen to impress that this does not deny the possibility of meaning, it simply reorientates the legal scholar's method of accessing meaning. Writers produce texts, readers produce meaning. Thus, as with literary texts, the real 'meaning' of a legal text 'is not in its message but in the experience it offers its reader'.[76] As we shall see in chapter 3, this type of reader-response theory lies at the heart of White's reconstitutive thesis.[77] The reading community thus constructs its own rationality by which it can establish meaning. Thus, although the judges' role is thoroughly 'creative', the creation is constrained by the 'shared experience' of reading, and the legal reader is able to construct 'solid judgments' about meaning.[78] It is in order to understand this process of legal reasoning that White suggests that law schools already emphasise, and should continue to emphasise, the teaching of culture rather than rules, and it is for this reason that they should embrace the possibilities that narrative texts can present.[79]

The arguments that White presented in 1982 have been forcefully repeated in his subsequent work. In both *When Words Lose Their Meaning* and more recently in *Justice as Translation* White has again placed the idea of a 'culture of argument' at the centre of his thesis.[80] The elaboration of this idea leads White to emphasise, perhaps more than before, the need to approach law, at all times, as an interdisciplinary study.[81] Judicial opinions, he stresses, are at once aesthetic, ethical and political.[82] He firmly aligns himself with Foucault's determination to isolate and as far as possible to break down 'specialised knowledges'. In stressing the 'post-structural' language of law, White's more immediate aim is to challenge Posner's economic analysis of law by attacking the very foundation upon which it stands, the 'conceptual' language and culture of economics. It is conceptualisation which structures language and prevents its creative and 'reconstitutive' potential. As far as any language can, the language of economics thus lies essentially outside the community, and outside the community's creative use.[83] What White is again trying to do is to bring to consciousness the 'internal', or already existing, 'cross-disciplinary' nature of legal

studies.[84] As authority for this thesis White makes much of
the metaphor for language creation used first by John Dewey and
then by Dewey's great admirer, Richard Rorty – language creation
as 'conversation'.[85] So a legal text is always a 'constitutive ... stage'
in a conversation, and it is this conversation which defines the
'culture of argument'. Jurisprudence becomes more than ever an
exercise in 'constitutive rhetoric' and the need to persuade the
reader and, like Rorty, White stresses that this culture determines
and is determined by a contingency of language, of self and of
the community:

> In this sense the law can teach all of us how to live in a world in which
> each culture is its own ground, made out of itself, as a language or a
> human life is made out of its beginnings ... The critical study of the judi-
> cial opinion in this way leads to the acknowledgment of the contingency
> of language and the self, and of the community too – for we are made by
> the very language that we use – and beyond that to a sense of the art by
> which life on such terms is possible.[86]

As ever, it is the 'integration' of disciplines, not just their identification, that White encourages. Thus it is not simply a case of advocating law *and* literature, but rather of impressing that law *is*
already literature, and thus any reading of either a literary or a
legal text is at once an act of 'creation' and of 'translation' between
discourses.[87]

To a certain degree, Richard Weisberg has lent support to
White's thesis. In one sense Weisberg, perhaps more than White, is
keen to stress the intellectual origins of 'law *as* literature'. In his
1986 essay 'Text Into Theory', Weisberg painstakingly traced these
origins back through the reader-response theories of Culler and
Fish, the deconstructionism of Derrida and de Man, and the
hermeneutics of Gadamer, through to Heidegger and ultimately to
Nietzsche – the position where he determined the locus of 'ressentiment' and the context for the narratives of the 'alienated' human
condition of the twentieth century, and, moreover, where he suggests that the origins of the CLS movement really lie.[88] Thus
Weisberg's position, at least in a textual sense, is considerably less
foundational than White's, and correspondingly more sceptical.
The Heideggerian antinomy leads inevitably to the conclusion that
interpretation is an exercise that we conduct against ourselves.[89]
The responsibility for interpreting legal texts lies, for Weisberg,
firmly with the reader, and Weisberg's final position is very much

in line with that taken by his mentor de Man, and with Culler and Fish.[90] Yet, at the same time, in *Poethics* Weisberg is equally keen to stress that too great a concentration on the intellectual intricacies of literary theory can distract law and literature from its primary engagement with literary texts.[91] The real hardened opposition to law *as* literature comes, once again, from Richard Posner. According to Posner, just as literary texts are unusable as legal texts, so the methods of literary theory are inappropriate for the interpretation of legal texts. Once again, Posner's primary argument is that this inappropriateness is rendered by the very different roles and ambitions of fictional and legal writing. In 1986 he concluded that 'the functions of legislation and literature are so different, and the objectives of the readers of these two different sorts of mental product so divergent, that the principles and approaches developed for the one have no useful application to the other'.[92] It was an assertion that he was to repeat two years later in his more developed *Law and Literature*, where he was particularly keen to stress the privileging of certain 'interpretations', most especially that of the speaker over the reader. Despite the relative virtues of pragmatic or utilitarian concerns, 'in legal interpretation the subordination of the interpreter to the "speaker" is a condition of legitimacy'.[93] In other words, if in any doubt, original intent enjoys an 'authority' over creative interpretation. The concession that Posner is prepared to make to the 'law *as* literature' position, and it is an important one, is that although lawyers have little to learn from the various techniques of literary theory they have much to gain from the study of rhetoric. In both his 1986 essay, and much more strongly two years later, Posner made much of the importance of improving the style of judicial opinion-making. 'Judicial opinions', he suggested, were 'unavoidably rhetorical'. The key concession is the statement that '[r]hetoric is important in law because many legal questions cannot be resolved by logical or empirical demonstration'.[94] Unsurprisingly, it is an essentially pragmatic concession, but it does invest literature with a role for lawyers, even in Posner's relatively structured vision of legal studies. He uses, in particular, Holmes's dissent in *Lochner* as an example of the power of rhetoric, and its ability to blind the reader to the relative virtues of the argument.[95] Thus, although he is keen to maintain the distinction between literature and politics, Posner is prepared to admit that 'there is still the possibility that immersion in literature might make a person a better judge by enlarging his knowledge of the human condition'.[96] Even the most sceptical of detractors is prepared to concede some virtue in the accommodation of literature in legal theory.

THE AMBITION OF LAW AND LITERATURE

As law and literature has indeed become more 'serious', so too has the debate with regard to its purposes. For some, such as Robin West, literature is only of value insofar as it can help to reveal the politics of law, and the purpose of studying literature is thus subservient to the overriding purpose of developing alternative political visions. There is, obviously, some validity in this thesis. It is certainly difficult to deny that law is to some degree both literature and politics. For others, such as Richard Weisberg, in similar vein literature is merely the means for representing a particular moral philosophy, which, in his case, is a Kantian one. There is a danger here which probably cannot be avoided, at least to some degree. It applies most immediately to West's political thesis, but in a sense applies equally to Weisberg's. Messing about with the politics of law is an inherently dangerous business, and if we are going to play with literature, then we must be very careful indeed. Legal thought has been down this path before, and recently. Law and literature is haunted by a very familiar ghost. The early socio-political CLS movement began with the very best of motives. Its primary ambition was to educate law students about the politics of law.[97] It has ended, not by reaching any particular goal, or indeed identifying one, but by going round in ever-decreasing circles, using up its dissipating energies in a multitude of various internecine disputes, and in the invention of increasingly pretentious and ultimately useless language which, rather than educating, serves only to mystify and then to alienate all but the most fervent of believers. The fate of the CLS can serve as a salutory warning to proponents of law and literature of what can all too easily happen. Using literature to illustrate politics is one thing, using it as an excuse to replace one political dogma with another is something else. In flirting with these same temptations, some of the leading current law and literature scholars, perhaps most obviously Robin West, but also to a certain degree Richard Weisberg, are dancing around the edge of the volcano. There is a clear temptation, and to a certain extent the law and literature enterprise, to have any point at all, must be prepared to flirt. It should not, however, permit itself to be seduced.

It is for this reason that I want instead to emphasise an alternative ambition for law and literature. We will, of course, continue also to flirt with politics but, primarily, we will concentrate, not on any political ambitions, but instead upon the educative ambition of law and literature. Of the many intriguing characteristics of the law and literature movement one of the most exciting and most valuable is that, unlike many other theoretical approaches to the problems of law, law and literature wants to better educate. Any political ambitions are necessarily secondary. Moreover, they are secondary in two ways; first, because the political manifesto is supposed to emerge from the educational force of literature, and secondly because politics was certainly not such a ranking ambition in the earliest days of the law and literature movement. James Boyd White's *The Legal Imagination* was written primarily as an educative tool. He suggested that the purpose of literature could be to better educate law students. More recently, Dunlop has suggested that the use of literature can educate both students and teachers, providing both with 'the opportunity to get beyond the technical and circumscribed study of legal rules, and to look at law as part of the broader civilization'. With regard to teaching law, Dunlop's suggestion that North American law schools have concentrated too much on law as a 'professional training', and too little on law as an 'exercise ... in liberal education', is at least as true in the UK as in the US.[98] In other words, 'what is important about literature is not only "what" it teaches but also "how" it teaches'. Concentrating particularly on the research potential of law and literature, Dunlop has also suggested that research 'about' law will inevitably address much bigger questions than research 'in' law. Literature is very much a shared interest for teacher and student and, he suggests, is the immediate direction in which both must go. Yet at the same time he also warns that the sudden interest in literary studies must not lead to an over-intellectualising of law and literature; the sort of over-intellectualising decried by Edward Said in literary criticism as a whole. The great virtue of law and literature is its potential to be user-friendly. That quality, above all, must not be lost. Too many long words are dangerous. As Dunlop suggests, law is already beset by far too many words that do not really mean anything, either to lawyers or to anyone else.[99]

In a recent essay Nancy Cook has re-emphasised the underlying anxiety which has been brought to the fore, but perhaps also to some extent allayed, by the advance of law and literature; the feeling that there are better ways of teaching and equipping law students for the real world.[100] According to Cook there is certainly no need to justify law and literature, which she suggests has sometimes seemed almost too shy of its own potential. The art of teaching, she suggests, has always lain in the use of analogy and metaphor. Rather like Richard Weisberg, who suggests that law and literature's most important claim, and one that was rare in law school, was that of being 'fun', Cook has stressed the virtue of literature as a teaching medium. Students, she suggests, like literature. The use of literature can break down the teacher–student barrier. Students can have an opinion about literature. It is not a right-answer/wrong-answer discipline, and so opinions are all that a teacher need ask. It is the '[n]on-threatening novelty, especially combined with humour' which can be so 'appealing' in a classroom situation. John Bonsignore has recently made precisely the same claim, suggesting that every legal theory course should open with a discussion of Kafka's parables.[101] Like Dunlop, Cook agrees that legal study has become too 'scientific', too bound by the casebook method advocated by Langdell, and then by realists such as Karl Llewellyn. But whereas Dunlop suggests that literature can somehow direct the law school away from an excess of professional training, Cook suggests that that training itself is in need of precisely the skills which literature can provide. Literature can present the student with a real-life situation, and concentrate the mind on the realities of case-resolution.[102]

The educative ambition of law and literature, and the perceived limitations of the traditional casebook method, was strongly re-emphasised in the recent colloquy entitled 'Human Voice in Legal Discourse', published in the *Texas Law Review*. In his keynote essay, Jules Getman identified a schism between the 'professional' and the 'human' voice.[103] It was this schism which, he suggested, was determined in the law school. Students become lawyers instead of, not as well as, people. This position is of course one that is familiar from the days of the CLS movement. In 1984, perhaps at the peak of their powers, CLS proponents like Peter Gabel were making precisely this point, suggesting that both conceptually and linguistically students in the law school experience a 'weird dissociation'.[104] The naked politicisation inherent in the CLS approach to legal education may now be more subdued but the basic problem remains, or so Getman suggests. Language, according to Getman, is 'dangerous to the lawyer's psyche' in that it removes him or her from 'the concerns of ordinary life'. This 'myopic focus on the professional voice does a major pedagogical disservice by preparing students for only a part of what lawyers do ... [s]uccessful lawyering frequently requires human understanding far more than it does intellectual rigour'.[105] In similar vein to Dunlop, Getman warns against the excessive intellectualism which captured the CLS earlier in the decade, and which became a virtually impenetrable discourse of meaningless words 'far removed from the emotions, language, and understanding of the great majority of human beings'.[106] Literature, Getman suggests, can do something that law never can, at least not in the classroom. It can present ethical dilemmas which demand resolution not by 'lawyers', but by people. By training lawyers to be lawyers, and not people, law schools singularly fail to equip their students for resolving the decisions which really matter.[107] In his closing comments, Getman concentrates particularly on the synthesis of both law's and literature's ambitions:

The need to address reality in words understandable to most of humanity is particularly great for those of us who seek to influence social policy in a more liberal direction ... I do not deny that the conveyance of complex ideas sometimes requires a special vocabulary, but such special circumstances occur far less frequently than many would like to pretend. In most cases, when we present our ideas in a form designed to separate us from the great mass of humanity, we are almost certain to obscure their meaning, limit their reach, and reduce their significance.[108]

His suspicions were shared by Elizabeth Perry Hodges, who noted that, when compared with non-law students, law students display 'a conscious effort on their part to erase any sign of non-professional discourse', although, at the same time, their 'language fails to reflect the unavoidable fact of their membership in a larger community from which they derive their fundamental linguistic abilities and to which, as mediators from the world of law, they must communicate'.[109] Hodges urges lawyers to recognise the dynamic force of language, and to release the peculiar constraints of legal language. Students, and law students in particular, must learn about the nature of language. At present the problem is that 'instead of understanding legal discourse as a dynamic product of complex historical, social, and personal forces', students 'treat it as an independent rational structure, built up of stable denotations that correspond to an objective reality'. Thus, crucially, 'they fail to recognize that discourse is itself a polyphonic construct, coloring and colored by human experience'.[110] Because language is dynamic there is a responsibility incumbent upon all members of the discursive community. More particularly lawyers have a responsibility with regard to the language of law. Language is the one thing which can activate the law, and change it. To fail to teach the language of law is to 'resign a vital part' of our 'authority' as both teachers and writers.[111] Most recently James Boyd White, who first signalled the educative potential of law and literature, has returned to re-emphasise the essential need to educate lawyers and law students in the use of language, and comments that it is the 'integration' of literature in legal study, and not its study as some sort of foreign field, which remains at the heart of the law and literature enterprise.[112] Throughout life, White suggests, we are 'learning languages' and continually moving between languages. What disturbs him is the unwillingness of lawyers and law teachers to acknowledge this movement.

Law and literature, then, and its ambitions, has received both approbation and condemnation. However, despite the warnings of those like Posner that both teachers and students should remain aware of the particular nature of legal as opposed to literary study, I would suggest that there is much to be said in favour of the 'renaissance' of law and literature and, moreover, regardless of its political potential, the greatest and least disputed virtue lies in its educative potential. It must be stressed, once more, that the two 'kinds' of law and literature – law *in* and law *as* – are in no way exclusive. Indeed, both facets are indistinguishable in text use. As Nancy Cook concludes, ultimately law and literature, in its use of texts that are not immediately 'legal', 'helps identify and clarify important issues in the legal realm that might otherwise remain clouded'. In this way, '[n]ew ideas sink into consciousness without the learner even necessarily realizing that the process is occurring or knowing to what to attribute changes in thinking patterns and attitudes'. The process is one of 'learning by osmosis'.[113] Even if the structural distinction between law and literature remains, as Posner suggests that it should, the functional distinction need not. The educative ambition of law and literature, it is suggested, is both a credible and a creditable one. Moreover, it is one which teachers of law should not seek to dispute, if they do indeed cherish the ambition of educating lawyers to be more than simply lawyers.

CHAPTER 2

The text, the author and the use of literature in legal studies

In 1968 the French semiotician Roland Barthes suggested that 'writing ... by refusing to assign to the text (and to the world-as-text) a secret i.e., an ultimate meaning, liberates an activity we may call countertheological, properly revolutionary, for to refuse to halt meaning is finally to refuse God and his hypostases, reason, science, the law'.[1] In Barthes's opinion, the concept of law, along with reason, science and God, in its peculiar claim to objective interpretive meaning, represented a threat to the text, and to the reader. Barthes concluded his essay by suggesting that 'the birth of the reader must be requited by the death of the author'.[2] It has become fashionable in certain areas of literary theory to dismiss the role of the author in the reading of texts. Here I want to assess the situation of the author in contemporary literary theory, and to suggest that in law and literature scholarship there is perhaps a case for reintroducing the author, if not in the interpretive enterprise at least in the pragmatics of text use. The reader may, as Barthes would suggest, control the interpretation, but the author retains control, at least in part, of the use of a text. In the first part of the chapter I examine the various approaches taken to the role of the author in recent literary theory, and as this review progresses it will be seen that attention to the functionalist role of the author has continued. In the second part I suggest that the author-function can play an important role in facilitating the use of literature in legal study by suggesting three identifiable 'discourses' amongst literature texts. Finally, I will seek to ally the emerging ambition of the law and literature movement with the idea of the pragmatics of text use and the author-function.

THE AUTHOR AND THE AUDIENCE

In his 1968 essay entitled 'The Death of the Author' Barthes suggested that positivism, as a capitalist philosophy, had championed the role of the author, and moreover that the author remained a revered figure in literary theory. This position, he continued, had first been subverted by Mallarmé, and then by Proust. The subversion had been continued by the surrealists and by linguistics, which had shown that the 'speech-act' does not need an author. If the author could be removed from the equation, then with him or her went any chance of 'deciphering' the text, that is, decoding the text in such a way as to find a true meaning. The very nature of writing destroyed the author, and so the future of literary theory lay only in an understanding of reading.[3] This has proved a popular position. Umberto Eco has used the same metaphor, suggesting that the writer of novels, in particular, writes precisely to preserve anonymity and to let the text come into itself.[4] Barthes himself repeated the thesis in an equally influential essay, 'From Work to Text', in which he suggested that literature as an inherently 'interdisciplinary' exercise demanded the breaking down of structures. Instead of the 'notion of the work', there was a 'need for a new object' of study, the 'text'. The 'text' is alive, whereas the 'work' is strangled by its association with, or 'filiation' to, an author. It is important to stress Barthes's concentration on the text as 'an activity, a production'. Texts are all about being used, and it is this empirical characteristic which led Barthes to acknowledge the 'problems of classification'. The pragmatics of text use demand some sort of classification. For Barthes, however, the ambition was to access a form of classification geared to the reader's approach, and not to the author's design.[5] In Barthes's final analysis, the only constraints on a text are previous texts. This is again another idea which has gained popularity. Stanley Fish, as we shall see in chapter 3, attacked Owen Fiss's notion of 'constrained interpretive objectivity' by suggesting that all such 'disciplining rules' were themselves texts, and so the idea of any constraints was immanently reductive.[6] Again, Umberto Eco has stressed that all books are merely the compendium of other books, a suggestion repeatedly used in his much-acclaimed novel *The Name of the Rose*.

A very similar position to Barthes's was taken by Michel Foucault, who also chose to concentrate on the role of the author, and sought to reveal its limitation on the free play of texts. The concept of the author, in Foucault's opinion, was a product of excessive 'individualizing'. Using exactly the same metaphor as Barthes, Foucault suggested that writing must be allowed to go 'beyond its own rules' and to 'transgress' its own 'limits', and it would do so because, in a text, 'the mark of the writer is reduced to nothing more than the singularity of his absence; he must assume the role of the dead man in the game of writing'.[7] The role for literary theory is to investigate the text *qua* text. Significantly, however, Foucault continued by suggesting that the concept of the author was very much alive, chiefly because of the pragmatic demands of text use: 'the notion of writing seems to transpose the empirical characteristics of the author into a transcendental anonymity'. In the absence of the author as God, writing itself had emerged as the sacralised transcendental force. Although the 'death' of the author as an individual may have released the creative possibilities of the text, text use had replaced him by the author as author. So again, like Barthes, the symbol of the author as author had a purely 'classificatory function,' which was used to determine forms of discourse:

The author's name serves to characterize a certain mode of being of discourse: the fact that the discourse has the author's name, that one can say 'this was written by so-and-so' or 'so-and-so is its author', shows that this discourse is not ordinary everyday speech that merely comes and goes, not something that is immediately consumable. On the contrary, it is speech that must be received in a certain mode and that, in a given culture, must receive a certain status.[8]

Foucault may have regretted any tendency to over-individualise the author-function, but as a historian of 'systems of thought' he acknowledged its functionalist force. What he called the 'author-function',

is therefore characteristic of the mode of existence, circulation, and functioning of certain discourses within society ... The manner in which they [modes of circulation or use] are articulated according to social relationships can be more readily understood, I believe, in the activity of the author-function and in its modifications, than in the themes or concepts that discourses set in motion.[9]

This is a constraining force, one which 'impedes the free circulation, the free manipulation, the free composition, decomposition, and recomposition of fiction'. But, as Foucault acknowledged, though it may be an evil, it is perhaps a necessary one. There has to be a constraint somewhere. Utility demands one. Foucault's plea is that the critical questions in literature should not be concentrated solely around the author-function, but should instead recognise that the theoretical, as opposed to functional, questions should investigate the text as a text.[10] More recently Terry Eagleton has reaffirmed the 'death' of the author. Eagleton's thesis, in considerable part due to his own progressive political agenda, is heavily historicist. The written word had always been a tool of social oppression. In his identification of the three essential stages of literary theory, authorial intent rose and then declined during the nineteenth century, to be followed by the New Critical concern with the text, and now the contemporary obsession with the reader. In Eagleton's uncompromising thesis, the text creates its own meaning. However, revealing some sympathy for the semiotic approach to speech acts, articulated perhaps most influentially by J.L. Austin, Eagleton does suggest that the author can place 'signs' with a text, which can act as functional guides towards meanings, or, in other words, as functional constraints.[11] Again like Foucault, Eagleton is willing to acknowledge at least an initial directional role for the author, even if it is strictly functional.

Whilst not readmitting the traditional notion of authorial intent, a number of contemporary literary theorists have taken positions similarly inspired by the demands of text use. A step in that direction has been taken by Umberto Eco, who has suggested, again not unlike Foucault, that there is an immanent relationship between the model author and the model reader of a text, determined in large part by text use. According to Eco, the text constrains because of its semiotic qualities; the concession made by Eagleton. In his recent Tanner lectures, Eco suggested that reading a text was analogous to being a detective; an idea which he then transformed onto a grand metaphorical stage in two novels, *The Name of the Rose* and *Foucault's Pendulum*. One of the principal ways of being led astray in attempting to decode a text is by paying too much attention to the author. However, Eco does not wholly dismiss the role of the author. In writing any text, the author envisages a model reader, or a series of model readers, of varying degrees of 'sophistication'. Thus, while it may be impossible to access the author's interpretive intent, the author still plays a key role in directing the use of a text.[12] The pragmatics of text use is central to Eco's theory of semiotics. Reading is always an active and contributive process.[13] The author, he suggests, retains control of what is 'talked about', even if he does not control what the discussion will resolve. The text is a device 'conceived' by the author in order to 'produce its model reader'. It both constitutes and constrains its audience. The reader in turn, when reading a text, constructs a model author, and does so by citing that author model within a functional discourse.[14] In similar vein to Foucault and Eagleton, Edward Said has suggested that literary theory as a whole has become both too privileged and too elitist, and also too obsessed by issues of 'textuality'. There has been a shift from a 'kind of objectivised historicity', which might have privileged the author, to an excessive 'intellectualism'. Literary theory, he suggests, has been dragged into a 'labyrinth of textuality' of French design, and is now no longer capable of finding its way out. It is a 'will to eccentricity'.[15] Said is keen to stress the power of the text and its politics. The written word is a weapon, and in order to understand the functioning of this weapon it is necessary to pay some attention to the writer of the word. Texts are always 'worldly', situated within a particular socio-historical context and contributing to it. Literary theory, by contrast, has become 'distanced' from the real world. Despite his explicit criticism of the excessive intellectualism of Foucault amongst others, Said presents a thesis which is, again, not dissimilar. Using the same concept of 'affiliation' he suggests that literary criticism has contributed to the privileging of certain texts and certain authors. In other words, it recognises discourses, and does so by means of recognising an author-function. As soon as a text is completed it goes 'beyond authorial control', but it 'retains the signature of its author's manner'.[16] In other words, it presents a discourse.

Perhaps the most influential interpretive theorist during the 1970s and 1980s, at least in jurisprudential circles, was Hans-Georg Gadamer, who took the historicity which Said, for example, insists must be returned to literary theory, and then radically subjectivised it. Gadamer's *Truth and Method*, published in English translation in 1975, proved to be an almost instant hit with critical legal scholars who sought theoretical justification for their impending political assault on the perceived 'myth' of liberal neutrality and objective interpretation.[17] Gadamer specifically addressed the respective roles of author, text and reader, and by constructing his hermeneutic theory of understanding granted each a mutually dependent role. More precisely he suggested that the historicity of all texts meant that the reader, himself subject to socio-historical 'prejudices' or 'fore-understandings', would read a text that was historical, and had been created by an author who was historically situated. This did not mean that authorial intent was possible provided the reader knew that the text was historically situated, but it did suggest that the text, as constructed by the historically situated author, was always a socio-historical product. In his essay the 'Universality of the Problem' Gadamer stressed that '[t]he consciousness that is effected by history has its fulfillment in what is linguistic'.[18] Moreover Gadamer, and it was this which served to deify his work in law faculties, specifically addressed the 'exemplary significance of the legal hermeneutic'. 'Legal hermeneutics', he suggested, was a peculiarly 'purposive' hermeneutic directed to 'practical measure[s] to help fill a kind of gap', and the practicalities of using legal texts, according to Gadamer, demanded the exercise of 'fidelity to the text'. The use and interpretation of a text demanded that the reader used the text honestly. The demands of legal use meant that the lawyer, in particular, should not release all to the free play of the text, but should instead seek to access the socio-historical constraints of the text and text-author. More than most readers who approach texts, the hermeneutic lawyers should be particularly inclined to read historically, and to think 'productively': 'Understanding, then, is for him [the historian] a matter of placing a given text within the context of the history of language, literary form, style etc, and thus ultimately within the totality of the living context of history.'[19] Such a suggestion, Gadamer admits, is really 'literary criticism writ large', and certainly it appears to be little different from Foucault's identification of the 'discourse' which, as an essentially pragmatic classificatory determinant, acknowledged the role of the author-function. The lawyer 'supplements' meaning, he does not create it, and neither, in isolation, does the text.[20] Fellow hermeneutist E.D. Hirsch immediately attacked Gadamer for denying the role of the author. Hirsch, like Gadamer, was essentially looking to extract some sort of interpretive constraint from the phenomenology of Husserl and Heidegger. In *Validity in Interpretation*, Hirsch suggests that the use of authorial

intent did not necessarily demand objective interpretation, but
that it did prescribe constraints of 'probable authorial meaning'.[21]
Hirsch's position obviously took the role of the author much
further than Gadamer in that he suggested that use of authorial
intent could help access interpretations of the text. The furthest
Gadamer ever went, like Eco, Said and even Foucault, was to
suggest that identification of the author-function could assist in the
use of the text as a discourse. The historicity of Gadamer's
hermeneutic could never permit authorial intent to go further.
Although he was perceived by many to be a potentially subversive
figure, as we shall see in chapter 3, Gadamer's work has been
seized upon by a number of interpretive foundationalists, perhaps
most strikingly by Owen Fiss and Ronald Dworkin.

USING THE TEXT

Why does the role of the author matter to law and literature? As
we have already noted, one of the most striking characteristics of
law and literature is that, unlike so many other approaches to legal
theory, its ambition is very much an educative one. Because of this
essentially functional ambition, from its earliest days law and literature has revealed an enthusiasm for categorisation; an unavoidable functionalist requirement, made unavoidable by its very own
ambition. It is the same requirement acknowledged by both
Barthes and Foucault. In his *The Legal Imagination* James Boyd
White immediately entered upon the task of categorising literature.
The purpose of this part of the chapter is to re-engage the process
of categorisation, and to do so in such a way as to reinstate the role
of the author in presenting the text. In other words, with regard to
those literature texts which are of potential use to legal scholars, it
is suggested that there are three distinct 'discourses' identifiable by
their author-function. The first category of texts are those written,
generally by legal theorists, for a primarily legal audience. In other
words, to use Eco's analysis, texts that were written for a sophisticated model reader. These texts are literary in the sense of the purpose to use literature to illustrate the nature of legal theory. The
best examples come from the pre-modern era, and in many cases
from outside the western tradition. As we noted in the last chapter,
'storytelling' is perhaps somewhat alien in modern western
jurisprudence. It has not always been the case. As Ricoeur has

pointed out, it is the western tradition which is peculiar in using 'scientific' discourse rather than a literary form to describe social and scientific concepts; other traditions do use literary forms.[22] Among the native peoples of North America parables remain the essential source of jurisprudence. The same is true in Islamic and in Jewish law, where both the Sharia and Talmud are constructed around a series of metaphors and parables. The use of 'storytelling' in a jurisprudential tradition is clearly more popular in cultures which remain strongly tied to a theological basis. One of the most striking examples of a jurist using a 'story' as the basis for an entire jurisprudence is in Maimonides' use of the Creation in the *Guide to the Perplexed*, the essential text in medieval Jewish philosophy. The *Guide* is a patchwork of various metaphors and parables, as is Maimonides' equally influential *Mishneh Torah*. The account of the Creation, and particularly Maimonides' interpretation of it, was picked up by Aquinas, and has thus remained to haunt western jurisprudence since the thirteenth century.[23] In Maimonides' account, Adam acquires knowledge and, with it, doubt and anxiety. In the Old Testament, Moses extolled language as the image of the law at the expense of discarded icons. Thus, to obey the 'spirit of the law' necessitated a knowledge of the language of the law. But, as Maimonides realised, this knowledge was defined by its doubt.[24] The problem which haunted Maimonides has continued to haunt writers as disparate as Francis Bacon and Franz Kafka. Bacon used the 'story' of the Creation, and its determination of truth and reason in law and government as in everything else, as the centrepiece of his philosophy. He also followed the pervasive trend in sixteenth- and early seventeenth-century England of presenting political and legal theories in the form of 'stories' or descriptions of idealised states. His *New Atlantis* followed More's more famous *Utopia*, and was itself followed by a whole spate of 'utopias', such as, perhaps most famously, Harrington's *Oceania*. As the seventeenth century tried to turn itself the right way up, it did so by telling stories.

The second and third categories concern literature which was not written with a specifically model legal reader in mind, or 'envisaged'. The first of these categories, and the most substantial in its variants as a discrete discourse, is made up of literature written to describe and comment upon law and society. In most, though not in all, cases this is literature written with an agenda, as well as an audience, in mind. To ignore the author in using these texts is to be deliberately obtuse. It is a failure of 'fidelity' or 'integrity' in the use of the text. There are innumerable examples of such texts and, as with the first category, it is only possible to present some of them. Dickens's *Bleak House* has proved to be one of the most popular texts, portraying as it does the notorious inadequacies of the English legal system, particularly the Chancery Division, in the nineteenth century. Not only does Dickens satirise the legal order, but he does so to a considerable extent by satirising those who work within the system, and thus who nourish it. Satire has always proved to be a popular means of attacking the legal order, revealing its barely veiled political agenda. A more contemporary example of such satire is Mordechai Richler's *St. Urbain's Horseman*, which not only castigates the lawyers and the clients, and the alleged victim of the rape, but also, as with all good satires, in the alternative treatment of the two accused suggests the most disturbing of conclusions. And, as we shall see in chapter 5, some of the most subtle examples of satire can be found in children's literature, including *Alice's Adventures in Wonderland* and *Gulliver's Travels*.

Although satire endures as a form of 'storytelling' popularly used by writers in an attempt to highlight the failures of the established legal order, there are a number of authors who have used a different and more directed discourse. The politics of literature is very much the politics of exclusion. Two sections of society which in particular have experienced continual exclusion from power have turned repeatedly to 'storytelling' as a means of articulating their position, or alternatively have had their position articulated by others in narrative form. The first of these groups is women. Here, the use of literature to highlight social and legal inequalities is not new. Jane Austen, always the most acute of social observers, laced her novels with commentaries on the condition of women in property and inheritance law. In both *Pride and Prejudice* and *Sense and Sensibility* the sophisticated model reader can find a plea for a recognition of a woman's equal right to inherit. The historical condition of women is also highlighted by Thomas Hardy, whose *Jude the Obscure* was immediately acknowledged as a plea to recognise a woman's equal rights with regard to divorce law, and attracted considerable criticism for doing so. In a similar vein, Nathaniel Hawthorne's *The Scarlet Letter* highlights the sexual hypocrisy of adultery laws in seventeenth- and eighteenth-century Massachusetts. If these texts are as much historical commentaries, the literature is still as useful today in revealing gender discrimination at the heart of contemporary legal systems. High on the agenda of feminist critical legal thought is the desire to stress the particular female experience of certain legal situations. One pertinent example is rape, legally, at least, a peculiarly female experience, and in reality predominantly so. The law merely acknowledges the event of rape, and the legal definition of the act if not the intent of rape is at once objective. In chapter 6 I return to feminist legal thought, and to the issue of rape, in an attempt to suggest how a law and literature approach can enhance our understanding of both.

The second socio-legal problem which has been addressed through the pages of fiction is racism. One of the most cited examples of a text which can convey both implicit and explicit racism is Mark Twain's *Adventures of Huckleberry Finn*. By using a specifically 'nigger' language for Jim, which then contrasts sharply with the discourse of the rest of the story, Twain can use language as a symbol of exclusion, which can then conflate all the ethical and legal issues which were encompassed by slavery. The delimited 'nigger' language impresses upon the reader, adult or child, the historicity of the text, and at the same time, more importantly, the series of moral dilemmas which Huck is forced to face. The text is thus both descriptive and constructive. As Robin West has suggested, the strength of *Huckleberry Finn* lies in its ability to make the reader part of the 'community of the text'.[25] Another text with a very obviously legal 'message', again concerned with the intersection of social and legal prejudice, is Harper Lee's *To Kill a Mockingbird*. Although the creation of various 'discourses' within the text is perhaps not as explicit here as in *Huckleberry Finn*, Lee's novel very effectively impresses upon the reader the exclusion of a section of society within a legal system that is unavoidably political. A final example of literature which can fight against legal prejudices as social prejudices, and which does so by directing itself against the exclusion of both blacks and women, is Alice Walker's *The Color Purple*, which represents black women suffering because they are women, and suffering because they are black. To know the discourse in which *The Color Purple* or any of these other texts are written is to operate more effectively as the kind of sophisticated model reader envisaged by Eco, or Foucault or Said. Both these discourses, the female and the black, must be understood as such. The text itself can of course speak for the discourse, but the author too unavoidably speaks through the text, and the use of a concept such as Foucault's 'author-function' can only aid the educative potential of these discourses and texts. The same is true of the third category: literature which uses law to describe something else. As suggested in chapter 1, this approach has proved to be most common in modern, usually twentieth-century, literature. A great deal of work has already been conducted into the texts of writers like Dostoevsky, Camus and Kafka. All three used the legal situation because it could best sum up what they wanted to convey, which was, essentially, the alienation of the human condition. The interrogatory nature of the criminal procedure in the civil tradition lends itself to the type of psychoanalytical picture which these authors wished to impart. According to Richard Weisberg, the use of the legal situation places the reader in the position of a juror, who is thus engaged creatively with the text. In other words the 'legal' discourse in literature is particularly suited to engaging the model reader.[26] Raskolnikov, Mersault and Joseph K. are the heroes of the modern world, all three isolated in a world which first Nietzsche, and then Heidegger, had identified as yearning for a new God. I will return to concentrate more fully on this approach, characterised in the modern novel, in chapters 7, 8 and 9.

WHAT THE TEXT CAN DO

One of the ambitions of this book is to stress the active nature of literature. It is this characteristic which makes law and literature such a necessary and exciting enterprise. As we suggested in chapter 1, this 'doing' ambition has two components: first it seeks to educate, and secondly it seeks to present a socio-political agenda. It is this very pragmatic ambition which demands a functionalist approach to literature, and which in turn then requires a reassessment of the discourse-forming role of the author-function as a determining factor in this use of texts. In this chapter's final section, I want to investigate what has emerged as the ultimate pragmatic ambition of the law and literature movement: the role of literature in reconstituting the community. Whether or not literature is always political and should always be political is, of course, a subject of great contention. According to Jean-Paul Sartre, literature has a duty to be political and literary analysis and theory have a complementary duty to reveal their political sub-structure.[27] More recently a number of literary theorists have taken up Sartre's challenge. One of the most influential is Terry Eagleton, who has repeatedly stressed that the 'rise of English' was the rise of a capitalist ideology. It is not that literature should somehow strive to be apolitical. It is rather that we should appreci-ate that literature is everywhere political, and moreover that it is political in a way which invariably reinforces the established social structures. Of course, it is the power to privilege texts, an immense power, which makes Eagleton so critical of authorial influence, but paradoxically so aware of it, and it is this which would make him wary of a suggestion that the use of author-function might assist the law and literature project. The use of literature, he would sug-gest, is just another form of politics. But then if literature is every-where and always political anyway, then we may as well take the responsibility for using it. Indeed, as Eagleton has himself sug-gested, the immediate ambition for literature studies is to embrace an interdisciplinary approach in order to reveal literature's political and historical substructure. It is this ambition which fires law and literature.[28] Edward Said is another who has repeatedly stressed the political nature of literature, most particularly its power as an imperialist force. Literature, like culture, is a 'system of discrimina-tions and evaluations'. Literature empowers. So does literary theory, chiefly by its tendency to concentrate on the 'great monu-ments of literature', and its bold claims to the 'power to show how things work'.[29]

One of the most influential figures in literary theory and one who has advocated the interdisciplinary and constitutive approach, which has become so beloved of critical legal movements, is Richard Rorty. In Rorty's opinion pragmatic philosophy demands an interdisciplinary approach, in which literature plays a central role, in determining a social and political agenda. Rorty uses certain authors and certain texts to justify his approach. In his *Contingency, Irony and Solidarity* he advocates the turn from theory towards literature in an attempt to create 'solidarity'; it is an attempt to create, and not, most importantly, to discover. It is Rorty's suggestion that the ultimate home of critical theory is in language and in literature.[30] This of course was the position reached by three intellectual figures whom Rorty places at the centre of critical theory: Dewey, Heidegger and Wittgenstein. According to Rorty, it was Dewey who, building on the discoveries of Kant and Hegel, first stressed that the community was defined by the patterns of linguistic behaviour which it created. Moreover, this creative potential is best illustrated in the individual's use of metaphors and, on a grander scale, use of 'stories'. It was Nietzsche who said that truth was simply a 'mobile army of metaphors'. According Rorty, life is a 'dramatic narrative' in a process of 'Nietzschean self-overcoming'. When the individual creates, he or she does so 'poetically'.[31] So if someone has a new idea or concept it is articulated as a metaphor, and whether or not the community determines it to be rational is really an assessment of the rationality of the metaphor. Similarly human ambition, whether it be classified as social, political or legal, is never just an idea or a theory. The end that is envisaged is always 'created' by a political literature. So the 'liberal charter' which Rorty seeks will be found within literature. The writer is never neutral, and so should always be prepared to take the responsibility of presenting literature as argument, and as a creative mechanism for persuasion.[32] For Rorty,

[t]he liberal society is one whose ideals can be fulfilled by persuasion rather than force, by reform rather than by revolution, by the free and open encounters of present linguistic and other practices with suggestions for new practices. But this is to say that an ideal liberal society is one which has no purpose except freedom, no goal except a willingness to see how such encounters go and to abide by the outcome. It has no purpose except to make life easier for poets and revolutionaries while seeing to it that they make life harder for others only by words, and not deeds. It is a society whose hero is the strong poet and the revolutionary because it recognizes that it is what it is, has the morality it has, speaks the language it does, not because it approximates the will of God or the nature of man but because certain poets and revolutionaries of the past spoke as they did.[33]

Rorty himself uses writers such as Dickens, Nabokov, Orwell and Proust in an effort to describe the creative potential of literature. They are the writers who can and do create our vocabulary. It is their language which the liberal must use in order to reveal the nature of society, and the direction which it should take. Literature will lend to the 'solidarity' of society, particularly in its ability to identify the 'marginalized'. The ultimate ambition of the liberal is the ability to 'share the same final vocabulary' which can enable us to ask whether a fellow individual is 'in pain'.[34]

If we are to use literature to understand the situation of our fellow (wo)man, most importantly we will need to understand the role of the author behind the texts. In making this statement, Rorty expressly approves the assertion made by Hirsch that the use of a text requires knowledge of the author. This is not, as Barthes would have us believe, an impossible and dangerously misleading illusion. It is important to realise that 'we can have some sort of objectivity about the mind of the author'. At the same time, Rorty is keen to align himself with the pervasive belief that the text itself cannot reveal an authorial intent, merely, at most, its own. Rorty's ambition is to 'convince Hirsch' that his position can be 'reconciled' with the Deweyan pragmatism that Rorty suggests. In other words, the concentration on the role of the author can be directed towards the author's control of the use of a text; the 'significance' of the text, if not its 'meaning'. There are for Rorty, of course, no hidden truths within a text, but there are possibilities, and those possibilities are created by the author. The author thus constrains the creative possibilities, as does the social condition of the reader and of course the text itself. What Rorty does essentially is to adopt a similar position to that taken by Gadamer with regard to 'constraints', and which of course distinguished Gadamer from Hirsch, and to that taken by Foucault who advanced the idea of the author-function.[35] Again there is no surprise in this. Gadamer and Foucault, like Rorty, have shared the same dream: to develop a pragmatic Heideggerian theory of language as a means of reconstituting society. As we have already noted, it is this pragmatic political ambition which has become increasingly important for a number of law and literature adherents. It demands more and more notice of the author. So the essay comes full circle. It was Barthes who in 1968 first suggested that it was the capture of the author for political purposes which had camouflaged the role of the reader, and which had to be reversed. It is Terry Eagleton and Edward Said who remind us that literature itself is always political, and so we should be at least aware of this 'secret' agenda, both of the text and the author. It was Foucault who developed the idea of 'classification' and suggested that the author-function identified functional discourses. It is law and literature which now fights over not whether there should be an agenda, but the form which the agenda should take. If law and literature is to maximise its potential as an educative and perhaps as a socio-political force, then it must acknowledge the functionalist author–text–reader relationship. Moreover, it is suggested that any classification is of value, because each of the groups of texts will play a particular contributive role, educative and socio-political, and this role can only be enhanced by a knowledge of the author, his or her socio-historical situation and the audience which was 'envisaged'.

CHAPTER 3

Cases in the laws of reading

Is there a given meaning to a text? Or is there just a meaning generated by a particular reader? These related questions are obviously of paramount importance to any literary or legal enterprise. Moreover, in the particular context of this book they take on an especial relevance. Having suggested that certain texts are of particular importance to lawyers, our next task is to discuss the extent to which they have a meaning which can be shared by a readership. The question of interpretive (in)determinacy has emerged as one of the most pressing in contemporary legal studies, and we will shortly discuss some of the various suggestions that have been made. However, the parameters of this debate are set in literary theory, and are commonly determined by the polarity of two rival theories of interpretation, hermeneutics and deconstruction. A whole series of 'debates' among legal and literary scholars have oscillated around these coordinates, and it is these 'cases' which I want to look at in this chapter.

The first piece of litigation is the Gadamer–Derrida encounter. These two litigants are the leading advocates in contemporary hermeneutic and deconstructionist theory respectively. To a certain degree, both share a common philosophical origin in the later work of Martin Heidegger, and what has become familiar as his 'linguistic turn'.[1] By following Heidegger's lead, both Gadamer and Derrida deny the possibility of a transcendental language-free idea of human understanding.[2] To the extent that there can be discrete definitions of the alternative theses presented by Gadamer and Derrida the difference between them is, therefore, one of degree. For Gadamer, hermeneutics preserves the possibility of unity of meaning. Although a text might give off a multitude of possible meanings, the intersubjective relationships of text and reader, and of reader and reader, create a bounded or 'constrained' meaning for every text. Thus a community of readers can share a meaning. In his *Truth and Method* Gadamer affirmed that there was always the possibility of an intersubjectively determinate meaning in any legal situation:

It is the work of interpretation to make the law concrete in each specific case, i.e. it is a work of application. The creative supplementing of the law that is involved is a task that is reserved for the judge, but he is subject to the law in the same way as every other member of the community. It is part of the idea of a legal order that the judge's judgment does not proceed from an arbitrary and unpredictable decision, but from the just weighing up of the whole ... This is the reason why, in a state governed through law, there is legal certainty.[3]

It is, Gadamer concluded, a matter of judges exercising 'fidelity' to the texts which they are set to interpret. For the deconstructionist, however, like Derrida and, as we shall see shortly, to a certain extent for his pragmatic counterpart, Stanley Fish, texts are radically indeterminate, defying the possibility of ever being securely constrained by any circumstance. The possibility of no shared meanings is, therefore, an ever-present reality.[4] Ultimately, then, the difference between the positions is considerable and goes to the very heart of any literary legal enterprise. The degree of disparity was revealed by the abortive 'Gadamer–Derrida encounter' set up in Paris in 1981. Rather than establishing any common ground between the alternative theses, the encounter has become famous precisely because it became apparent that neither party really understood what the other was talking about.[5] According to Gadamer it is the extra-textual factors which determine understanding, to such a degree indeed that *contra* Derrida he suggested that 'what makes understanding possible is precisely the forgetfulness of language, a forgetting of the formal elements in which the discourse or the text is understood'. Repeating his statements in *Truth and Method*, Gadamer again cites judicial hermeneutics as exemplary. The pragmatics of legal interpretation, he suggests, demand the abandonment of the legal text itself.[6] Derrida responded by accusing Gadamer of being an unreconstructed Kantian transcendentalist, and refused to accept the hermeneutic distinction of circularity as opposed to transcendence. For Derrida, there is only the text.[7] Gadamer, in turn, simply expressed himself as wholly unable to understand what Derrida was trying to say.[8] It quickly became obvious that there was absolutely no possibility of any common ground, and thus our first 'case' was universally judged to be something of a mistrial.

The Gadamer–Derrida encounter has been repeatedly played out in specifically jurisprudential fields. The two most articulate proponents of the hermeneutic approach have been Owen Fiss and Ronald Dworkin, whilst the deconstructionist (op)position has been championed most influentially by Stanley Fish. It is to these 'cases' that we should now turn. In a 1982 essay, 'Objectivity and Interpretation', Fiss presented a classical hermeneutic theory of interpretation, directed expressly against the deconstructionist tendencies which he perceived in critical legal studies.[9] 'Interpretation', he affirmed, 'whether it be in the law or literary domains, is neither a wholly discretionary nor a wholly mechanical activity. It is a dynamic interaction between reader and text, and meaning the product of that interaction.'[10] Fiss denied that the CLS attack on interpretive objectivism necessarily meant interpretive indeterminacy. The interpreter, he suggested, was 'constrained' by 'disciplining rules' and by his existence in an 'interpretive community':

The idea of an objective interpretation does not require that the interpretation be wholly determined by some source external to the judge, but only that it be constrained. To explain the source of constraint in the law it is necessary to introduce two further concepts: One is the idea of disciplining rules, which constrain the interpreter and constitute the standards by which the correctness of the interpretation is to be judged; the other is the idea of an interpretive community, which recognizes these rules as authoritative.[11]

Echoing Gadamer's comments *contra* Derrida, Fiss added that the 'idea of objective interpretation accommodates the creative role of the reader' by 'recognizing that the meaning of the text does not reside in the text'. 'Viewing adjudication as interpretation', he continued, 'helps to stop the slide toward nihilism. It makes law possible.' It also, he added, helps to make law moral, because the creative reader interprets in accordance with moral values. What prevents the creative reader from interpreting in an uncontrolled fashion, and the judge from adjudicating in an equally uncontrolled fashion, is 'an argument of necessity': that the judge will judge with 'integrity'. Fiss concluded that the 'issue seems to be one of faith, intuition, or maybe just insight'. Critical legal studies, he suggested, represented the 'deepest and darkest of all nihilisms', whereas 'the

idea that the Constitution embodies a public morality and that a
public life founded on that morality can be rich and inspiring'.[12]

The most immediate response to Fiss's article came from Stanley
Fish. Fish has emerged as the leading proponent of an American
pragmatic deconstructionism, distinguished from its continental
counterpart mainly by its willingness to embrace what Fish terms a
philosophy of 'common sense'.[13] Like Derrida, Fish has repeatedly
insisted that interpretation is the text, and that the reader's response
to a text is the meaning, and is the only meaning. Thus it is the
reader who 'creates' the text, and although the reader is determined
by the 'situation' of his 'interpretive community', he remains wholly
free with regard to the text itself. There is, it follows, only interpretation, and likewise any 'constraints' which either the reader or the
text might suggest are themselves only texts and thus exercises in
interpretation. As Fish says in *Is There a Text in this Class?*:

Because we are never not in a situation, we are never not in the act of
interpreting. Because we are never not in the act of interpreting, there is
no possibility of reaching a level of meaning beyond or below interpretation ... What I have been saying is that whatever they [readers of texts]
do, it will only be interpretation in another guise because, like it or not,
interpretation is the only game in town.[14]

Fish has continued to develop this thesis in a number of subsequent
essays, and on a number of occasions has sought to stress the
shared origins and similarities of the hermeneutic and deconstructionist enterprises. However, what remains crucially to separate
them is Fish's refusal to accept that any position can be taken outside the text. Because the 'interpretive community' is itself textually determined, the exercise of reading is thus irredeemably
fluid.[15] Fish re-presented this thesis in his reply to Fiss, stressing
that the constraining or 'disciplining rules' suggested by Fiss are
themselves 'texts', and thus 'are in need of interpretation and cannot themselves serve as constraints on interpretation'.[16] It was
Fiss's, and Gadamer's, determination to objectify the text, if not its
meaning, which Fish could not accept. There is nothing, including
rules, which lies outside the text. Accordingly,

rules, in law or anywhere else, do not stand in an independent relationship to a field of action on which they can simply be imposed; rather,
rules have a circular or mutually interdependent relationship to the field
of action in that they make sense only in reference to the very regularities
they are thought to bring about.[17]

Constraints are not, then, external. Rather the reader, by his very existence, is always and everywhere in a constrained situation, and thus the constraints which guard against the nihilism which Fiss fears are 'always already in place'.[18]

Fiss's central tenets were, unsurprisingly, those articulated also by Ronald Dworkin. For Dworkin, too, legal practice is legal interpretation, and legal interpretation is an exercise in hermeneutics. Thus, he began his 1982 article 'Law as Interpretation' by stressing that such interpretation 'is not a matter of personal or partisan politics, and that a critique of law that does not understand this difference will provide poor understanding and even poorer guidance'.[19] Legal interpretation, he suggested, could best be understood as an exercise in literary criticism, one which denied the supremacy of the author's intention and instead championed the authority of the text and the reader, and the relationship between them.[20] Dworkin's 'constraints' on the reader are those presented by the text, and he famously used the idea of the 'chain novel' as a metaphor for the kind of historically constructed 'constraint' which he had in mind. The meaning of a text was thus constrained by its past, and the shared past of the reader.[21] Dworkin has subsequently developed this thesis, most strikingly in *Law's Empire*, where it is championed as the 'integrity' thesis, and is replete once again with the historicity of the 'chain novel' and its associated concepts. The integrity thesis is, precisely, Gadamer's concept of judicial 'fidelity'. Indeed, Dworkin specifically acknowledges his debt to Gadamer, though perhaps not the depth of it. *Law's Empire* reaffirms the centrality of interpretation in the adjudicative process. Law as integrity is 'relentlessly interpretive'. It is, however, 'constructive' as opposed to 'conversational' interpretation, and thus respects the objectivity of the text as a text. Moreover, it is this interpretive process which confirms the morality of law, because the interpreter is always interpreting in accordance with the 'constraints' of 'principle'.[22] In the final chapter of *Law's Empire* Dworkin stresses that Hercules, his ideal judge, is guided above all by the moral 'god' of interpretive fidelity. Law as integrity 'makes the content of law depend not on special conventions or independent crusades but on more refined and concrete interpretations of the same legal practice it has begun to interpret'.[23] Perhaps not surprisingly Fish's critique of Dworkin was essentially the same as his critique of Fiss. Whilst admitting the initial attraction of the chain novel metaphor,

if only because of its superficial affinity with his own idea of 'interpretive communities', Fish suggests that ultimately it does not
really help, simply because, as with Fiss's 'disciplining rules', it
depends upon some sort of original textual foundation. But nothing, of course, grounds the text, because there is nothing else
but the text. There is thus no distinction between the first novelist
and any subsequent reader-novelist. They are all reader-inter-
preters, engaged in the same task. Thus Dworkin is right, but
pointlessly so. What Dworkin fears, the unconstrained judge, is the
same as what Fiss fears. But in fact such a judge does not and cannot exist, and there are, therefore, no constraints which could
possibly be, or need to be, invoked in order to 'ensure' judicial
integrity. The integrity thesis itself, moreover, is simply an alternative 'version' of a continuing thesis, which despite its initial
curative ambitions, is nothing more than a placebo. Integrity is
simply everyday interpretation, no more and no less.[24]

As I intimated before, the debate in legal circles with regard
to interpretation and the possibility of extracting shared meanings
of texts has not been restricted to the apostles of the hermeneutic
and deconstructionist theories. Indeed, the problem of interpretive
indeterminacy has emerged as perhaps the most burning issue
in contemporary legal scholarship. Affinities and allegiances have
been taken up along fairly predictable political lines. The supporters of the hermeneutic approach, who maintain the possibility of
a 'constrained' interpretation of an objectified text, have been
those of a liberal tendency such as Fiss and Dworkin. They also
fear that with radical interpretive indeterminacy will come,
inevitably, political nihilism and the death of theory. Thus Ken
Kress has adopted the pervasive tactic of acknowledging a core of
deconstructive truth but, at the same time, stressing that indeterminacy is nothing like as damaging to the liberal critique as its more
radical proponents would like to think. The deconstructionist critique is characterised as mere 'mischief'.[25] At its more defensive
extreme, the whole value of interpretivism in legal scholarship has
been challenged. Michael Moore has suggested that interpretivism
is irreducibly anti-philosophical, and thus has no place in jurisprudential debate. Moore is an avowed legal realist, and it is no
surprise that the extreme anti-interpretivist stance should be an
extreme realist one. In Moore's opinion, indeed, ultimately both
deconstructionists such as Fish and hermeneuticists such as

Dworkin are tarred with the same brush, and present merely variants of the same threat to the essentially experiential realist theories of adjudication.[26]

Unsurprisingly, in contrast, the interpretivist thesis, and particularly its more radical deconstructionist variants, has proved to be more popular among critical legal scholars. The extent of this popularity, however, tends to vary. For some, textuality remains a dubious accompaniment to political and legal radicalism. The tension which critical legal scholars felt in the earlier forays into textualism can be sensed in Mark Tushnet's 'Following the Rules Laid Down', which sought to subvert the liberal Dworkinian premise that a constitutional clause might be neutrally interpretable. In classically critical legal vein, Tushnet emphasised that any interpretation was merely the championing of a political dogma, often in the guise of historical precedent. Liberal interpretivism, he suggested, was merely the denial of the reality of the creative reader-interpreter. Yet ultimately, geared by his pervasive socio-political interest, Tushnet's argument was, in fact, the same as Moore's. Where Moore suggested that the text distracts us from philosophy, Tushnet suggested that the text distracts us from the politics of law.[27] Recently Robin West, who has flirted much more obviously with law and literature than Tushnet, has expressed reservations about the present concern with interpretivism. Like Tushnet, she too sees it as being distractive. As suggested in chapter 1, West brings with her an especial sympathy for the politics of critical legal scholarship. The 'analogy' between law and literature, she suggests,

has carried legal theorists too far ... Adjudication is in form interpretive, but in substance it is an exercise of power in a way that truly interpretive acts, such as literary interpretation, are not. Adjudication has far more in common with legislation, executive orders, administrative decrees, and the whimsical commands of princes, kings, and tyrants that it has with other things we do with words, such as create or interpret novels. Like the commands of kings and dictates of a majoritarian legislature, adjudication is imperative. It is a command backed by state power. No matter how many similarities adjudication has with literary linguistic activities, this central attribute distinguishes it. If we lose sight of the difference between literary interpretation and adjudication, and if we do not see that the difference between them is the amount of power wielded by the judiciary as compared to the power wielded by the interpreter, then we have either misconceived the nature of interpretation, or the nature of law, or both.[28]

What is needed is not subtle literary analysis, but 'a truly radical critique of power'. Ultimately, Fiss, Fish and Dworkin betray an 'undue optimism' in the nature of the interpretive community, and this prevents them from truly critiquing legal practice. The meaningful critique of law lies outside the text 'in the text we didn't write – the text of our true needs, our true potential, our utopian ideals'.[29]

Despite these doubts, in recent years a number of other critical legal scholars have increasingly recognised that any critical approach is at root a textual one. The literature of law is unavoidable. More than that, it is now more readily appreciated that such an approach actually enhances the nature of political-legal critique. At an extreme, scholars such as Jerry Frug and Peter Goodrich emphasise that law is simply language and rhetoric.[30] One of the more committed converts to the textual approach, and one of the most vigorous 'litigants' in interpretive debate, is Allan Hutchinson. According to Hutchinson:

We are never not in a story. History and human action only take on meaning and intelligibility within their narrative context and dramatic settings. There are many stories being imagined and enacted, but we can only listen to them and comprehend them within the vernacular contexts of other stories. Our conversations about these narratives are themselves located and scripted in deeper stories which determine their moral force and epistemological validity ... The life of the law is not logic or experience, but a narrative way of world-making ... Like all tales, legal stories gain meaning and significance from the selective emphasis of certain features of our always complex and frequently ambiguous experience. As a narrative, legal stories favour some aspects of our experience at the expense of others, thereby empowering some individuals and disenfranchising others. Most importantly, it is the stories themselves that come to comprise the reality of our experience. In this sense, legal stories mediate our engagement in the world and with others: they provide the possibilities and parameters for our self-definition and understanding.[31]

The nature of Hutchinson's interpretivism can be further understood through a series of engagements with Dworkin, Fish, James Boyd White and Richard Rorty. In each of these, Hutchinson employs textualism to better effect his political-legal critique. Thus his critique of Rorty is not so much a critique of Rorty's conversationalist thesis, which is not unlike Fish's, but rather that Rorty's innate liberalism prevents him taking his thesis to its radical political extreme. It is from conversational-interpretive

indeterminacy that Rorty advocates social and political construc-
tionism. According to Hutchinson, what Rorty fails to do is 'take
seriously his historicist insight'. What Hutchinson wants to do is
pursue the 'radical spirit rather than the liberal letter' of Rorty's
thesis. The political model which, he suggests, complements the
textual ambitions which he shares with Rorty is the Foucauldian
idea of 'participatory democracy'.[32] The aim of Hutchinson's thesis
is thus similar to that of Tushnet and West, for example: to recognise the politics of law, but, by acknowledging that this can only be
effected by acknowledging the politics of texts, the tenor is wholly
more sympathetic to the critical worth of textualism. Hutchinson's
critique of Fish is essentially the same as that of Rorty. It is Fish's
failure to acknowledge the historical import of legal discourse
which condemns him to pragmatic liberalism, not itself so dissimilar from the politics of precisely those whom Fish is keenest to
criticise, Fiss and Dworkin. Hutchinson's affinity lies much more
with the continental Derridean and Foucauldian brand of deconstructive interpretivism, because, unlike the pragmatic variant,
it embraces the full import of textual criticism, historical, social
and political.[33]

The most aggressive critique is undoubtedly that
which Hutchinson reserves for the doyen of liberalism, Dworkin.
According to Hutchinson, Dworkin does not take literature
seriously, essentially because he champions the text and refuses
to recognise the irreducibly participatory nature of language
and interpretation. Dworkin, he suggests, ignores the ordinary
reader. Despite appearances to the contrary, Dworkin's thesis,
he suggests, is thus anti-textual, and remains the most influential of
current 'liberal formalist' theses.[34] The same liberal foundationalism which serves to condemn Fiss, Dworkin and even Fish
also serves to condemn James Boyd White. According to
Hutchinson, White's more promising attempt to reconstruct
participatory politics through reading texts is flawed precisely
because of the foundationalism, which, he suggests, haunts
any such hermeneutic enterprise. The 'search for the hermeneutic
grail', in Hutchinson's opinion, inevitably introduces a political
morality of reading. Therefore White's attempt to understand
the meaning of texts is merely another exercise in flawed 'metaphysics'. In a review of White's *When Words Lose Their Meaning*,
Hutchinson suggests that the

whole book is a sophisticated attempt to justify and apologize for the present chaotic practice of adjudication ... White's pluralism is typical of the
predicament and practice of contemporary scholarship. Although eschew-
ing any reliance on or search for absolute truth, it remains haunted by
Pilate's question, 'What is truth?' White cannot escape or discard the
logocentric urge for objective and original meaning.[35]

Subsequently, Hutchinson has renewed his critique of White's
theory of reading, emphasising White's failure to consider the
'historical situation of particular acts of writing', and, as with
Dworkin, the failure too to fully appreciate that language is always
necessarily 'lived'. For 'all its polish and erudition' White's more
recent work 'paradigmatically and powerfully illustrates the ambition and failings of contemporary legal and literary theory.
Enslaved to the logocentric desire for objective truth and meaning,
White refuses to deal with the political determinants and beneficia-
ries of language, legal discourse and scholarly endeavour. He flags
these crucial matters, but only to ignore and sideline them.'[36]

There is no doubt, as I suggested in chapter 1, that amongst the
law and literature scholars, White has emerged as the most concerned with regard to how we read literature. For him, law *as* literature is the crucial debate. In his 1982 essay 'Law as Language'
White interwove both hermeneutic and deconstructionist techniques in order to suggest a discrete 'culture' of legal argument,
suggesting that 'reading a legal text is often not so much reading
for a single meaning as reading for a range of possible meanings.
Law is in a full sense a language, for it is a way of reading and
writing and speaking and, in doing these things, it is a way of
maintaining a culture, largely a culture of argument, which has a
character of its own.'[37] Reading is a communal enterprise. As we
noted in chapter 1, White thus suggests that the indeterminacy
debate is an irrelevance. What matters is how we write, and how
we read, and not whether or not there is some discrete meaning.
Reading becomes an 'interactive experience', interactive with text,
community and 'life experience'. This may all seem very sceptical,
but White does not abandon meaning, and it is at this that
Hutchinson's critique is directed. In language which at times
echoes both Gadamer and Fish, White suggests that the reading
community constructs its own rationality, by which it can then
construct its own meaning. Thus, although the judge's role is
thoroughly 'creative', the creation is constrained by the 'shared

experience' of reading, and the legal reader is able to construct 'solid judgments' about its meaning.[38] This theory of constitutive language and the establishment of 'cultures of argument' has continued to lie at the heart of White's theory of interpretation. In *When Words Lose Their Meaning* he reasserted that

whenever we speak or write we define ourselves and another and a relation between us, and we do so in words that are necessarily made by others and modified by our use of them ... Unlike any other conversation, it has an unlimited number of anonymous but necessarily individual partners, located in an unlimited set of cultural contexts. It offers its reader an experience of cultural reconstitution that can be repeated in the imagination at any place and time. In this sense it is a part of culture that transcends its own immediate location in space, time and social context.[39]

More recently, in *Justice as Translation*, White has again stressed that the solution is not simply to 'borrow' someone else's technology, such as hermeneutics or deconstruction, but rather to create and formulate 'new ... communities of discourse', and to be aware of doing so.[40] Jurisprudence, then, becomes more than ever an exercise in 'constitutive rhetoric' and the need to 'persuade' the reader. Law is already literature, and thus the reading of any text is always an act of 'creation' and of 'translation' between communities of discourse. There is no possibility of ultimate translation, but by suggesting that the 'appropriate' test for translation is that it 'be judged by its coherence, by the kinds of fidelity it establishes with the original, and by the ethical and cultural meaning it performs as a gesture of its own', White is making a statement that does indeed smack of Kantian discipline.[41] The more White concentrates on method, the nearer he approaches Gadamer, and, of course, Fiss and Dworkin.

White's thesis has attracted criticism not only from critical legal scholars such as Hutchinson. As we have already seen, Robin West has criticised White for presenting a theory of interpretation which, because of its hermeneutic underpinning, she characterises as 'conservative' and anti-communitarian. West subverts White's premise that we can at least 'know' the interpretive community as a text-creating entity.[42] It is the distractive intellectual pretensions of interpretivism which she rejects so fervently. Law, in the final analysis, for West is politics not text, a matter of power, not interpretation. A quite different, but in its way equally condemnatory, critique of White has been articulated by Richard Weisberg. For

Weisberg, unlike West, it is not the presence of foundationalism and ethics in interpretivism which is problematic, it is the absence of a substantive ethical vision which serves to condemn White. As we noted in chapter 1, Weisberg has concentrated primarily on the analysis of law *in* literature, but as ever, of course, this is never fully separable from law *as* literature, and thus from the problem of meaning. As we also noted in his earlier writings, Weisberg revealed a clear sympathy for the deconstructionist teachings of Paul de Man. In a sense, Weisberg's particular interest in the modern existential novel perhaps demanded such a sympathy. The Heideggerian antinomy which underpins such literature suggests that interpretation as an activity is an exercise which we conduct against ourselves. Thus it is the reader and not the text, which, ultimately, is the arbiter of meaning.[43] This thesis has been refined quite strikingly in Weisberg's more recent *Poethics*. Here, like West, he accuses White of allowing himself to become over-intellectual, of producing an 'upper-class' book. But whereas West advocates a re-emphasis on the politics of law, Weisberg demands a return to the philosophy of law. According to Weisberg, what White presents ultimately is a pure 'rhetorical theory', devoid of any 'ethical effect'. Such a purely textual theory is wholly internal, and ultimately useless. Weisberg concludes:

Ultimately, we are left with a familiar question, but one that has little to do with ethics, at least not in White's sense ... if there is nothing to law except linguistic constitution and reconstitution, and if the lawyer is always seeking the metalanguage of the nonlawyer's rhetoric, what constrains the legal actor from ignoring the discourse of the other altogether? Too much emphasis placed on language as the end of law threatens to silence (or to puppetize) the other, to bring about an elegant 'translation' of a text that has been ignored ... Although little that White says is objectionable ... little helps us to mold an ethics of law.[44]

In the final analysis, Weisberg implies that White's purely rhetorical thesis is akin to Fish's deconstructionism. There is more to interpretation than rhetoric. Applauding Owen Fiss, Weisberg's ethical amibitions lead him inexorably to advocate the value of external interpretive constraints.[45] The better alternative, Weisberg suggests, is the reconstructive ethics of Derridean postmodernists such as Drucilla Cornell.[46] In its earlier forms, Cornell's postmodernist 'dialogism' often seemed strikingly reminiscent of a Rortian conversationalism. Thus she suggested: '[d]ialogism involves a

commitment to universality: we are all to be recognized as partici-
pants in our collective conversation, and we are to hold it out as a
possibility that generalizable interests will emerge in the course of
that conversation'.[47] In more recent writings Cornell has identified
herself increasingly with Derrida and the idea that the deconstruction of a text by a reader will always be itself an ethical activity,
and will thus be the essential means of reconstructing an ethical
vision. 'A legal verdict', she suggests, 'is a creative supplement to
the text, which once again brings the meaning of the text to life by
telling us how we should guide our conduct in the future.'[48] At the
same time, Cornell is quick to distance herself from any trace of
foundationalism. Ethical interpretivism is not foundational or
objective interpretivism, as presented by Fiss or Dworkin. Rather,
it is the fluidity of postmodern interpretivism which, she suggests,
can actually realise a transformative ethics:

The Law of Law calls us to interpretation through an appeal to justice,
and this process of interpretation also projects the good of the community, which is itself only an interpretation and not the last word on what
the good of the community actually should be ... Interpretation is transformation. Thus, we need to remember that we are responsible, as we
interpret, for the direction of that transformation. We cannot escape our
responsibility implicit in every act of interpretation.[49]

The call to interpretive responsibility is a call to interpretive
fidelity, but it is not the Gadamerian or Dworkinian fidelity to
the text, but a fidelity to fellow readers. Again, in a different essay,
she suggests that the reading is the only means to realising ethical-
transformation. In this sense 'legal interpretation must be both
discovery and invention because there can be no simple origin of
meaning'.[50] This is the postmodern conception of meaning. It
is Cornell's hope that this thesis, the 'philosophy of the limit', will
finally undercut the hermeneutic–deconstructionist divide, which
characterises current legal-literary debate. The jury, here, is
still out and, I would suggest, we have certainly not yet heard all
the evidence. The jury for the 'case for the postmoderns' is likely
to be recalled on many occasions, and if postmodernism is right,
whether it be ethical or pragmatic, it will never need to reach
a verdict. By turning to Cornell we are returning to Derrida, and
thus once again, as in chapter 2, to a certain extent coming full
circle. There is ultimately no resolution to this debate. These
are not 'cases' that can be won or lost. They are simply arguments

and counter-arguments. Is there a meaning to this text, this chapter? Well, I hope so but, if not, how will I ever know, so why should I worry about it? It is you, not me, who really matters, and you, as reader, must reach your own conclusions.

PART II

Perspectives

CHAPTER 4

Shakespeare revisited

In the light of the growing controversy over the 'political' ambition of law and literature, perhaps the least controversial area in which it can be suggested that literature is of value in legal studies is that of legal history. I would suggest that the study of historical literature as an educative supplement to the study of law in history is unarguable. Rather curiously, perhaps, it is not an approach which has attracted much attention from the law and literature scholars whom we have already discussed. Possibly this is precisely because of its relatively uncontroversial, and un-philosophical, perspective. This is not to say, of course, that historical literature has not already been used precisely as such a supplement. There are numerous examples of such usage.[1] Potentially the richest of such sources is, of course, Shakespeare. Again, Shakespeare is certainly not virgin territory for the law and literature student. The comedies in particular have already been much used as a mechanism for readdressing such familiar jurisprudential concepts as justice.[2] In a more legal historical vein, *Hamlet* has been used as a vehicle for studying the law of homicide, *Henry V* for the study of international law in medieval and early modern Europe, and a whole range of plays, including comedies and histories, for an exploration of the controversy which surrounded the Oath of Allegiance and the role of ecclesiastical courts in the effecting of the Elizabethan Settlement.[3] In this chapter I want to present a similar study, which I hope will at least suggest the potential educative value of using contemporary literature as a means to better understanding a certain legal historical issue. In particular, I will look at three of Shakespeare's history plays, *Richard III*, *King John* and *Richard II*, as a way of supplementing the study of late sixteenth- and early seventeenth-century constitutional thought. In the first part of this chapter I provide an introduction to early modern constitutional thought, and in the second section show how these three plays illustrate the various tensions which characterised the contemporary debate.

THE TUDOR CONSTITUTION

Shakespeare's histories were studies of kings and subjects, and they were all titled as such. The observation may seem obvious, but it is no less important for that. Whatever else we may think of his understanding of constitutional and political matters, in this Shakespeare was absolutely right. In medieval and early modern England, at least until the early seventeenth century, kings (and of course queens) mattered more than anyone else, and by a considerable margin. Indeed, although criticism of individual monarchs and theories of monarchy was various, and at times vociferous, no one, at least until the mid-seventeenth century, really contemplated an alternative.[4] This is not to say that the monarchy was an icon of stability. As recent scholarship has re-emphasised, the monarchy by the sixteenth century was in crisis, right across Europe.[5] From an English perspective the seeds of 1649 were already well sown and rooted. By the end of the fifteenth century the English monarchy was financially crippled, and the need to finance government became an obsessive characteristic of successive monarchs. Moreover, their failure to raise revenue led to an increasing complaint of 'lack of governance'. In practice, as Lander suggests, the English monarchy was a minimalist monarchy, its ability to effect government increasingly 'limited, restricted, and precarious'.[6] By the 1590s, as recent scholarship has re-emphasised, England was thoroughly unstable.[7] This instability was concentrated on three issues, each of which, to some degree, was caught up in the crisis of monarchy. The first issue was one which, by its very nature, was becoming ever more pressing: succession. By the 1590s it was quite clear that there would be no natural succession, and the nightmares of the fifteenth-century dynastic disputes became increasingly vivid. The consistent outbreaks of factionalism at court, in part a response to the queen's own increasingly irascible nature, did nothing to alleviate concern. The Essex rebellion, to which we shall return later when we consider *Richard II*, threatened the realisation of everybody's bad dreams.[8] The second cause of instability was the continuing inability to effect the Elizabethan Settlement of 1559. The problem of the church was, of course, at once the problem of monarchy. Building upon her father's determination to strengthen the quasi-divine association of monarch and God, which he had inherited from medieval theology, and which we shall consider in greater depth below, Elizabeth determined to present herself as the Protestant godly princess. The publication of the Marprelate pamphlets in 1587–9 articulated open opposition to the settlement, and by the 1590s both Puritans and, less surprisingly perhaps, Catholics were openly counselling disobedience of the Crown. The publication of Richard Hooker's *Laws of Ecclesiastical Polity* revealed a defensive Anglicanism, sensitive to its own theoretical inadequacies and keen to try to present a first coherent theological statement. The crisis of monarchy in late sixteenth-century England was at once the crisis of the Anglican church.[9] The third issue in the 1590s was perhaps more intermittent, but no less disconcerting. Indeed, it was probably most disconcerting of all. Exacerbated by a series of poor harvests, the obedient subjects were, with increasing frequency, becoming less obedient. The 1590s was a decade of general economic difficulty. For those who wished to fuel dissent, there was an increasing number of potential dissenters.[10]

Given this degree of unrest during the last decade of Elizabeth's reign it is not at all surprising that there should be renewed interest in redefining the relationship of monarch and subjects. One of the most immediate responses was an intensification of Elizabethan propaganda. The inevitability and desirability of monarchy was impressed upon the people. As it had been for centuries, ceremony and ritual was the bedrock of Elizabethan England. By the 1590s, the court was consciously fostering an almost transcendental image of Elizabethan mythology.[11] We shall, shortly, consider the quasi-divine portrayal of monarchy which the Tudors were so keen to support, and its position in constitutional debate, for it was the increasingly vociferous nature of this debate which, by the turn of the century, more than anything else betrayed the widening concern regarding the constitutional settlement. Yet, paradoxically, it is almost commonplace to suggest that the fifteenth and sixteenth centuries were something of an intellectual dark ages.[12] The fact that there was no substantive theoretical alternative to monarchy presented can thus be comfortably explained by the complementary fact that there was nothing of real

theoretical substance being presented at all. The seventeenth
century is always seen to be the dawning of identifiable English
political and constitutional thought. Jurisprudence, it is generally
asserted, was born with Thomas Hobbes. There is some truth in
this consensus, but, at the same time, we would be unwise to so
readily dismiss the late sixteenth century, for although there may
have been little that was fresh or original there was a theory of
constitutions, and, increasingly, there was a desire to debate. There
had to be. This suggestion has been forcefully articulated in two of
the most recent studies of political and constitutional thought in
the seventeenth century which have both emphasised that whilst
constitutional debate became ever more vociferous as the century
progressed, the parameters of that debate were already in place by
the second half of the sixteenth century.[13]

The parameters were set by two dominant theories of the
Constitution, the mixed monarchy and the absolute monarchy, and
by two philosophies of government, providentialism and humanism. To a considerable degree the idea of a mixed monarchy, the
centrepiece of what has become familiar as the Ancient
Constitution, was a peculiarly English invention, bred from the
particular weaknesses of English monarchy already discussed.[14]
The original advocate of this suggestion, and the foremost
medieval advocate of mixed monarchy, was Sir John Fortescue,
Lancastrian Chief Justice to Henry VI. It was Fortescue who first
articulated the suggestion that the late medieval English monarchy
was accelerating into crisis, and the pragmatism which has
emerged as the dominant characteristic of English jurisprudence
was already at the heart of Fortescue's thinking. As a matter of
constitutional theory, Fortescue distinguished the English mixed
monarchy from continental monarchies in that the former was
dominium politicum et regale, as opposed to the latter, which was
simply *dominium tantum regale*.[15] Three characteristics flowed from
this distinction. First, as a 'political' monarchy it was an institutional, as opposed to purely natural, construct. This constructed
idea of monarchy led to a second characteristic: the monarch was
determined in relation to law and constitution. In this way, governance was firmly divided between monarch and subjects, and thus
determined by the common law. There has been some debate
about the precise nature of Fortescue's thinking here. For some,
Fortescue advocated a putative thesis of parliamentary sovereignty.

Others have suggested that the continued presence of natural law militates against such a radical portrayal, and that Fortescue was instead advocating a species of absolutism trimmed by a rule of law, but which was itself subject to natural law, and as such superior to any human law. Certainly, Fortescue was no democrat. Governance was shared by the king and a very few select subjects.[16] The third characteristic which Fortescue emphasised was that, given its institutional origins, and its balanced nature, the English monarchy ruled well when it was well counselled. The counsellors, of course, were the nobility and aristocracy, the very select subjects with whom the monarchy was mixed.[17]

The theory of mixed monarchy continued to be developed during the sixteenth century, though in an increasingly defensive fashion, and a number of treatises in its support were published by, for example, Thomas Starkey, John Aylmer and John Ponet, the Puritan scholar who suggested that the monarch was simply the 'trustee' of the realm, Sir Thomas Elyot, William Tyndale, and Queen Elizabeth's secretary of state, Thomas Smith.[18] By the time of Smith's treatise *De Republica Angolorum*, published finally in 1583, English constitutional thought was being openly allied with humanist impulses. Any government of men, Smith asserted, was unavoidably mixed, and like so many English humanists, he cited Aristotle as his authority.[19] The congruence between the more defensive mixed monarchists and the emerging English humanism is far from exact, but it is one which can be defended.[20] Certainly Tuck's recent study of sixteenth-century humanism has done much to reveal the degree to which the 'new humanism' had taken root in England by the late sixteenth century. Tuck further suggests that the ecclesiastical theorist Richard Hooker, often presented as the definitive late Elizabethan mixed monarchist, can be more clearly understood as an Aristotelian humanist.[21] Hooker composed his *Laws of Ecclesiastical Polity*, published between 1593 and 1597 as already mentioned, primarily to fill the vacuum left by the absence of a substantive theory of Anglicanism. However, despite its theological ambitions, Hooker's thesis is essentially constitutional, with the law as its very keystone. In suitably Thomist fashion, all law was derived from divine law, whilst human law was employed as the mechanism by which divine law is accessed. Both monarch and subject were thus limited by the rational discovery of human law. Monarchs did not discover law themselves, they merely enforced

natural laws discovered by human reason. Monarchs were thus
limited methodologically, if not in extent. What Hooker ultimately
presented was a kind of social contract, one which was less a
historical event, and more morally and philosophically implied.
The binding upon the monarch, therefore, was moral only. There
was certainly no right to rebel. No one, at least not an Anglican,
even bothered to contemplate that possibility. Although one or two
vociferous but essentially marginalised Puritans, such as George
Buchanan, urged open disobedience, the rhetoric of Levellerism
lay half a century and a bloody civil war away. Mixed monarchy
protected against tyrants, and humanism denounced tyranny, but it
was left to God to remove them.[22] In many ways, Hooker's thesis
can be justly presented as the definitive theory of mixed monarchy
in the final decade of the sixteenth century.[23]

The fear of the English humanists was one which was shared by
the common lawyers – a fear of tyranny. The danger of tyranny
was of course greatest with absolutist monarchs. The reason why
the presentation of mixed monarchy became rather more defensive
in the sixteenth century was that the earlier Tudor monarchs had
increasingly moved towards, if not absolute monarchy, one that
was certainly more obviously absolutist in sympathy. The ultimate
fear, then, was Tudor tyranny.[24] The precise nature of the Tudor
monarchy has long been the subject of dispute, but few would
dispute its tendency towards absolutism. Burns suggests that by
the mid-sixteenth century, the English monarchy was wholly absolutist.[25] Certainly, as Elton has emphasised, obedience to the will of
a Tudor monarch was uncompromisingly absolute.[26] The strongest
intellectual support for absolutist monarchy was continental.
Perhaps most influential of all was the Frenchman Jean Bodin who
suggested that, given the impossibility in reality of king, lords
and commons being in agreement over anything, the idea of
mixed monarchy was a 'logical absurdity'.[27] Perhaps rather
curiously, given the suggested propensity of Tudor monarchs for
absolutism, though not given the relative paucity of any political
thought, English absolutist theory was conspicuously insubstantial
in the sixteenth century. There was, of course, Scottish absolutism,
as articulated by King James VI, soon to be James I of England, in
his *The Trew Law of Free Monarchies*. Although, paradoxically, James
was to prove, in practice at least, to be far less of a spiritual
absolutist than his Tudor predecessors, the publication of this

treatise in 1598 did little to calm sensitive common law consciences amidst the anxiety of the succession debate.[28]

The two great proponents of absolutism to emerge in the early and mid-seventeenth century were, of course, Sir Robert Filmer and Thomas Hobbes.[29] But in the late sixteenth century, as Somerville has recently affirmed, English, as opposed to continental, absolutism was firmly and unswervingly identified with the divine right of kings. It is, thus, not too surprising that the marriage of monarchy and church in the Henrician and Elizabethan Settlements should feel most comfortable when founded upon the divine right thesis. Taking its authority, like the mixed monarchists indeed, from Aristotle and Aquinas, absolutist divine right theory affirmed that monarchial power was derived from God alone. The monarch was God's anointed. Thus the monarch, although subject to divine law, was the sole interpreter of divine law, which remained unquestionably superior to human law, and which thus rendered the monarch outside, or, more accurately perhaps, above the common law of the realm. It was the final development which so sharply distinguished absolutism. There was, of course, no question of disobedience, even if the actions of a monarch were patently counter to divine law. It was for God to deal with tyrants, not man. Indeed, the popularity of absolutism to the Tudor mind, yearning for good order above all else, was that it represented the strongest form of hierarchical government against any perceived threats of civil disobedience.[30] The philosophical construct of absolutism was providentialism. That God should design the ends of human life was of course wholly in accordance with divine right theory. It was providence which visited tyrannical monarchs upon the commonwealth, and disposed of them. The marriage of constitutional absolutism and providentialism was articulated most forcefully in the various homilies published during Elizabeth's reign.[31] Recent scholarship has suggested, however, that providentialism is itself almost impossible to identify, and the essentially pragmatic nature of early modern English political thought tended to leave the resolution of philosophical niceties, such as providentialism, to continentals such as Bodin.[32] Divine right theory displayed its more obviously constitutional teeth most openly in the exercise of prerogative. It represented the right of the monarch, under law, to operate outside the law in certain key areas, including most importantly church government and Crown revenues. For

Elizabeth, and particularly the early Stuarts, it came to represent even more, being the unquestionable right of monarchs to operate, not alongside the law, but above it. As Elton suggests, for them it represented 'true absolutism – freedom to disregard the law because that was under the king'.[33] It was this redefinition of prerogative along the lines of continental, as opposed to the more familiarly acceptable Tudor, absolutism that Coke, as James's Chief Justice, so significantly rejected in 1610.

Theoretical debate was one thing, but it was the breakdown of constitutional consensus, threatened during the 1590s, which really mattered. Burgess suggests that it was the anachronistic insufficiency of the medieval thesis of the 'king's two bodies' which caused the polarisation of constitutional positions towards the end of the sixteenth century.[34] As I suggested before, the ceremony of kingship was the foundation upon which monarchy resided. In moments of crisis, as in the 1590s, this symbolism was ever more urgently emphasised. The 'king's two bodies' thesis, as rearticulated by Kantorowicz, was the epitome of this ceremony of kingship. According to the thesis the king had two personas, the quasi-divine representative of God on earth, replete with suitably quasi-divine constitutional rights, and at the same time a rationally endowed civil magistrate. Symbolically the king, being quasi-divine, remained above the law, but in practice, as a political institution, he remained subject to it. In such a way the rule of law, as it was itself derived from nature, could in no way be perceived as a challenge to the king's quasi-divine persona. According to Kantorowicz, although its origins lay in continental medieval theology, the 'two bodies' thesis reached its apogee in England under the Tudors. It was their particular design for effecting the quasi-absolutist monarchy which they sought to effect.[35] The Tudor interpretation of this thesis was, of course, akin to the mixed monarchy thesis of Fortescue, and as long as the practical political niceties of the exercise of prerogative remained resolvable then there was, to use Burgess's term, a 'constitutional consensus'. It was this delicate consensus to which, despite his own propaganda, James I carefully adhered, but which Charles I was to so cavalierly disregard. Charles's fate lay half a century ahead, but it was at the dawn of the intensification of this crisis that Shakespeare wrote his histories, and in them articulated the dilemmas which fashioned it.

SHAKESPEARE'S REPUTATION

Before embarking upon a particular study of *Richard II, Richard III* and *King John*, I think that there is value in undertaking what once again must be a necessarily brief review of the recently burgeoning literature surrounding Shakespeare's 'politics'. The place to begin such a review is unquestionably with Tillyard. The evolution of subsequent scholarship has very much been a history of a retreat from Tillyard.[36] In his *Shakespeare's History Plays,* Tillyard allied the history plays to the grand theme of the Elizabethan world picture. According to Tillyard, Shakespeare composed the plays to mirror the Tudor orthodoxy of hierarchy and order, and providence. Tillyard's thesis leant much on the cultural icon of the great chain of being, where everything and everybody occupied a predestined and inescapable place in the natural order. Necessarily then, what Tillyard suggested was that Shakespeare wrote against the lures of disorder, scepticism and the unnatural, the epitome of which was Machiavellianism. Shakespeare was thus an Elizabethan propagandist, the natural heir of such as Polydore Vergil, Edward Hall and to a degree Holinshed, constantly stressing the value of history as an education against the dangers of rebellion, and the necessity of unswerving obedience to strong monarchy, orthodox Anglicanism and the natural order of things.[37] In presenting such a thesis, it has been suggested that Tillyard was simply articulating the political vision of English intellectualism of his time which, like the 1590s, was high on sovereignty, nationalism and civil order.[38] Despite this suggestion, or perhaps indeed because of it, Tillyard's thesis has continued to attract at least qualified approbation. In one of the more influential studies Reese has developed the Tillyard thesis, suggesting that the histories reveal the pervasive Elizabethan concern with the challenge of new humanism against the received wisdom of providentialism, and the overarching desire, especially acute in the 1590s, to somehow effect a political accommodation which could continue to preserve strong authoritarian government.[39] A number of commentators have detected a sea change in Shakespeare's histories, from a presentation, if not a belief, in providentialism in the earlier plays to a presentation of humanism in the later plays – the bridge from the first to the second tetralogy, which encompasses the three plays which we shall shortly consider, is often presented as the watershed for this development.[40]

The more recent revisionist approach to Shakespeare's 'politics' has tended to evolve through two schools, new historicism and cultural materialism.[41] New historicism asserts that history is always an 'activity' of narration, and thus the language of the elite and correspondingly the literature of oppression.[42] Cultural materialism, which has itself in large part developed from the historicist approach, emphasises the polyphonic pluralism of literature, and suggests that it is impossible to access any totalising picture of Shakespeare, political or otherwise. This pluralism, the separation of Shakespeare from a particular Tudor myth, is common ground in revisionist criticism, as is the conclusion that not only is it impossible for us now to access a precise understanding of Shakespeare's politics, but similarly that there never was, and anyway could not have been, any uniform political vision in the plays.[43] The question still remains, of course, whether Shakespeare can be thought of as an active political thinker, and this revisionist approach has itself spawned diametrically opposite conclusions. On the one hand Kiernan has recently reaffirmed that Shakespeare was first and foremost an active 'political poet' and, moreover, while following the line that it is impossible to derive a 'cut-and-dried gospel' from the plays, has tended to suggest that they can be read at times, *contra* Tillyard, as politically and socially subversive. The histories, as pieces of interpretation rather than mere chronicles, Kiernan suggests, articulate the pervasive feeling of uncertainty and dissatisfaction which culminated in the events of 1640–60.[44] At the other extreme commentators like Melchiori have tended to minimise not the political import of Shakespeare's plays, but the degree to which we should be thinking of Shakespeare as an active political propagandist. Shakespeare, Melchiori suggests, was first and foremost a man of the theatre, not of high politics.[45] A middle position was taken, albeit nearly forty years ago, by Knights, who suggested that while Shakespeare showed a 'lively concern' with matters political, it would be a mistake to read into his plays too great an interest, or knowledge, in the niceties of philosophical and constitutional debate. Shakespeare, he suggests, was above all a political realist.[46] This might, at least in part, explain why specific discussion of the constitutionalism in Shakespeare's plays, as opposed to wider socio-political concerns, in relative terms has been so strikingly sparse. Constitutionally, Shakespeare is still very much up for grabs.

RICHARD III

By all contemporary accounts Richard III was a good king. Recent historical scholarship has reinforced the view that he was a good administrator, politician and soldier, and a devout man of God. In short, precisely the godly monarch that the Tudors were so keen to applaud. Moreover, his claim to the throne was at least as viable as any at the time, and certainly not exceptional in the often uncertain world of medieval monarchical succession.[47] Yet the Richard who emerges from Shakespeare's portrayal is infamous as the archetypal tyrant and villain. Shakespeare could have portrayed Richard in the same way as he was to portray Henry V. But instead he chose to make life difficult for himself, although not, as we shall see, as difficult as he was to do in his succeeding two histories. The reason, of course, is that Shakespeare was rewriting a story which had already been told by previous Tudor propagandists, most notably Sir Thomas More and Edward Hall.[48] Richard was already typecast. According to Tillyard, his fate was determined by the grand design which lay behind the entire first tetralogy. Richard was visited upon, and symptomatic of, the sinful and unnatural state of fifteenth-century England. His tyranny and evil were part of God's design, and only providence would remove him, as it did in 1485 when Henry Tudor restored law and order to the dislocated realm. The Tudors were thus God's chosen dynasty. In suggesting this theme, Tillyard concludes that Richard is 'the vehicle of an orthodox doctrine about kingship'.[49] A complementary reason for the portrayal of Richard which Shakespeare presented in his play was the genus of the character which emerged from the *Henry VI* plays, primarily part 3, and at the same time the intensification of a particular theme which pervades all three parts – insufficient kingship.[50] It is quite clear that Shakespeare was increasingly interested in the inadequacies of individual kings, and all of the histories in varying degrees, and indeed many of the tragedies, question the validity of the central thesis in medieval and Tudor kingship: the 'king's two bodies'. The ideal monarch was ideal in both personas: such monarchs were Henry V and Henry VIII. But every other king portrayed in the histories is in some way deficient in one or other of the two bodies.

Richard is particular in being defective in both and it is this, ultimately, which made Shakespeare's job, constitutionally at least,

easier. Shakespeare's Richard is a plain tyrant, and can thus be
treated as such.[51] It has been suggested that in his desire to effect a
more subtle approach to the problems of politics Shakespeare
realised the need to concentrate upon the development of key
characters. *Richard III* thus represents an evolutionary stage on the
way to the greater complexities of *Richard II*.[52] As a number of
commentators have noted, the Richard described in the play thus
tends to be a more one-dimensional figure, and one familiar to
Shakespeare's audiences. The 'stage Machiavel' was certainly
familiar in Elizabethan literature, and provided Shakespeare with a
ready-to-hand and popular character with which he could portray
the Richard which Tudor culture demanded. At the same time
Richard could be represented, as by Sir Thomas More, as the
Antichrist. He could also represent Vice, a figure familiar to audiences from the morality plays, which was synonymous with
decayed public morality.[53] Richard's Machiavellian persona was
introduced in the final scenes of *Henry VI* part 3, where his 'dreams'
of sovereignty betray a raw and evil ambition, and a determination
to achieve all by subverting God and nature, and by setting 'the
murderous Machiavel to school'.[54] Later he urges Edward to be a
pragmatic king, and to ignore constitutional niceties in favour of a
raw politics of power.[55] Monarchy, he advises Edward, must be
absolute and unprincipled. In other words, it must be tyrannical.
At the close of *Henry VI*, as he murders God's anointed King,
Richard's unnatural character, having 'neither pity, love, nor fear',
has already been established.[56]

In declaring himself to be Machiavellian Richard is declaring
himself to be self-determined and not determined by providence.
At the same time the route which he maps for himself in his very
first soliloquy in *Richard III* is a contradiction of nature and good
government. Richard is 'determined to prove a villain'.[57] He is a
wholly ungodly and unnatural prince, but, for a while, a
thoroughly effective one.[58] Subsequently, having established his
ambition, the realisation of it reveals to Richard the tenuous
nature of unnatural government, standing as it does on 'brittle
glass'.[59] The hypocritical puritanism with which Shakespeare
colours Richard's speech reinforces the presentation of a man and
a king deceiving of both his subjects and his God, as Richard is
only too well aware.[60] He thus denounces Edward's excesses as
king, and sends Hastings to his death in a fit of Puritan rhetoric.[61]

Yet Anne knows that Richard acknowledges 'no law of God nor man', and thus, of course, potentially could be a king in neither of his 'two bodies'.[62] Clarence, at the moment of his death, makes precisely the same observation.[63] Similarly Margaret, too, appeals to providence to reveal the dishonesty of Richard's puritanism.[64] Because Richard is so evil, God strikes him down. This is achieved by Richmond, who Shakespeare very carefully portrays as the hand of God. Richmond works with heaven and the angels. His men go forward in 'God's name'.[65] In sharp contrast to Richard, Richmond is a barely developed character.[66] He does not need to be. His function is merely to serve as the mouthpiece of good and Godly princely government. He is, by his own reckoning, merely the 'captain' of God.[67] The orthodox providential theme here, as Tillyard rightly suggested, is pervasive in *Richard III*.[68] This has its advantages, and it certainly makes Shakespeare's task easier. It does not, however, tackle the crux of contemporary early modern constitutional debate. Rather it serves to deflect it. By unambiguously describing God's vengeance upon an equally unambiguously evil and insufficient Richard, Shakespeare was able to negate the need for anyone else to remove him. There is no need for rebellion, at least not a self-determined rebellion. This perhaps is the central constitutional message in *Richard III*.[69] It is the problem of what to do with the more ambiguously insufficient kings, John and Richard II, which really catalyses much deeper constitutional themes in the subsequent histories. Shakespeare's concentration on Richard's character has led, understandably, to critical concentration more upon philosophical themes, most obviously those of providentialism and Machiavellian humanism, rather than upon mixed and absolute monarchy. However, despite the fact that *Richard III* is very much more about providentialism than the niceties of constitutional debate, and is a play about character rather than kingship, there are certain more obviously constitutional issues in the play which warrant our attention. The first issue has already been suggested. Tyrants were subject to providence. Although Shakespeare could graphically portray the misery which tyrants visited upon their realms, it was not for subjects to rebel, unless so instructed by God.[70] This, as I have already suggested, was Tudor orthodoxy.

A second and not unrelated constitutional issue is the question of legitimacy. Richard is consistently conscious of the issue of

legitimacy, and it has been suggested that this is the dominant
constitutional issue in the play.[71] Of course, Shakespeare ensures
that Richard does not appear to be legitimate, and moreover that
Richard realises this. For him legitimacy is power. Yet here
Shakespeare was presented with an unavoidable dilemma.
Although he is quick to condemn Richard's legitimacy, his
approach to Richmond's is more ambivalent.[72] Tudor orthodoxy
was itself ambivalent here, championing a long dynastic genealogy
right back to Cadwallader, yet at the same time concentrating far
more on Henry Tudor as the unifying force above the dynastic
struggles and claims of legitimacy which characterised fifteenth-
century England. As the ghost of Henry VI suggests, it is the invasion of the King's 'anointed body' which serves to condemn
Richard, not merely the insufficiency of his genealogy. Richmond,
in contrast, is the epitome of the godly prince.[73] Interestingly, in his
oration to his soldiers in 5.3 Richmond makes no particular claim
to genealogical legitimacy, appealing instead to God and justice as
his right: 'Yet remember this: / God, and our good cause, fight
upon our side; / The prayers of holy saints and wronged souls,
/ Like high-rear'd bulwarks, stand before our faces.'[74] Richard's
appeal, which follows, conspicuously makes no reference to any
form of legitimacy, save for possession.[75] However, in the final
scene Shakespeare does make more overt reference to legitimacy,
but then again only to strengthen the more important theme
of inter-dynastic unity, and moreover as an adjunct to divine
providence:

> And then, as we have ta'en the sacrament,
> We will unite the white rose and the red.
> Smile, heaven, upon this fair conjunction,
> That long have frown'd upon their enmity
>
> ...
>
> O now let Richmond and Elizabeth,
> The true succeeders of each royal House,
> By God's fair ordinance conjoin together,
> And let their heirs, God, if Thy will be so,
> Enrich the time to come with smooth-fac'd peace,
> With smiling plenty, and fair prosperous days.[76]

Legitimacy, as far as it is important, is only so as a symbol of divine
providence. It is the 'divine' right of the king which seals his
legitimacy.

Elizabeth's long litany of Richard's wrongs in 4.4 concludes by suggesting the 'greatest' wrong of usurpation is not against the usurped, but against God.[77] As well as the issue of legitimacy, there is the associated question of Richard's relation with his subjects. Shakespeare portrays his attempt to secure the throne by popular acclamation as a reflection of his insufficient legitimacy, something about which Richard, and his followers, seem to be only too aware.[78] At the same time as trying to stress his legitimacy, in 3.7 Buckingham and Richard also make much of Richard's godliness. Richard knows what a king should be, and knows the extent of his own insufficiency. Shakespeare appears to make two particular observations here. First, Richard is himself deceitful in his claim to be a desirable monarch. Indeed, Richard is advised by Buckingham to be deceitful, and Catesby deliberately lies in his description of Richard's holiness.[79] As Richmond later emphasises, Richard has been a suitably unnatural and thoroughly destructive king.[80] The second observation seems more ambiguous. As Shakespeare suggests elsewhere, most obviously in his treatment of Cade's rebellion in *Henry VI* part 2, the people are fickle, and certainly are not the wise counsel which the godly prince requires. Popular democracy is not favourably portrayed in Shakespeare. Yet this is not to say that all the people are so incapable. Buckingham's attempt to woo the people in 3.7 is met in silence, and only the Mayor ultimately urges Richard to take the crown.[81] Moreover, in the scene immediately preceding Richard's appeal to the common people, the Scrivener wisely emphasises the wrongness in perjuring the law.[82] The common Englishman can understand right and justice, but he can be misled by rhetoric, as a few are by Buckingham.[83] Ultimately, Shakespeare seems to suggest that it is a matter of both principle and good government. It is the danger of popular acclamation of princes which must be avoided, not the inevitability of their misunderstanding. Kings should not seek approbation from their subjects, only from God. Richard's desire to be, in effect, crowned by the populace, as McNeir has commented, makes a mockery of the sanctity of legitimate coronation, something which will not have been lost on an Elizabethan audience.[84] The same would have been true of Richard's loss of control at the end of his own coronation.[85]

Richard III, then, though certainly a less obviously constitutional play than either *King John* or *Richard II*, should not be dismissed too lightly. A treatise discussing the merits of providentialism is to some degree always a constitutional treatise. The approbation of providentialism does not itself tell us, however, whether mixed or absolute monarchy was more desirable. Although providentialism tended in Shakespeare's day to sit more neatly with absolutist theory, as we have seen the peculiar nature of the 'consensus' which characterised Tudor absolutism could just as well align it with mixed monarchy. Certainly, Reese suggests that in its portrayal of the dangers of the tyrant _Richard III_ presents Shakespeare at his most anti-absolutist in constitutional terms.[86] Given the play's relatively restricted and rather one-dimensional approach to constitutional issues, concentrating almost exclusively, as Carroll has recently affirmed, on variations on the question of legitimacy, it may not be possible to draw any grand conclusions from _Richard III_. However, aside from the issues which it raises with regard to kingship, as Prior suggests there is a virtue in beginning an examination with _Richard III_ of the much more subtle constitutional problems which develop in the subsequent histories. _Richard III_ in a sense opens the constitutional debate, and it is the retreat from the tidy orthodoxy of Tudor providentialism and a reopening of the question of humanism that characterises Shakespeare's treatment of things constitutional in the next two plays.[87] Although the play proved, and continues to prove, to be one of the most enduringly popular of Shakespeare's corpus, in _Richard III_ it might reasonably be suggested that we can detect a Shakespeare who is, if not actually dissatisfied, certainly not entirely satiated by the neat and tidy providential theory of kingship which he inherited in the story of Richard III.[88]

KING JOHN

The fact that _King John_ is the natural development of _Richard III_, and the natural precursor of _Richard II_, at least as a political play, has attracted growing support. Despite one or two lingering doubts it is now generally suggested that _John_ was composed between _Richard III_ and _Richard II_.[89] Similarly, although for so long one of the more neglected plays, in recent years _King John_ has been perceived as representing a crucial stage in the development of Shakespeare's politics.[90] It is certainly the first time that Shakespeare addresses more overtly constitutional political themes.[91] Once again it is perhaps important to begin with the origins of Shakespeare's *John*. John was treated variously by different Tudor chroniclers, but the dominant influence was undoubtedly the anonymous play *The Troublesome Raigne of John King of England*, which set the scene for a thoroughly incompetent and wicked king.[92] What is remarkable about Shakespeare's characterisation of John, in sharp distinction from his characterisation of Richard III, is the extent to which he modifies this poor image. In *John*, Shakespeare is trying to create ambiguity.[93] At the same time, the most striking similarity between *John* and *Richard III* is the development of the Machiavellian theme. Unlike the two *Richard* plays there is no one dominating character in *John*. That role is shared by John, whose character declines as the play progresses, and the Bastard, whose role correspondingly rises. Both are to some degree Machiavellian, but at the same time neither is so patently evil or tyrannical as Richard III.[94] For this reason, Shakespeare's ambition is greater, and his task more difficult: tyrants like Richard were easier to deal with. Although there is, of course, the matter of his right to the throne, John's wickedness really only emerges in an unambiguous form in his decision to kill Arthur. Even then, in sharp contrast to Richard's treatment of the Princes, he shows remorse. In his discourse with Philip, the French king makes much of John's unnaturalness as king, but there is not, at least initially, any evidence of his unnaturalness as a person.[95]

However, by 3.2, as well as ordering Arthur's murder he is ordering the Bastard to 'skin the fat ribs of peace' but even here, given that John refers to 'hoarding abbots' it might be inferred that the audience would treat such a command with sympathy.[96] Indeed, John's presentation as the champion of England against the papacy was perhaps the greatest ambiguity of his character.[97] Again, it is one which Shakespeare inherited from the chronicles, but it was also one which he was careful to exacerbate. In his defiance John suggests that the Pope is a usurper of the realm.[98] His resulting excommunication, of course, takes John and his subjects outside the law of God.[99] Yet, once again, the audience could just as well read this as a victory for the law of the realm. Constance suggests that heavenly justice is always superior to civil justice, but then Constance is the mouthpiece of popery, and the proferred example of such supreme godly law is French absolutism.[100] However, it is following his order to murder Arthur in the following scene that John's fortunes, and indeed his importance in the play, decline. By 4.2, he is a figure of indecision and inconstancy, belatedly seeking, but still failing to execute, the advice of his counsellors.[101] It is significant that, as in *Richard III*, Shakespeare chooses to reveal the pretender's inadequacies at the moment of his coronation. As a king without ceremonial trappings of kingship, it has been suggested that John is presented as the king with 'one body', devoid of the divinity which 'doth hedge a king'. His survival thus depends purely upon his success as a politician.[102] The seriousness of his situation is revealed later in the scene, when he is informed that a considerable French army is already approaching. Ultimately he merely tries to escape responsibility for his own insufficiencies, both as a person and as a king.[103] The Machiavellian monarch, the supreme pragmatist, depends on the constant enforcement of his possession. He must be the man of action. In 5.1, in contrast to his earlier patriotic defiance of the Pope, John is a humble supplicant resigning his realm to Rome, under the threat of deposition by the French king and his own nobles. As the Bastard notes, he now appears to be wholly unfit to rule, and incapable of action.[104] Later, in scene 7, John dies, symbolically as sick as his realm, burnt up by 'tyrant fever'.[105] It is a tyranny bred not just of illegitimacy, but of incompetence and weakness.

As John's situation weakens from 3.2, his place is taken by the Bastard. Recent scholarship has championed the role of the Bastard as pivotal, although opinions as to what that character is vary enormously.[106] It has been variously suggested that as the high priest of 'Commodity', the Bastard is a direct evolution of Richard III, and the precursor of Henry V.[107] It has also been suggested that in his presentation of the Bastard, Shakespeare is making his first tentative critique of the 'king's two bodies' thesis; a critique which emerges as central to *Richard II*.[108] The Bastard's character announces itself with force as early as the first scene. Aligning himself with John's 'strong possession', the Bastard declares himself for power in politics, as well as bastardy in lineage, and his ensuing ridicule of the trappings of form and ceremony strike echoes of certain of Richard's early comments in *Richard III*.[109] Reacting to John's incompetence, the Bastard reflects on the chaos brought by a usurped and ineffective monarchy.[110] His 'conversion', in Act 3, is one of the most important turning-points in the play. Though the epitome of illegitimacy, he increasingly emerges as an ideal kingly figure.[111] When John resigns himself to the will of Rome, it is the Bastard who appreciates the unkingliness of this act, and its subversive effect on the realm.[112] In 5.2, it is again the Bastard who gives voice to the English riposte to Lewis and the invading army.[113] Thus, it is the Bastard who assumes John's mantle and his rhetoric as England's champion.[114] In his final act of fealty to the new king, Henry, the Bastard completes his conversion, and with it marries 'Commodity' to honour and duty.[115] It was of course his Machiavellian capabilities as a politician and soldier that secured Henry's crown. The Bastard is the supreme exponent of politics in a world without absolutes. More than that, he is successful and ultimately loyal. It has been suggested that in creating the Bastard, Shakespeare is thus creating a figure for the new world, as opposed to the old medieval one.[116] If this is so, then the Bastard can be seen as the prototype of Bolingbroke in *Richard II*. A similar comparison between John and Richard II, of course, is less viable. If anything John, too, is akin to Bolingbroke. At times, certainly in the opening scenes, John and the Bastard appear to be complementary characters.[117] As Machiavellians and pragmatists, though one is more competent than the other, they often think alike. Both abandon legitimacy as a creed in favour of power. Both thus agree to abandon constitutional debate before the citizens of Angiers, and instead attack the town.[118] They both also decide to bleed England in order to finance further warfare.[119] It is only following the Bastard's conversion that their characters and roles diverge.

The greater ambivalence in the portrayal of less obviously tyrannical Machiavellianism has the inevitable result of casting a shadow across the role of providence which had, of course, been the philosophical keystone of *Richard III*. Constance and Eleanor exchange divine curses, but neither do so with the avowedly holy conviction of the female characters in *Richard III*.[120] Constance continues intermittent cursing of 'perjur'd kings' such as John and, in the sense that John dies, her appeal is successful.[121] Yet they do not affect the fortunes of Arthur. Whilst the fortunes of the illegitimate and similarly 'perjur'd' Machiavellian Bastard improve, those of the only character of undoubted virtue, Arthur, decline. Nature is on Arthur's side, but providence abandons him in much the same way as it abandoned the Princes in *Richard III*.[122] Of course order is restored, both to the country and to the succession, with Henry and the Bastard's submission to him. But if God has engineered Henry's unifying succession, as he did Richmond's, he has chosen the supreme Machiavellian as his instrument to do so.[123] The other constitutional themes, along with the issues of providence and humanism, are the same in *John* as in *Richard III*.[124] First there is the question of legitimacy and rights of succession.[125] The very first scene opens with Chatillon's comment on John's 'borrow'd majesty'.[126] John himself is inclined to stress his 'strong possession', and Eleanor confirms that it is 'Your strong possession much more than your right.'[127] It has been noted that in John's time, lineal descent was not such a recognised necessity of succession, but it is reasonable to assume that Shakespeare was writing less about medieval problems of succession and more about those which were troubling Elizabethan audiences in the 1590s.[128] The matter of legitimacy is immediately reinforced by the ensuing discussion regarding the Bastard's legitimacy. Although it is perhaps significant that John is correct in law in his pronouncement, and thus is well aware of the legal repercussions of illegitimacy, what is really important about this episode is the Bastard's conscious decision to renounce legal legitimacy in the cause of John's political legitimacy of 'possession'.[129] In his discourse with Philip in 2.1 John certainly speaks the rhetoric of legitimacy, together with a somewhat unconvincing appeal to providence.[130] It is, however, Philip of France, a truly legitimate monarch, who is able to furnish a convincing appeal to divine right legitimacy.[131] In reply, John can only seek recourse to the reality of his 'authority'.[132] As we have noted, France was recognised in the 1590s as being the archetypal absolutist monarchy, and, of course, Shakespeare effects a dilemma by making John appear to be the patriot in his and the Bastard's defence against the papist French. The audience is to support 'strong possession' against Catholic absolutism, no matter how legitimate. John may have committed 'rape / Upon the maiden virtue of the crown', but at least he is not French or Catholic.[133] Once again, in the scene before Angiers, whilst Philip discourses richly on Arthur's divine right to the throne, John concentrates on his 'lawfulness' and his military strength. 'Doth not the Crown of England prove the king?', he asks.[134] The answer is much less certain than in *Richard III*.[135] It just might.

Given the diminished certainty with which Shakespeare presents providence there is also the problem of disposing of tyrants. This introduces one theme in particular which is central in *John*, that of oaths. Subjects' oaths are constantly being compromised, not least by John's insistence on demanding new ones to abrogate earlier oaths. Thus, ultimately, John undermines his own legitimacy as king.[136] The dilemma that repeatedly faces various subjects in *John* is that there are clearly times when it is worse to keep an oath than to break it.[137] It has been suggested that Shakespeare creates ambiguity with regard to the status of oaths in an attempt to undermine the 'capstone' of divine right theory, which thus develops further the critique of absolutism. Particularly in a Machiavellian world of politics, oaths themselves can no longer be taken as guarantees of obedience, unless they enjoy an independent rational force.[138] Although there is a greater ambiguity with regard to the issue of obedience, as in *Richard III* it is clear in *John* that Shakespeare recoils from the idea that subjects should really be trusted with the task of selecting monarchs. The scene before Angiers when the rival kings, John and Philip, bid for the throne of England would have been disturbing to the Elizabethan audience. More unsettling still would have been the citizens' resolution that until the two rivals could make up their minds, there would be no king at all.[139] The kings, not surprisingly, merely go off to fight. This might seem to be all very providential, because after all God would grant victory to the righteous. Indeed, Hubert suggests that a 'greater power than we' can resolve the issue.[140] The problem is that, unlike in *Richard III*, nothing really gets to be resolved. Moreover, the Bastard seizes the opportunity to recommend 'wild counsel', and a combined assault on the impertinent and chronically indecisive citizens.[141] The Bastard, at least, appreciates the unnaturalness of allowing subjects to select monarchs. This applies, too, to noble subjects. Thus Salisbury muses on the dilemma of whether to support the French in order to enforce what he perceives to be right.[142] The error of his reasoning can best be seen when it is compared with York's attitude in *Richard II*. Salisbury's inability to act positively sums up the inadequacies with which Shakespeare portrays the treasonous nobles hoodwinked to such a degree that they almost fight to ensure their own destruction, saved only at the last by the Bastard.[143] Providence might be a weaker force in *John* than in *Richard III*, but it is far from clear as to how else the responsibility of effecting good government can be taken. It certainly is not for the subjects to decide. The role of the perfect subject is played,

ultimately, by the Bastard, and he recoils from the horror of
rebellion, but only because he rationalises that John is not a tyrant.
As Womersley suggests, it is not the decision that the Bastard
makes which threatens constitutional orthodoxy, it is the manner in
which he reaches it which is heterodox.[144] This, of course, is the
essential dilemma which Shakespeare has added to his *John* – the
problem of the incompetent king who is not a tyrant, and who
cannot safely be left to the whim of providence.[145] The Bastard
thinks for himself. It has been suggested that *John* is thus a
much more subversive play, and one which questions the very
foundation of English constitutionalism.[146] Certainly *John* represents a more overt turn towards the peculiar characteristics of
English humanism, but as we have noted this was not in itself a
challenge to English constitutional orthodoxy. Indeed, English
mixed monarchy theory deliberately evolved to accommodate it.
Thus, more moderately and, I would suggest, more persuasively,
Hamilton proposes that in *John* the particular treatment of oaths,
and the complementary critique of absolutism, shows Shakespeare
confirming his allegiance to mixed monarchy theory.[147] The
play does then operate within the boundaries of constitutional
orthodoxy, revealing a very conscious shift in Shakespeare's
thinking towards a more obviously mixed and balanced polity.
Certainly, given what was shortly to follow in *Richard II*, this is
what we might expect to find.

RICHARD II

Richard II is Shakespeare's most compelling investigation into
constitutional thought. In the same vein as *Richard III*, in *Richard II*
he created a play around one dominating character. Indeed, such
is the depth and subtlety of that character that it has been
suggested that *Richard II* is a precursor of the tragedies which were
shortly to follow.[148] As with *John*, Shakespeare took a common history and transformed it. The history of Richard II had been
covered by a number of chroniclers, and, being generally
approached as the catalyst for the Wars of the Roses the events
of his reign were recorded in a light which varied with the political
affiliation of the chronicler.[149] Shakespeare, however, ignored
such a one-dimensional approach. The reign of Richard was
simply a vehicle. Instead he concentrated upon presenting a

substantive discourse on the nature of the constitution, employing all the concepts which he had been developing in *Richard III* and *John*.[150] Once again, moreover, as with *John*, he did so while at the same time clothing the debate in the dilemmas made inevitable by the weakness of human nature.[151]

The character of Richard represents the epitome of an absolutist monarch, or at least one who harboured such absolutist ambitions.[152] Recent scholarship has suggested that Richard's reign was indeed noteworthy for its attempt to introduce a continental absolutist style of monarchy, in place of the kind of mixed polity which Fortescue had observed half a century later.[153] The ambitions which Shakespeare's Richard holds are evident from the very first scene, where his court is defined by its ceremony and formality. Indeed, the entire scene is an enactment of ritual.[154] It is Richard's consciousness of what a divinely ordained monarch must do which forces him to permit, against his better judgement, the trial by combat of Bolingbroke and Mowbray. As becomes clear in scene 2, it is Richard who has caused Gloucester's death, and so recourse to divine justice, though a kingly duty, is likely to be counter-productive.[155] It is the first example of many which see Richard as kingly in status but not in person.[156] Richard's ambitions are not only absolutist, they are portrayed as being ultra-medieval.[157] The Elizabethan audience would also have been struck by this first example of Richard's preference for divine justice over the natural course of the law.

The legality of Richard's decision to halt the combat in scene 3 is much contested. It is certainly unorthodox, and can only be justified, at best, as an extreme exercise of royal prerogative. It would certainly have appeared to the audience as a sign of Richard's inclination to override judicial form in order to achieve his personal ambitions.[158] The abruptness of Richard's behaviour is emphasised when it is compared with his earlier commitment to the immanent rightfulness of such a combat. Gaunt, very much a symbol of the old order, immediately appreciates that Richard's actions have condemned Gaunt himself, and the constitutional theory for which he stands. Moreover, Gaunt suggests, Richard's extra- or at best quasi-legal behaviour serves to condemn the king himself, and his realm. The denial of justice to his subjects is the most serious abrogation of monarchial responsibility.[159] It is Richard, Gaunt notes, who is exiled, not Bolingbroke, who now goes to a 'fresher clime'.[160] Gaunt's doubts with regard to Richard's kingliness are quickly confirmed: we learn of Richard's reckless extravagance, his determination to 'farm' his realm, his propensity for continental fashions and his determination to follow his will, regardless of reason and good counsel. Richard, indeed, has consistently sought bad counsel from favourites rather than seeking counsel from his barons – the mark of the absolutist and the tyrant.[161] He is, as even his Gardeners are aware, a thoroughly incompetent monarch.[162] Ultimately Richard seeks Gaunt's death in order to seize his estates.[163] Gaunt's death, of course, and Richard's subsequent unlawful seizure of the Lancastrian estates will herald the return of Bolingbroke to exact justice, and the arrival of a new political order. Richard wishes and causes his own demise. Berated by Gaunt, Richard is well aware that he is abandoning his inheritance, and in 'farming' out his own realm is subjecting himself to the vicissitudes of the common law. As Gaunt says, 'Landlord of England art thou now, not King / Thy state of law is now bondslave to the law.'[164] As soon as Gaunt dies, Richard himself abandons his realm to fight the Welsh.[165] Richard is very conscious that he is moving into fresh political waters. Indeed, as neither he, nor, of course, Bolingbroke, espouses the constitutionalism represented by Gaunt, Shakespeare makes an alternative and new polity inevitable.

Richard appreciates the novelty, and weakness, of his position in 3.2, when the Bishop of Carlisle, whilst approving his confidence in his position as God's anointed ruler, suggests that in the real world of politics being anointed ruler is not always enough. Richard clings to his quasi-divine status, reassuring himself that:

> Not all the water in the rough rude sea
> Can wash the balm off from an anointed king;
> The breath of worldly men cannot depose
> The deputy elected by the Lord
>   ...
> God for his Richard hath in heavenly pay
> A glorious angel: then, if angels fight,
> Weak men must fall, for heaven still guards the right.[166]

Angels are all Richard has, for the whole country, he is told, has turned against him. As the seriousness of his position, and misapprehension with regard to the nature of kingship, sinks in, Richard temporarily loses his reason, which is then followed by the realisation that he is ultimately just a human being, and then, finally, by the acknowledgement of his own despair. Rather than defend his realm, Richard decides instead to 'sit upon the ground / And tell sad stories of the death of kings.'[167] A growing self-awareness emerges as Richard's dominant characteristic during the closing acts. Like Richard III and John before him, Richard is left to muse upon his own question, 'How can you say to me, I am a King?'[168] It is Carlisle who immediately replies by suggesting that he will only be a secure king if he can win battles.[169] Richard's despair, however, pervades 3.3. Initially his rhetoric is that of God's anointed, demanding of Northumberland, 'show us the hand of God / That hath dismiss'd us from our stewardship.'[170] But he is quick to submit to Bolingbroke's demands, shortly after enquiring of Northumberland, 'What says King Bolingbroke? Will his Majesty / Give Richard leave to live till Richard die ?'[171] It is only now that Bolingbroke can emerge as a major character. Though for the most part overshadowed by Richard, Bolingbroke, 'the silent king', is presented as an equally unambiguous figure. He is the Machiavel first introduced in the character of Richard III, and then developed in a non-villainous, and thus more ambiguous, guise in the Bastard.[172] His first appearances, however, reveal little other than his disillusionment as Richard refuses him the justice to which he was entitled under either divine or civil law. Indeed, much of what we learn about Bolingbroke in the early scenes is hearsay. Richard fears Bolingbroke's 'courtship to the common people', and his political abilities.[173] Bolingbroke reappears in 2.3 seeking, he maintains, merely the legal restoration of his estates. It is Richard's refusal to effect the law of the land which has prompted his return.[174] His ambition for the crown only becomes apparent in 3.3, where he threatens rebellion if Richard fails to effect justice.[175] There are three occasions in *Richard II* where Richard and Bolingbroke interact, and each goes to the heart of the issues of kingship and obedience. The first is the protracted matter of the combat between Bolingbroke and Mowbray, which we have already considered. The second is this scene at Flint, in 3.3, when Bolingbroke effectively takes power. Here Bolingbroke begins by demanding the return of the estates and ends by being hailed 'King Bolingbroke' by Richard, and by ordering his king's return to London.[176] The command contains only four words, but it signals the triumph of power over rhetoric.[177] The Machiavel has finally usurped the old order.

The third occasion on which Richard and Bolingbroke interact is in the ceremony of deposition. It is noteworthy that, unlike similar ceremonies concerning Richard III and John, Bolingbroke's is the first such ceremony to be effected with the active approval of Parliament and, moreover, is one of the scenes which Shakespeare chose to invent. The occasion gives rise to a direct confrontation between alternative theories of monarchy. Carlisle gives voice to the divine right of the monarch, whilst Bolingbroke typically stays silent.[178] Bolingbroke espouses no constitutional theory. Events have spoken for him, and others have chosen to 'crown' him, most notably and most literally Richard, who assumes the role of both 'priest and clerk'.[179] Throughout the scene which was to represent his triumph, Bolingbroke is reduced to occasional one-line orders. Such is the depth of his new-found appreciation of kingship and its demands that Richard quite steals the scene from Bolingbroke. Paradoxically, this is to be Richard's greatest moment. The ceremony of kingship is still his, and it ill-suits Bolingbroke.[180] Shakespeare chooses this moment to re-emphasise Bolingbroke's illegitimacy, at least as an anointed ceremonial monarch. Revealing the falsity of an abdication effected by duress, Richard berates the new king and his supporters. When Northumberland demands of him a confession of his guilt, he responds by re-emphasising the constitutional nakedness of their actions: 'If thou wouldst, / There shouldst thou find one heinous article, / Containing the deposing of a king, / And cracking the strong warrant of an oath, / Mark'd with a blot, damd'd in the book of heaven.'[181]

Following his deposition, Richard continues to muse, with far greater insight, on the paradoxes of kingship, and particularly of the 'king's two bodies'. At the moment of his abdication and his 'crowning' of Bolingbroke, Richard comments that although Bolingbroke might now be king of his realm, he is still 'king' of his own 'griefs'.[182] Still pressed by Northumberland's concern to satisfy the 'commons', Richard calls for a mirror so that he can look at the new 'unking'd' Richard. Kingship, he notes, using the same metaphor as Richard III, is always a reflection of 'brittle' glass. His smashing of the mirror symbolises the destruction which he has effected of his own kingship, and, he also realises, that of kingship itself.[183] It is he, ultimately, who has served: 'T'undeck the pompous body of a king; / Made glory base, and sovereignty a slave; / Proud majesty a subject, state a peasant.'[184] It is this presentation of Richard which, Kantorowicz suggested, represented the classic portrayal of the 'king's two bodies'.[185] What is Richard without a crown, and what is the crown without Richard?[186] The nature of Bolingbroke's kingship can only emerge once Richard has departed. As Richard suspected, Bolingbroke proves to be a popular king, capable of wooing the commons, and displaying other suitable kingly abilities, revealing the quality of mercy in his treatment of Aumerle, and his instinct for swift action in the defence of his realm.[187] At the same time, in wishing for Richard's death, he also reveals the darker side of the competent Machiavellian.[188] As the play closes, he further betrays a sense of guilt and responsibility, and a growing appreciation of the 'burdens' of kingship which Richard had suggested would be his.[189] In sharp contrast, while Bolingbroke remains the man of action rather than words, Richard continues to achieve new poetic heights. The rhetoric of nobility is still his. In the soliloquy before his death Richard continues to muse on the nature of kingship, and the inadequacies of absolutism and divine right alone. A king, he realises, must be so much more than a symbol or a ceremony:

> Thus play I in one person many people,
> And none contented. Sometimes am I king,
> Then treasons make me wish myself a beggar,
> And so am I. Then crushing penury
> Persuades me I was better when a king;
> Then I am king'd again, and by and by
> Think that I am unking'd by Bolingbroke,
> And straight am nothing.[190]

In a final act of self-assertion and understanding, Richard refuses to meekly take the poison, and with previously undisplayed vigour attempts to defend himself against his murderers.[191]

Although Richard and Bolingbroke, and the interaction between them, provides the heart of the play, three other characters play important supporting roles. The first of these is the Bishop of Carlisle, who consistently articulates the theory of divine right, even when Richard himself comes to doubt it. Carlisle is thus the mouthpiece of providentialism, advising Richard, 'Fear not, my lord. That Power that made you king / Hath power to keep you king in spite of all.'[192] It is he, alone, who defends Richard's position in the deposition scene.[193] It is noteworthy that, as in *John* especially, the representatives of the church appear to be particularly subversive characters, and particularly duplicitous ones. It is the Abbot of Westminster, along with Carlisle and Aumerle, who hatches a plot to oust Bolingbroke. Men of the church should not be entrusted with affairs of state, or given the opportunity to meddle.[194] The two other characters both represent the old order, and are essentially Shakespeare's inventions.[195] The first of these is Gaunt, who consistently articulates the medieval providential approach to kingship. He thus refuses to act against 'God's substitute', even though he knows him to be responsible for Gloucester's death. It is for heaven to effect 'revenge'.[196] Providence, however, can no longer be relied upon. The failure to act actually serves to condemn Gaunt, who appreciates Richard's incapabilities, and the threat which he thus poses to his own realm, but steadfastly refuses to act. Most famously, of course, there is Gaunt's speech in 2.1, where the image of England is invoked as

> This royal throne of kings, this scept'red isle,
> This earth of majesty, this seat of Mars,
> This other Eden, demi-paradise,
> This fortress built by Nature for herself...

This Eden has now been compromised by Richard's continental, and thus of course absolutist, ambitions, so that now

> This land of such dear souls, this dear dear land,
> Dear for her reputation throughout the world,
> Is now leas'd out – I die pronouncing it –
> Like to a tenement or pelting farm
>   ...
> That England that was wont to conquer others,
> Hath made a shameful conquest of itself.[197]

No one appreciates the fate of the old, and the old order, better than Gaunt himself. Gaunt dies, and with him dies the culture of medievalism, bled dry by Richard.[198]

Gaunt's role is, however, taken up by other characters of the old order, including Northumberland, who ferments rebellion in his desire to throw off the 'slavish yoke' which Richard has introduced, and by York, whom Richard entrusts with government of the realm whilst he is in Wales, and who in constrast to Northumberland, agonises over the question of obedience.[199] York's is the classic dilemma:

If I know how or which way to order these affairs,
Thus thrust disorderly into my hands,
Never believe me. Both are my kinsmen:
Th'one is my sovereign, whom both my oath
And duty bids defend; th'other again
Is my kinsman, whom the king hath wrong'd
Whom conscience and my kindred bids me to right.[200]

The dilemma is reinforced in the following scene when Bolingbroke again forces York to acknowledge his right.[201] York, indeed, emerges as a key figure constitutionally, because it is his character which serves to describe the changing role of the obedient subject.[202] Prior to deposition York, like Gaunt, had obeyed the anointed monarch. Such a monarch might be wholly inadequate, like Richard, but, despite constant misgivings, ultimately there was no question with regard to disobedience. Thus, despite acknowledging the wrong done to Bolingbroke, York warns both him and his supporters that they are 'rebels all' if they attempt to force justice upon the king.[203] York switches his allegiance only when Richard conveys his intention to abdicate; until then, he determines to remain 'neuter', and refuses to lift a hand against his king.[204] Despite his acknowledgement that it is not providence but power which has effected Richard's deposition, York becomes Bolingbroke's most dutiful subject to the extent that he is prepared to reveal his own son's involvement in fermenting rebellion.[205] York is the ideal Hobbesian subject, content to serve whoever is monarch without regard for their achievement of that position, and equally regardless of their capabilities. Rebellion, against either Richard or Bolingbroke, is not to be contemplated.

The story of the performance of *Richard II* on the eve of Essex's rebellion is now familiar. According to Lambarde's account, the Earl of Essex requested that Shakespeare's players should put on a performance of the play at a fee of 40 shillings. Subsequently hearing of the event, Queen Elizabeth is reported to have said: 'I am Richard II. Know ye not that?'[206] But was Shakespeare really a subversive and dangerous constitutional thinker? The ever-sensitive Elizabethan authorities thought not, and decided not to take action. Indeed, there is no real evidence that they even contemplated doing so.[207] Having said that, it is a fact that the deposition scene was cut, either by the censors or by Shakespeare, from the 1597 and 1598 quartos.[208] Is it that the written word mattered more than the performance?[209] Certainly, both Elizabeth and an Elizabethan audience would have appreciated that *Richard II* was a play with a 'political' message.[210] But it was also a piece of tragic drama. The extent to which the constitutional debate would have fermented or effected civil unrest must remain doubtful. The inconsistencies of the play's treatment by the authorities probably simply reflect the inconsistencies of confidence which characterised government during the 1590s. This should not detract, however, from the importance of *Richard II* in helping us to access Shakespeare's understanding of matters constitutional. In this it remains, by a considerable margin, his most important play. It is also his clearest statement. By the end of *Richard II* it is quite clear that Shakespeare has committed himself to a thoroughly anti-absolutist stance in constitutional thinking. Absolutism represents the past, the medieval world of Gaunt. The new world is that represented by Bolingbroke.[211] This does not, of course, necessarily make Shakespeare a subversive thinker, although it does confirm his increasing uncertainty with regard to certain of the fundamental tenets of earlier quasi-absolutist Tudor thought, most obviously providence and divine right.[212] Neither does his more ambiguous portrayal of providentialism necessarily make him ungodly. What it does reveal is Shakespeare's growing sympathy with a position more akin to that taken by the English humanists, and to the type of mixed monarchy to which Queen Elizabeth herself subscribed; absolute to a degree, but subject to the common law of the realm, and limited by the common law determination of kingship. It is Bolingbroke who rules in accordance with Parliament, who exercises the prerogative propitiously, and determines to subject himself to the law of the realm. It is this which, as Holderness notes, makes Bolingbroke's victory one against constitutional innovation, and marks the 'return' to pre-Tudor. mixed monarchy.[213] Shakespeare's 'constitution', at least that presented by the close of *Richard II,* was certainly not subversive. Though not thoroughly providential, or absolutist in the strict continental or Ricardian sense, it was entirely orthodox in that it remained unquestioningly godly and monarchial. Shakespeare's 'constitution' reflected the evolving redefinition of constitutionalism in the England of the 1590s. As we noted earlier the redetermination of mixed monarchy, and the accommodations with absolutist themes, such as divine right, was a tortuous task, which took decades, and two seventeenth-century rebellions, to work through. The fact that its thematic evolution proved, at times, to be difficult in Shakespeare's histories, and that doubts and dilemmas clearly remained, only serves to reinforce the impression that Shakespeare shared, and articulated, many of the uncertainties of his time.

CHAPTER 5

Children's literature and legal ideology

The literature which we read as children is the most influential and important that we ever encounter. In this chapter I want to examine the extent to which children's literature is jurisprudence. W.H. Auden suggested that with regard to children's literature there are essentially two questions: 'what insight do they provide as to how the world appears to a child?; and, to what extent is the world really like that?'[1] Auden's questions will serve as our guide in this chapter.

CHILDREN'S LITERATURE AND IDEOLOGY

As with the law and literature movement, academic study of children's literature is very much an emerging discipline.[2] Indeed, much of the debate surrounds the issue of whether children's literature can or should try to establish itself as a discrete discipline. As children's literature has striven to establish itself from the middle of the nineteenth century, there has been a particular anxiety in stressing its differentness, as a counter to its often alleged inferiority as an academic discipline.[3] The perceived 'simplicity' of language and 'triviality' of subject-matter in children's literature has encouraged its dismissal without the full appreciation of the relativity of a child audience. Although one of the great strengths of children's literature is its inter-disciplinary nature, in the past regrettably this strength has only added to its dismissal.[4] It is its inter-disciplinary nature which makes children's literature a particularly appropriate subject for law and literature study, and it is the affective importance of children's literature which surely elevates the subject from the desirable to the necessary. Everyone has read *The Tale of Peter Rabbit*. Not everyone has read *The Metaphysics of Morals*. The problem of differentness is, of course, at once the problem of definition. What precisely is children's literature? It is not an easy determination, in part because of the inherent instability of defining what 'children' are.[5] The demise of authorial intent has militated against a determination on the grounds of what the writers of children's books might have thought. The inadequacy of determining children's literature from the text itself has also been often and forcefully asserted. According to Felicity Hughes, for example, a concentration on the subject-matter of children's literature encourages a 'realist' intellectual 'prejudice against fantasy'.[6] Style is a more viable possibility. Nicholas Tucker has supported this position, suggesting that '[i]f a writer is aiming at a young audience he must of necessity restrict himself in certain areas of experience and vocabulary'.[7] A number of critics have agreed that children's literature is indeed 'recognisable' by its style of language and presentation.[8] But whether that is sufficient as a means of substantive definition is more doubtful. Aidan Chambers has gone an important step further. Using Wolfgang Iser's 'doctrine of the implied reader' around the idea of the author's 'use' of style in addressing particular readers, Chambers has orientated the investigation towards the particular nature of the reading audience.[9]

The common position now is to determine children's literature by its audience, and by audience use. According to Peter Hunt, children's literature 'uniquely' defines itself in terms of its audience.[10] Thus 'classic' children's texts are defined less as classic because of their being 'better' than other texts, but because they are more 'useful'. Such a definition, in its concentration on the 'use' of the text by the audience is, of course, a very pragmatic one, and, as we saw in chapter 2, is immediately reminiscent of the position taken, for example, by Foucault and Eco.[11] Moreover, by determining itself in relation to audience use, children's literature presents itself once more as a particularly appropriate subject for law and literature. At the same time as stressing the differentness of children's literature, it is important also to recognise that many of the positions taken in literary and critical theory also apply, and it is the extent to which the various positions apply that is the distinguishing factor. Unsurprisingly, given its tendency to determine itself in relation to its audience, theories of the reader-response type have been popular in children's literature criticism. In addition to Wolfgang Iser and the implied reader, Roland Barthes and the idea of a specific linguistic 'code' in

children's literature has enjoyed considerable support. Lissa Paul
has tried to advance a semiotics of children's literature. Peter Hunt
has referred to 'oral discourse markers' which are used as 'signifiers'
in children's literature. As well as the advance of semiotics there is
also, equally unsurprisingly, the inevitable sprinkling of deconstructionism amongst critical essays. Iser and Barthes have been joined
by Culler and Derrida.[12] The use of such high-and-mighty figures of
literary theory in children's literature criticism has generated something of anti-intellectual backlash. This determination to avoid
over-intellectualising is of course paradoxical, given the long and
strenuous attempts to assert children's literature as an academic discipline. In recent years, the 'problem' of over-intellectualism has
risen to the fore across literature studies as a whole.[13] More than a
century ago writers such as Dickens, Ruskin and Chesterton were
warning of precisely the same dangers, and most particularly of the
advances of the moralising intellectual.[14] As recently as 1988 Peter
Hollindale has made many of the same points, suggesting that any
attempt to intellectualise children's literature is often simply the
attempt to replace one ideology with another.[15]

Intellectualism is not, then, a means of establishing legitimacy.
However, it is suggested that the critical-ideological approach,
though it should not be overplayed, has force. By using Iser and
Barthes, and Culler and Derrida, children's literature critics are
unavoidably joining a critical position which suggests that words
are power. Peter Hunt has suggested that the linguistic style of C.S.
Lewis's writings present 'an example of the covert "control" of the
audience so common in children's books'.[16] For Hunt, children's
literature presents a 'very obvious power relationship between
writer and reader'.[17] Lissa Paul has stressed the similarities between
children's literature and feminism, in that the two share the experience of exclusion through 'closed' texts. Both are gender conditioned, and present an aura of subservience to dominant male
adult figures.[18] In a similar vein, Hollindale has suggested that we
must accept the presence of ideology and 'fragmentation' in any
children's literature. Like Eagleton, Hunt and Paul, Hollindale
recognises that words present power, and moreover that the child
audience is a particulary receptive and impressionable one.
According to Hollindale, there is an implicit, which he terms 'passive', ideology in all children's literature. At the same time,
however, he also stresses the 'constraints' upon ideology,

represented by the need to write within specific contexts which the child can understand. For Hollindale it is not, then, a matter of recapturing children's literature for the cause of democracy, but more a matter of recognising the presence of ideology rather than trying to either constrain or promote it – the reason being, of course, that the two alternatives are essentially the same.[19] Once the inevitability of this 'fragmentation' is appreciated, children's texts can at the same time both subjugate and liberate.[20] This 'fragmentation' is very much fragmentation between not only text and audience, but between texts and between audiences. The idea that there can be a 'double vision' in children's texts, between what the child gets from the text, and what the more politically aware adult gets, has been forcefully suggested by a number of children's literature critics, including Hunt, Paul and Townsend.[21] It is of course a central one for us, as adults, attempting to understand and assess the significance of children's literature, both for ourselves and for children. The inevitability of this 'fragmentation' has been rearticulated by Mitzi Myers in her appeal for a New Historicism.[22] Following the work of Ricoeur, Clifford Geertz and particularly John Thompson, Tony Watkins has advocated the use of a 'depth hermeneutical framework' for a New Historicist model. This would stress the historicity of language, the characterisation of society as an expression of power struggles, the socio-cultural nature of the subjective, the nature of reading as a communicative discourse and above all the centrality of ideology in all children's texts. The child's identity, Watkins suggests, is determined by a narrative and communicative experience:

Stories contribute to the formation and re-formation in our children of the cultural imagination, a network ... of patterns and templates through which we articulate our experience. So the stories we tell our children, the narratives we give them to make sense of cultural experience, constitute a kind of mapping, maps of meaning that enable our children to make sense of the world. They contribute to children's sense of identity, an identity that is simultaneously personal and social: narratives, we might say, shape the way children find a 'home' in the world.[23]

LITERATURE AND PSYCHOLOGY

Having suggested the appropriateness of an interdisciplinary approach to literature and politics, which is already familiar in legal studies, I now want to suggest another interdisciplinary approach, which may be less familiar to lawyers, that of literature and psychology. The interdisciplinary association of literature with psychology is more familiar within literary circles. Reader-response theory demands the association. Terry Eagleton has made much of the influence of Freud and then Lacan on the development of critical literary theory, stressing particularly Lacan's assertion that children's literature in particular is a charting of children moving 'from one signifier to another, along a linguistic chain which is potentially infinite'. For Lacan this chain is geared by the child's 'desire' to establish itself 'within the symbolic order'. According to Freud and Lacan it is a desire generated by the child's 'severance' from the Oedipal tie.[24] The psychological interpretation of literature is now established alongside the socio-historical.[25] The latter is perhaps more familiar to legal theorists, stated famously in Marcuse's *Eros and Civilization*, and much more recently in Roberto Unger's *Passion: An Essay on Personality*. Like Marcuse, Unger suggested that psychological development is geared to social and above all to literary experience. The 'reconstitutive vision' that Unger presents will be established by a 'communicative ethics', and determined as a 'psychology of empowerment'. For Unger the key to solving the problem of the human condition lies in the association of politics, ethics and literature with a revitalised social psychology.[26]

Given the stress in children's literature on the role of the reader, it is perhaps no surprise that psychology should emerge to play a significant role in children's literature criticism. The most important work to date in this field has been presented by Nicholas Tucker with his application of Jean Piaget's theories of child psychology to children's responses to texts.[27] According to Piaget, if we want to access the cognitive and moral development of the adult, we can do so only by looking at the experience of the child.[28] Most famously in *The Moral Judgment of the Child*, and mainly using empirical evidence drawn from an investigation into how groups of children establish the rules of games, Piaget charted the evolution of children's ability to form moral judgements. Morality, for Piaget, was a system of rules.[29] Piaget was convinced that children developed experientially. Moreover, children are constantly trying to make sense of what is going on around them, and although literature itself is only a constituent of life experience, as a constituent it is potentially of the greatest importance.[30] In their first formative years, between birth and around the age of 7, Piaget suggested that children are almost solely subject to parental influence, and as a group have no unified comprehension of rules. It is only between the years of 7 and around 10 that children develop the need for common understanding of rules to which they are subject; although, at this stage, such rules are still 'regarded as sacred and untouchable, emanating from adults and lasting forever'.[31] At this point children have no sense of possessing rules. They are merely passive receptacles for them.[32] Similarly, for many children justice is immanent within nature. It is not a matter of social or individual responsibility: justice just happens.[33] From around the age of 10 children begin to reveal an evaluative capacity, and it is only then, between the ages of 10 and 14, that they show any concern for principles such as equality or fairness.

According to Piaget, there were then 'three great periods in the development of the sense of justice in the child'. The first, up until the age of around 7, during which 'justice is subordinated to adult authority'; the second, between 8 and 11, when there is a crude sense of 'progressive equalitarianism'; finally, the third period, from around 11, when a more mature sense of justice as fairness and equality 'sets in'.[34] This evolution in the child's capacity to form moral judgements is in part due to the gradual loosening of parental ties and in part to the corresponding influence of social bonding. The obligation to the parent is gradually subverted by an obligation to society.[35] At the same time, this conception of obligation becomes disturbed by the contradictions and contingencies inherent in life experience. Whereas the child aged from 3 to 11 still treasures the neat and ordered existence which the family unit can provide, the more mature child becomes increasingly influenced by the less stable environment of society. Along with an appreciation of the distinction between rules and principles, inevitably this brings with it an understanding of responsibility.[36] Most importantly, children begin to assert their wish to change rules, and are prepared to exert power to do so. In their desire to ascertain the situation of power, they begin to recognise a concept of 'sovereignty', and then a countervailing idea of 'democracy'.[37] They also begin to evaluate the responsibilities of others. From an initial belief in objective responsibility, the more mature child begins to develop a sense of subjective responsibility. Rather than assessing an action alone, the child begins to assess the moral culpability of the perpetrator of acts.[38]

This evolution in children's understanding of political conceptions and the nature of morality has been reaffirmed more recently by Joseph Adelson in his empirical research on the political understanding of young adolescents. Adelman, like Piaget, charted a development in political awareness, geared by the transferal of interest from parent to society, which intensified between the years 12 and 16.[39] Ultimately Piaget asserted that the child's conception of justice was determined, not mainly by the parent, nor even by other adults, but primarily by his or her association with other children, and with alternative forms of education. These associations, of course, could be both in reality or, indeed, in fiction. The potency of this particular assertion is underlined by the fact that children, often until a relatively late age, do not display an immediate capability to distinguish reality from fantasy.[40] Indeed, according to Sarah Gilead, the adult experience of literature is often characterised by the 'ability' to blur the fantasy–reality distinction.[41]

Tucker has broadly adopted Piaget's three-stage evolution of the child's understanding of ethical and moral issues and applied them to children's literature. The child's experience of literature is, according to Tucker, a complementary drift from an acceptance, indeed yearning, for moral absolutes and neatly structured texts towards a more open-ended and inquisitive approach. In essence, very much in response to his or her increasing association within society, the child becomes critical of literature. So, for example, as the child grows older it becomes more capable of handling and assimilating unhappy endings to stories, and less reliant on strong, unambiguous statements of responsibility reflected in happy endings and neat 'closures'.[42] Up until around the age of 3 children simply recognise, rather than cognise. From then until around 7 years the child becomes ever more capable of understanding cause and effect, and becomes capable of understanding stories sequentially. Children's literature used by children between these ages, and Tucker specifically uses Beatrix Potter as exemplary, tends to be suitably structured: basic storylines, simple moral absolutes boldly stated, with neat and, on the surface at any rate, 'happy' endings.[43] At this stage, children's literature is characterised by the assumption that readers cannot consistently distinguish reality from fantasy. The literature thus consciously collapses it. As early as the fourteenth century Chaucer, like Beatrix Potter was to do, interwove animals and humans in stories without any attempt to delineate closely the roles played by each. Children thus perceive little practical distinction between the two. As such, morality remains firmly an external force, often a magical one, and certainly not one which the child itself can exercise. Both Freud and Jung have suggested that the child's pre-occupation with fantasy during this period reflects its capacity to develop both sides of its personality, the good and the evil. Whether this is so, or whether, as C.S. Lewis suggested, this was a classic example of over-intellectual hogwash, is a matter for conjecture. Tucker reserves judgement.[44]

Between the ages of 7 and 11 Tucker suggests that children and children's literature undergo an important change. The much-savoured order of the earlier literature is disturbed. Texts portray children as exercising independence and as capable of making moral judgements. This is interesting becauses this literature implies that the child's individual capabilities develop a stage earlier than was suggested by Piaget. Piaget recognised that children of this age were perhaps capable of making such judgements, but refrained from doing so because they were not yet sufficiently subject to the experiential forces of society. At this age, according to Piaget, although the child was becoming aware of a crude sense of equality and fairness, it was still prepared to accept moral absolutes from parents, with little question. According to Tucker, Lewis Carroll and Enid Blyton offer particularly acute examples of children 'going it' alone, and more often than not using their own ingenuity to defeat adults. Tucker even goes so far as to suggest that the period between ages 7 and 11 is represented in literature as one of 'social iconoclasm'. Part of the explanation, he suggests, lies in the gradual awakening of the child to his or her sexuality. But a part lies also in the increasing seriousness with which the child is reading its literature. The 'morals' that stories represent at this stage in the child's cognitive development are still more real than fictional.[45] The final stage that Tucker delineates is between the ages of 11 and 14. By this time children are capable of thinking in the abstract and, in line with Piaget, Tucker suggests they are also capable of making subjective moral judgements. Children are no longer satisfied by the cosy structures of earlier literature, and desire something that is different and challenging. Rather than just accepting good and evil, they begin to ask why certain people are good or evil, so the literature for these ages and beyond is laced with moral dilemmas, and situates these dilemmas in realistic conditions. Happy endings are no longer guaranteed. As Piaget had noted, during these crucial formative years children are themselves confused and uncertain about how to use their mature cognitive capabilities. The literature they read is suitably confused and confusing. Frequently, novels portray the danger of lawless societies, devoid of normative structures. Rudyard Kipling's *Jungle Books* and William Golding's *The Lord of the Flies*, both of which will be considered shortly, offer striking examples of this danger and confusion.[46] Children between the ages of 11 and 14 are particularly unsettled and particularly impressionable, and more than ever they are searching for a stability that they can cling to. Much of the literature that they read exacerbates these uncertainties, stresses the dangers and in the relative virtues of law and order suggests the stability that is sought.

SOME TEXTS

In this section I am going to adopt a working distinction between two sets of authors, whose writings might be termed 'pre-adolescent' and 'adolescent'. This follows the divisions used by Tucker that are taken originally from Piaget. 'Pre-adolescent' encompasses those texts read by children between the ages of 3 to 11, and 'adolescent', those read by children of 11 to 14 years and beyond. It is not merely a distinction of convenience (although it is that as well). As we have just seen, Piaget's research in particular stressed a very real alteration in a child's pyschological condition as he/she moves from the 'pre-adolescent' to the 'adolescent', and so those scholars like Tucker who have applied psychological analysis to literature studies have tended to stress a complementary shift in the child's ability to comprehend literature. At the same time as following Tucker's and Piaget's substantive distinction in the categorisation of children's literature into pre-adolescent or adolescent, it is perhaps important to take note of the guidelines of the National Curriculum Council, not because they may be inherently right or wrong, but because essentially these are the guidelines which will be followed in schools and in the education of children in the UK. The pre-adolescent texts which will be considered are

Beatrix Potter's tales (the texts of which are not actually in the NCC guidelines), *Alice's Adventures in Wonderland* and Kipling's *Jungle Books*. The adolescent texts are Golding's *The Lord of the Flies*, Twain's *The Adventures of Huckleberry Finn* and Swift's *Gulliver's Travels*. Clearly this is only a selection of children's literature and certainly makes no claim to be comprehensive, or indeed perhaps even representative; but it might, at least, be suggestive.

PRE-ADOLESCENT TEXTS

The tales of Beatrix Potter

It is reasonable to assume that there are very few children (or indeed adults) who are not familiar with at least some of the tales of Beatrix Potter. In one sense, then, it is potentially a most influential jurisprudential text. It is also, undeniably, children's literature. Furthermore, according to Roger Lancelyn Green, Potter was 'the only writer for very small children to produce works of real literature which adults can still enjoy'.[47] Tucker has used the tales as the exemplification of literature for children aged under 7. He particularly notes Potter's careful use of language, and equally careful use of illustration. For children of this age the illustration is very often as important, if not more so, than the text. The particular care that is required in constructing a piece of literature for younger children requires, as Tucker suggests, far greater literary skill than that which is ever likely to go into a jurisprudential text (or indeed an academic essay).[48] The audience direction has to be infinitely more exact. Potter's storylines themselves are precisely what the psychology of the child aged 3 to 7 would require. There are no tragedies, but plenty of adventure and danger, lots of near-escapes, lots of happy endings. Above all there is a concurrent sense of both order and disorder in the world; the ordered adult world and the potentially disordered world of the younger animals, with which the child can identify. When a young animal misbehaves and leaves the ordered security of the adult world, there is an immediate sense of danger. Just as Potter uses a particular language to describe this change in circumstance, so the illustrations change. In the ordered world the animal is always dressed in human garb, but when in danger the animal looks precisely like an animal and will often move like one, on four legs rather than two.

The existence of these two worlds, and the movement between them, is the fulcrum in Potter's tales.[49]

The Tale of Peter Rabbit, the first of Potter's tales, is also perhaps the most famous. It is also probably the first jurisprudential text that a young child will ever encounter. In this tale, Potter immediately determines two worlds: the safe world where Peter lives with his Mother 'in a sand-bank, underneath the root of a very big fir-tree', and the dangerous world of Mr McGregor's garden, where Peter's father 'had an accident' and 'was put in a pie by Mrs McGregor'. With his Mother's warning ringing in his ears Peter, wearing his coat, trots off, on two legs, to commit trespass to property and criminal theft. Potter does not of course use this language, but she describes it in a language, and with pictures, that a child of less than 7 years can understand. Peter, 'who was very naughty', 'squeezed under the gate', and promptly started to eat Mr McGregor's vegetables. The use of the word 'squeeze', and the picture of Peter 'squeezing' under the gate, very effectively portrays the act of going surreptitiously into someone else's property, and moreover, somewhere where small rabbits should not go. The description of Peter's ensuing misery when first chased by Mr McGregor, and then when trapped in the gooseberry net, hiding in a watering can and then scurrying back under the gate, can be almost too harrowing for the young child.[50] Potter was, by her own admission, most deliberate in her construction of the conclusion to a tale. In *Peter Rabbit*, the tale concludes with Peter losing his coat, which is used by Mr McGregor for a scarecrow, and although restored to the sanctuary of the adult world Peter 'was not very well during the evening' and so, unlike his sisters, has to go to bed and suffer a 'dose' of 'camomile tea'. The 'moral' of the tale is clear: if you enter other peoples' property, and you take things, then you are removed from the familiar adult world, and placed in a more dangerous one. Trespass and theft are offences that should not be committed, either by small rabbits or by small children.[51]

Trespass and theft are the recurring 'offences' in Potter's tales. Whenever either is committed there is immediate danger and frequently much anguish before the ultimate return to the adult world. Often, as in *The Tale of Benjamin Bunny*, it is an adult figure which comes to the rescue. In *Benjamin Bunny*, Benjamin makes precisely the same mistake as Peter in entering Mr McGregor's garden. This time Peter, who falls into the garden, along with

Benjamin, 'did not seem to be enjoying himself' in the garden, did not eat anything, and informed Benjamin that he really wanted 'to go home'. Once again, their intrusion results in distress, with both Peter and Benjamin trapped for 'five hours' in a basket in the 'dark', which made them both 'cry'. When finally rescued by Mr Bunny, Benjamin was duly chastised, 'taken by the ears ... and whipped ... with the little switch'.[52] The rabbit tales, because they tend to revolve around the same 'offences' of trespass and theft, present themselves repeatedly as moral and jurisprudential tales. *The Story of a Fierce Bad Rabbit* presents the simple tale of a bad rabbit being punished for stealing a carrot from another rabbit and then eating it.[53] The Flopsy Bunnies are made famously 'soporific' by eating the lettuce that they steal when entering Mr McGregor's garden. Once more the young rabbits are saved by their parents, but not before witnessing Mr and Mrs McGregor discussing what they do with the rabbits that they catch.[54] These misfortunes are not, of course, reserved to rabbits. Samuel Whiskers, who also goes where he should not have done, suffers a similar fate and as a result for the rest of his life remains scared of rats.[55] *The Tale of Two Bad Mice* is similar, with the two mice entering the dolls-house, behaving naughtily and committing criminal damage. In the end, though, 'they were not so very very naughty after all, because Tom Thumb paid for everything he broke ... And very early every morning – before anybody is awake – Hunca Munca comes with her dust-pan and her broom to sweep the Dollies' house!'[56] Finally, and by way of a sharp contrast, a rather different and certainly more complex tale is *The Tale of Ginger and Pickles*. The story of the cat and the terrier, who go broke because they try to run a shop without ever being paid, says precisely what the law and economics movement has been suggesting for two decades, and is as jurisprudential a tale as Posner's *Economic Analysis of Law*, though certainly more fun to read and, some might suggest, truer to life.[57]

Alice's adventures

Alongside Potter's tales, probably the most immediately identifiable pieces of children's literature were written by Lewis Carroll. *Alice's Adventures in Wonderland* and *Through the Looking Glass*, as well as *The Hunting of the Snark*, contain passages of particular jurisprudential interest. As far as it is possible to categorise children's literature,

Carroll's writings are for children of the 7 to 11 age group. Certainly they bear many of the characteristics that Piaget or Tucker associate with this genre of literature – the self-assertive child, social iconoclasm, the use of nonsense and playing with words – and it is the extent to which Carroll offers these ingredients that has identified his writings as children's literature *par excellence*.[58] Moreover, such is the subtlety of Carroll's writings that, perhaps unlike Potter's tales, in using them we must begin to recognise the presence of two distinct audiences, and employ what is now familiarly received in the interpretation of texts as 'double vision'. On reading Carroll the child and the adult can gain, potentially, radically different understandings. The adult, for example, will be able to ignore the seemingly infantile emotions displayed not only by various animals, but also by the 'adult' figures, such as the Queen of Hearts. A child, on the other hand, may find these emotions deeply unsettling. Gone, certainly, is the secure adult world that Potter portrayed.[59] The ultimate security is provided in the Alice stories by 'framing' the text; by placing the events within a dream and restoring Alice to her 'normal' world. As such it is a mechanism for the child which at once can provide both escapism and a secured return to reality. Yet, for adults Carroll's use of dreams has proved to be a particularly rich source of fascination, and it may be that Carroll himself was well aware that ultimately he was trying to address two audiences, yet at the same time, perhaps, was also trying to collapse the distinction.[60]

In *Adventures in Wonderland* the most immediately relevant passages are the 'Trial of the Jack of Hearts' and 'Alice's Evidence'. Some commentators, like Kathleen Blake, have particularly stressed these passages because in them they perceive Alice to be finally overcoming her obedience to the fantasy of the adventures. In the trial scene Alice invokes the need and importance of rules, and thus banishes the disturbing anarchy and nonsense of the earlier passages. The scenes represent Alice's triumph.[61] She is not afraid to tell the jurors that they are 'stupid things' because they fear that they may forget their names. She snatches away a squeaky pencil and thus leaves Bill the Lizard to continue writing without leaving a mark. Alice's rebelliousness reaches its peak when she is called to give evidence and refuses to leave the court for an infringement of 'Rule Forty-Two'; 'All persons more than a mile high to leave the court.' She refuses to go for three reasons

(i) because she is not a mile high, and so the rule does not apply to her, (ii) because it is an arbitrary rule, and not created in accordance with any norm, and so cannot be binding, and (iii) 'I shan't go, at any rate.' Moreover, rather than just leaving the scene Alice determines to destroy it. She declares the whole proceedings and evidence to be meaningless, and when the Red Queen suggests that the sentence should precede the verdict, declares 'Stuff and Nonsense', refuses to hold her tongue when ordered, and, when the Queen 'turning purple', orders 'Off with her head!', Alice retaliates, 'Who cares for you?' 'You're nothing but a pack of cards!'[62] The dream ends with Alice's ultimate act of self-assertion.

Apart from the use of a trial scene to facilitate Alice's self-assertion, and to enable the restoration of right reason over nonsense and rules over anarchy, Carroll also presents a number of satires and metaphors that can appeal to a more informed audience. Indeed, the uncertainty and inconsistency of the entire proceedings has led some to compare the Trial of the Jack of Hearts to Kafka's *The Trial*.[63] The opening lines to the trial immediately stress the pomposity of the occasion: the judge's wig, the length of the trial, the fact that the King is also the judge and above all the ineptitude of both judge and jury.[64] Many of these satires are repeated elsewhere in both *Alice* and in other writings. The length of legal actions was of course notorious in the nineteenth century. Carroll, who had read Dickens's *Bleak House* and *The Pickwick Papers*, used this particular satire on a number of occasions earlier in *Alice*, in Father William's nonsense and perhaps most explicitly in the Barrister's Dream in *The Hunting of the Snark*.[65] Not only does the Dream satirise the length and officiousness of legal action, echoing the Trial of the Jack of Hearts, but at the same time it stresses the insular nature of the law, where judge, jury and lawyers are as one. Again there is the satire of the pompous bewigged judge, the incompetent jury and the nonsense of legal jargon. The ultimate nonsense of the final three verses of the Dream, when it is discovered that the convicted pig 'had been dead for some years', bears a striking resemblance to the final passages of *Bleak House*.[66] The idea of the immanence of the legal persona and its implied denial of justice occurs again in the Mouse's Tale in *Adventures*.[67] The Barrister's Dream, and perhaps also the Trial of the Jack of Hearts, were more precisely satires of the infamous Tichbourne case of the mid-nineteenth century. However, in making this informed observation

we have very definitely moved into the realm of interpretive
'double-vision'.[68] Whilst the text may say one thing to children,
perhaps about the slightly ridiculous nature of an improper legal
process and the need for sensible rules, for the adult reader
Carroll's writings provide many contemporary and enduring
satires. Perhaps most subtle of all is Carroll's satirical use of legal
language. The Trial of the Jack of Hearts is very much a game of
words, from the play between the King and the Hatter on the letter T to Alice's witnessing of the 'suppression' of the audience.
Perhaps most important of all is the express importance of being a
good speaker in a legal situation; the Hatter was condemned by the
King as a 'very poor' one.[69] The symbolism of words, like the more
obvious symbolism of the chess-game, also plays a pivotal role in
Looking Glass, where the exchange between Alice and Humpty
Dumpty can be said to represent so much of the anxiety of contemporary legal discourse: '"When I use a word," Humpty
Dumpty said, in rather a scornful tone, "it means just what I
choose it to mean – neither more nor less." "The question is," said
Alice, "whether you can make words mean so many different
things."'[70]

The 'Jungle Books'

The third pre-adolescent text is Rudyard Kipling's *Jungle Books*.
The precise nature of 'Kipling's Law' has already been the subject
of academic controversy, and the alternative positions taken are
ones familiar to jurisprudence: whether Kipling present a 'Law'
that is natural or one that is positivist. Shamsul Islam suggested
that Kipling's own experiences and beliefs led him to present an
ultimately ordered, rational and immanent law of the jungle.[71] In
the *Jungle Books* this 'Law' was much more than just a juristic
expression, and represented an entire social order. Islam perceived
three sources for Kipling's 'Law': the 'moral order', the 'imperial
order', and the 'doctrine of action'. The first, the 'moral order',
was derived from the various religious influences which Kipling
encountered, the Judaeo-Christian, the Islamic and the Buddhist.[72]
At the same time, Kipling was quite convinced by the essentially
pragmatic missionary destiny of the British Empire and western
civilisation.[73] However, in philosophical terms the primacy of the
former 'order' meant that there could always be 'circumstances

under which the Law ought not to be invoked, when the breach of it represents a more profound justice'. It is this order which thus tempers Kipling's repeated insistence on the importance of obedience, which emerges as the governing concept of the second, 'imperial', order.[74] The final 'order' which Islam identifies, the 'doctrine of action', is also interesting because, for Kipling, it represented man's ultimate control of his own destiny, even inside a world which operates as a natural order.[75] In presenting this third position, Kipling presents something which is not only, as Islam suggests, particularly consonant with the Buddhist influence, but also something which to western legal theorists might be more familiar as a neo-Kantian position than as either a natural law or a positivist one. The extent of the 'controversy' over the nature of Kipling's 'Law' lies less in the dispute with regard to the possible influences upon it and more in the assessment of which law dominates in the actual texts. Whereas Islam suggests that ultimately the 'moral order' is the pervasive influence, more recent scholarship has suggested the opposite. Martin Seymour-Smith suggests that Kipling's final months in India were characterised by a disillusionment with the possibilities of natural order, brought about by the upsurge in civil unrest which he witnessed, so that when he returned to England he took with him a final, essentially negative impression of 'Law and Order' which was to remain with him. In other words, when Kipling wrote the *Jungle Books* it was the pragmatic rather than the philosophical approach to law and society which was pervasive.[76]

The Kipling 'controversy' is of course essentially an adult academic argument. The important question, at least for us, is the extent to which children appreciate it. Kipling was well aware that he was writing first and foremost literature for children, and according to Islam, one of the principal aims of the *Jungle Books* was to impress upon children the centrality of the order–anarchy dichotomy.[77] Kipling presents a world of order which has emerged from a state of lawlessness, but which is constantly threatened by another descent into disorder: the same themes, of course, as those worked by both Potter and Carroll. The most important chapter here is the first chapter of the second Book, 'How Fear Came', wherein the myth retold by Hathi is clearly a reworking of the biblical story of the Fall. The 'tale' that Hathi tells is a 'tale older than the Jungle', and returns to a paradisical state when there was food and

water aplenty, and all the animals 'walked together, having no fear
of one another'. Then evil entered the jungle, the fruits and trees
withered, the animals became hungry and began to dispute. Tha,
the 'First of the Elephants' deputed the 'First of the Tigers' to be
the 'master and judge of the Jungle'. However, when two disputing
bucks came to the Tiger for a 'settlement', the Tiger leapt on one
of the bucks and killed it. That was the first time that the animals
had encountered death, and with the Tiger having fled, 'left without a judge' they immediately 'fell to fighting among ourselves'.
Eventually Tha returned and determined that in place of rulers,
there should be a 'Law' of the Jungle to counter the 'Fear' that
they now knew.[78] If Hathi's tale describes the ultimate 'Law' of the
Jungle, as a revealed divine law, other tales in the *Books* flesh out a
series of complementary rationalised natural and positive laws.[79]
'The Law of the Jungle', presented in verse, is itself a system of
norms describing a series of positive laws. The actual verse frames
the positive laws with overriding norms:

> Now this is the Law of the Jungle – as old and as true as the
>   sky;
> And the Wolf that shall keep it may prosper, but the Wolf
>   that shall break it must die.
> As the creeper that girdles the tree-trunk the Law runneth
>   forward and back–
> For the strength of the Pack is the Wolf, and the strength of
>   the Wolf is the Pack...
> Now these are the Laws of the Jungle and many and mighty
>   are they;
> But the head and the hoof of the Law and the haunch and
>   the hump is – Obey![80]

The first three stories in Book One are particularly important
for their impression of law and justice in the Jungle. The first
tale, 'The Mowgli Brothers', immediately presents an immanent
and rational sense of order in the jungle; a 'Law' which 'never
orders anything without a reason'. This is complemented by the
laws by which the Wolves live, and which preserve them as a 'free
people'. These laws are repeatedly articulated by Akela.[81] The legal
academic can translate this into a Kantian moral order whereas a
child, perhaps, will perceive a community that constructs and
preserves itself, and functions purely because it observes certain
rules. The concept is the same, but the perception might differ.

Mowgli's conflict with Shere Khan, and his ultimate emergence as leader of the Wolf Pack, in the first and third stories, impresses very strongly the need for leadership in the Jungle; the Law needs a sovereign body to interpret and to enforce. More than that, it needs a capable, strong and just leader who will fulfil his responsibilities.[82] At the end of the first tale, Mowgli banishes Shere Khan and banishes danger, and at the same time asserts natural justice for Akela.[83] Even though Mowgli is the sovereign in the jungle, he remains bound by the law and its rational force. Kipling emphasises this in the final paragraphs of the very last Book, and again in the 'Outsong'.[84] The hierarchal nature of sovereignty in the Jungle, a concept beloved of legal positivists, is repeatedly stressed in the various tales: Rikki-Tikki-Tavi is sovereign in the garden, Kaa in the Middle Jungle and so on.[85] They are sovereign because they represent the forces of order and security against those of danger. The constant presence of danger and the need to maintain both natural and positive law recurs throughout the *Books*, most obviously perhaps in 'Kaa's Hunting', and in 'Red Dog', where the order of the Jungle is threatened by lawless forces, the bandar-log and dhole.[86] Kaa's tale contains a number of interesting statements about the nature of law and morality: Kaa's assertion that people use law for their own good, without ever bothering to understand it; the importance of law in preserving freedom and respect: the shame of lawlessness, and its danger; the demands that punishment must be meet and, as ever, the imperative of obedience.[87] The *Jungle Books* can thus provide the jurist with endless hours of academic debate, but for the child the message, as with Potter's tales, and with Carroll's Alice, is less confused. Although the stories are all clothed in a world of adventure and happy endings, fun and frolic, there is a clear order–anarchy contrast: the security of the ordered adult world and the presence of danger if this order is abandoned. The irony, of course, is that only we, as adults, find anything unclear in Kipling; because we assume that there must be so much more than is written in the text, and that the *Jungle Books* must be presenting either natural law, or positivist law or a Kantian order and so on, and we assume this because, deep down, we suppose Kipling somewhere had a preference. But for children at this pre-adolescent stage the text is not questioned. As Piaget and Tucker suggest, questioning only begins seriously as the child develops psychologically from around the age of 11 onwards, and is then reflected in more complex texts which demand the judgement and interpretive decisions of the reader. It is to this genre of literature which I now turn.

ADOLESCENT TEXTS

The demands made upon the child to take responsibility for moral judgements is one of the fundamental characteristics in adolescent literature which children encounter between the ages of 11 and 16. The treatment of law and justice becomes inextricably bound up with these demands. Furthermore, an additional twist is provided by the frequent presentation of morality issues, and issues of law and justice, in satirical form. In this section I will briefly consider three texts that are popularly associated with adolescent children, and which present both children and indeed adults with these demands.

'Huckleberry Finn'

Although texts identifiably written for children have received scant attention by law and literature scholars, a partial exception is Mark Twain's *The Adventures of Huckleberry Finn*. What has impressed these scholars is not Twain's specific treatment of issues of law and justice so much as his ability to create or delimit languages. The ability to create new discourse is a much-treasured virtue in critical legal scholarship. In his *The Legal Imagination*, James Boyd White uses *Huckleberry Finn* as an example of the type of 'constitutive text' which could be used by a community as a mechanism for the 'formation of a community's values'. As White emphasises, just as lawyers have to learn a certain legal language, so readers of *Huckleberry Finn* must learn a series of languages.[88] Most obviously, Twain presents one 'children's' language for Huck and another 'nigger' language for Jim. Although, as White suggests, the liberal conscience may struggle with the conception of a 'nigger' language, because of the symbolism which it carries, it was precisely essential for Twain to use this symbol because this one word can identify the conflation of ethical and legal issues which were encompassed by slavery. The delimited 'nigger' language impresses upon the reader, adult or child, the historicity of the text, and at the same time and perhaps most importantly the series of moral dilemmas which Huck is forced to face. The text is thus both descriptive and constructive. It describes a whole series of dilemmas, ethical and legal, and requires the reader to construct a meaning and make a judgement, as Huck himself was forced to do. As Robin West has suggested, ultimately *Huckleberry Finn* is all about 'interpretive competency'. The ability to understand different languages is the particular skill of the lawyer, and is the skill demanded by the reader of *Huckleberry Finn*. However, West is, above all, keen to emphasise that the text, like any text, will constrain the reader. In other words, although the reader may identify with Huck's moral dilemmas, he or she will only find resolution within the text, because he or she is by definition part of the 'community of the text'.[89] Any child, or indeed adult, who encounters Huck's world, and then identifies with him and his dilemmas, is already constrained by that community and that text.

When the novel presents specific legal issues Twain presents them in a specific legal language. Huck's discussion with Judge Thatcher is a discussion between someone who is comfortable with legal language, and someone who is not. Huck can only transfer his money to the Judge for 'consideration', a term that has to be explained to him.[90] A few pages later, when Judge Thatcher goes to court to contest Huck's guardianship with his father, Twain portrays a remote and distant legal system. The intrusive power of the 'new judge' in Huck's community is striking, and reinforces the impression of an almost transcendental force.[91] Yet the ability of Huck's father to use the legal system to fund his alcoholism presents a sharp counterpoint to the image of the supreme inalienable authority.[92] On either account it is useless to Huck, and offers him no recourse to justice.[93] For Jim, of course, the forces of law represent and enforce what seems, to the modern reader and seemed to Twain, to be an injustice: slavery. Yet in another skilfully presented juxtaposition, Huck's father aligns the freedom of a 'nigger' with the injustices which he perceives he has suffered. Both represent the failings of the law.[94] The law serves no one. Huck's father abuses it, and both Huck and Jim rebel against it by escaping its authority. The difference between Huck's disobedience and Peter Rabbit's is that for the former authority presented no form of security. Whereas Peter was just 'naughty', Huck, beset with ethical dilemmas, embarks upon a journey of self-discovery which will force upon him unavoidably moral decisions. In a lawless world, constantly threatened by danger, Huck has no choice but to make his own rules and to determine the moral validity of his own actions. In the initial stages he has no compunction in robbing a dead man's home, or being a party to fraud.[95] The crux is reached, of course, when Huck has to decide whether or not to return Jim, whom he terms 'my nigger', to 'its rightful' owner. Huck's decision not to do so is reached only after much agonising and indecision.[96] There is no doubt that Twain presents a conception of natural justice bounded by an ethics which lies above the positive law. Yet, as Huck realises this conception the positive law is reasserted in the person of Bell the lawyer, who investigates the fraud and brings the King and the Duke to justice.[97] Order is restored. The moral of the story is presented, and then framed by the controversial closing chapters, which can serve to focus the fact–fiction interplay of the narrative.[98]

'Lord of the Flies'

Golding's *Lord of the Flies* has remained one of the most revered texts for children. Again, it is the use of symbolism which has elevated *Lord of the Flies* into the realms of 'classic' children's literature. Whereas Twain employed the symbolism of distinct languages, in *Lord of the Flies*, as indeed in all his novels, Golding uses material symbolism. Throughout the story ethical dilemmas are constantly aligned with symbols.[99] The island, of course, is itself a symbol, and a symbol very familiar to legal theorists. It is, once again, the metaphor of the descent from the Garden or from Paradise, which has long lain at the heart of theological jurisprudence, Christian, Jewish and Islamic.[100] *Lord of the Flies*, as a piece of literature, speaks to distinct audiences. Whilst the adult academic audience might make much of the descent theme, children are more likely to be immediately impressed by the more familiar portrayal of the anarchy–order conflict which pervades the story, and the symbolism by which it is presented. The most powerful symbol that Golding deploys is the initial establishment of the conch shell as the symbol of sovereignty. It is, of course, when the conch is destroyed that the boys' existence dissolves into savagery.[101] Golding presents a much bleaker story than Twain, or, of course, than Kipling, Carroll or Potter. The putative attempts to assert law and order and the presentation of a leader trained by a concept of the rule of law are gradually eroded by the growing fear that some of the boys experience. The initial attempts do give rise to some optimism. A social hierarchy is evolved, with 'hunters', guardians of the fire, 'bigguns' and 'littluns'; a common 'schoolboy' language is shared; and there is great excitement at the possibility of instituting 'Lots of rules'.[102] However, it is not the immanent justice of the rules which attracts the children, but the collateral possibility of using rules as a pretext for punishment.[103] This, of course, is precisely the conception of justice that Piaget suggested was gradually questioned as the child matures.

At this point in the story the children are still restrained by the lingering influence of the adult world. Roger cannot bring himself to throw stones at Harry: 'Round the squatting child was the protection of parents and school and policeman and the law.' But, Golding adds ominously, Roger was 'conditioned by a civilization that knew nothing of him', and moreover that was now 'in ruins'.[104] The 'taboo' that prevents Roger from harming Harry is shattered shortly afterwards as Jack strikes Piggy – just as when, in Kipling's story of the Fall, the animals first 'tasted' death.[105] Ralph's position, and of course Piggy's, is quickly eroded as the fear grows and, with it, Jack's power. Ralph realises that the fear of 'ghosts' has banished the 'understandable and lawful world'. When he makes a last emotional plea for reason, that 'rules are the only things we've got', he is met by the unanswerable 'Bollocks to the rules!' When Piggy asks 'What's grown-ups going to say?', he is met by the equally unanswerable sound of 'hysterical laughter'.[106] The descent into anarchy and savagery is swift. Jack rules by fear, effecting sanctions and openly refusing to give reasons for punishment.[107] Ralph is hounded out, and then finally hunted down like an animal.[108] The demise of Ralph is symbolic, of course, but the ultimately tragic fate of Piggy is perhaps the most important. Golding deliberately presents an array of multi-faceted characters; characters with whom a child readership can easily identify, but which at the same time can represent aspects of any human character, child or adult. Piggy, unprepossessing and asthma-ridden, represents the ambition of reason. It is he who insists on meetings and order, on leadership and rules, and it is he who first invests the conch with its symbolic authority.[109] When he is crushed, the apparent inevitability of a rational order is crushed with him. Ralph is left to weep for his failure.[110] An adult might recognise the pathos of the human condition. A child might appreciate the tragedy of Piggy's death, and the terror of anarchy. Either way, Golding has made the same impression.

'Gulliver's Travels'

As with *Huckleberry Finn* and *Lord of the Flies*, it is the ability of *Gulliver's Travels* to speak to different audiences which has popularly elevated it to the status of classic adolescent children's literature. From its initial publication, the *Travels* was an immediate success. According to Michael Foot, it is a story which can and should be read by everyone, 'from the cabinet council to the nursery', adding as a further suggestion: 'everyone standing for political office in Dublin, the United States or London, should have a compulsory examination in *Gulliver's Travels*'.[111] Its success, according to David Nokes, lies precisely in its 'deceptive simplicity'.[112] Yet of all the texts considered in this chapter, the *Travels* makes the greatest demands upon its audience. The more advanced or complex the text the greater is the need to exercise an interpretive double vision. The subtle satirical nuances of *Gulliver's Travels* have been worked and reworked by generations of students of Swift, and even today much of the symbolism of the *Travels* remains uncertain.[113] Recent scholarship has suggested that Swift's prime ambition was precisely to determine different audiences, whilst at the same time constraining their particular interpretations of the text. Unsurprisingly, F.R. Leavis made much of identifying Swift's literary intent.[114] More recently Liz Bellamy, advocating a New Historicist approach, has suggested that the methodical symbolism that Swift wanted to employ was himself as a monarch and the audience as a fragmented polity, or 'commonwealth', of readers. Certainly Swift wanted to 'inform' his readers, and the *Travels* is very much a morality tale. But at the same time he also wanted to 'destabilise' his audiences, and this he could do precisely by encasing his satire in the fantasy of a children's adventure story, which could both liberate and constrain it. The ultimate paradox is that Swift intended to subvert the 'narrative dictatorship' which he perceived as lying in any text, including his own.[115] The thesis that Swift deliberately employed the method of children's literature, in his concentration on a language of games and play, to construct his satire, has been forcefully reasserted by John Traugott.

The Lilliputian customs of rope-dancing and 'leaping and creeping' as a method of deciding between candidates for government office emphasises not only the innate childishness of the political game but also, at a deeper level, the fact that political success will always depend upon the aspirant's ability to invoke skills learned as a child.[116]

Before embarking on an examination of some of Swift's particular uses of law and justice in the *Travels*, it is perhaps worth re-emphasising that the very fact that Swift wanted to speak to different audiences militates against too rigid an interpretation of any of the symbolism in the *Travels*, political or otherwise. David Nokes has wisely warned of the dangers of academic over-interpretation, and it is a warning that must be especially heeded in considering the *Travels* as a piece of children's literature.[117] Swift is keen to create particular languages. James Boyd White has used both *Gulliver's Travels* and Swift's *A Tale of a Tub* as examples, like *Huckleberry Finn*, of an author creating linguistic communities.[118] Apart from the use of words that can have different meanings for different audiences, Swift also uses language as a tool of satire. His own low opinion of lawyers was in part a distaste for their invoking 'a peculiar cant and jargon of their own that no other mortal can understand'.[119] Swift's use of legal 'jargon' is perhaps most explicit in Gulliver's 'Impeachment' and condemnation for breaking the law by entering the royal palace and 'pissing out' a fire. Gulliver is condemned without a hearing and 'the formal proofs required by the strict letter of the law'. The 'formal' law is as distant from Gulliver as it was from Huck, metaphorically and literally. It is also too often corrupted by the demands of politics. Swift was very much a critical legal scholar. Gulliver decides not to take a chance on a just trial, and instead flees:

I sometimes thought of standing my trial, for although I could deny the fact alleged in the several articles, yet I hoped they would admit of some extenuations. But having in my life perused many state trials, which I ever observed to terminate as the judges thought fit to direct, I durst not rely on so dangerous a decision, in so critical a juncture, and against such powerful enemies.[120]

It is this first book, the 'Voyage to Lilliput', which contains the greatest concentration of constitutional and legal satire, although there are passages in each of the other three books which have a jurisprudential perspective. The actual pissing out of the fire is thought to represent a satire on the Treaty of Utrecht, and the impeachment of Gulliver is thus a critique of the British government's position regarding Utrecht. Indeed it has been suggested that much of the first book is a satire on this Treaty, including Swift's comments on the injustice of slavery and despotism articulated by Gulliver's reasoned refusal to accede to the Emperor's demands that he should destroy the Blefescudians and reduce their country to dominion status.[121] The commentary on the Treaty of Utrecht speaks to one audience, the ethical rejection of slavery to another, and the silliness of over-ambitious governments and nonsensical laws to still another.

The tyranny of monarchical absolutism is a recurrent theme.[122] The Emperor's title is as comically ridiculous as the Emperor himself, and the Emperor's laws. The egg-breaking law will suggest the silliness of certain laws to one audience: certainly to children. To the more academic audience it represents a satire of the Test Acts. Gulliver's own reasoned conclusion that the wording of the law means that anyone can interpret it as they see fit says much to contemporary legal scholars who suggest that any piece of legislation is the subject of interpretive creation.[123] Whilst many of the Lilliputian laws appear to be individually absurd, there is certainly a pioneering intent behind Gulliver's approval of reward as well as punishment in the administration of justice, and his particular condemnation of corruption and fraud and the unnecessary complexities of law and government. Gulliver demands the rationalisation which Swift demanded in his political essays.[124] The satire of the monarchy and of government is continued in the second book, the 'Voyage to Brobdingnag'. It is as a jurisprudential as much as a legal historical satire that the second 'Voyage' is of especial interest, because Swift juxtaposes a common-sense politics with politics as a rational and positive science. In Gulliver's relation of a series of laws 'expressed in the most plain and simple terms' and which can only 'discover ... one interpretation', Swift is again satirising the language of law. The Brobdingnagian law seems to Gulliver to be thus devoid of 'skill': anyone can understand it.[125] This critique of science is continued in the third 'Voyage', wherein Gulliver voices Swift's own political ideals: the division of constitutional power and the ownership of property alone can bind the commonwealth.[126] It is in the final book, the 'Voyage to the Country of the Houyhnhnms', that Swift immerses himself most deeply in the dominant contemporary philosophical controversy; Hobbes v Locke, or nature v reason.[127] In discussing the relative virtues of reason, Swift uses the law as an immediate weapon of satire. It is worth quoting this section at length. Nowhere in English literature is there a more biting satire of the legal process, and nowhere is one presented in a manner which can better speak to any audience:

I had said, that some of our crew left their country on account of being ruined by the law; that I had already explained the meaning of the word; but he was at a loss how it should come to pass, that the law which was intended for every man's preservation, should be any man's ruin ... I said there was a society of men among us, bred up from their youth in the art of proving by words multiplied for the purpose, that white is black, and black is white, according as they are paid. To this society all the rest of the people are slaves. For example if my neighbour hath a mind to my cow, he hires a lawyer to prove that he ought to have my cow from me. I must then hire another to defend my right, it being against all rules of law that any man should be allowed to speak for himself. Now in this case, I who am the true owner lie under two great disadvantages. First, my lawyer, being practised almost from his cradle in defending falsehood, is quite out of his element when he would be an advocate for justice, which as an office unnatural, he always attempts with great awkwardness, if not with ill-will. The second disadvantage is, that my lawyer must proceed with great caution, or else he will be reprimanded by the Judges, and abhorred by his brethren, as one who lessens the practice of the law ... Now your Honour should know that these Judges are persons appointed to decide all controversies of property, as well as for trials of criminals, and picked out from the most dexterous of lawyers who have grown old or lazy ... It is a maxim among these lawyers, that whatever hath been done before, may legally be done again: and therefore they take special care to record all the decisions formerly made against common justice and the general reason of mankind. These, under the name of precedents, they produce as authorities to justify the most iniquitous opinions; and the Judges never fail to direct accordingly.

But it is perhaps the final paragraph that speaks loudest:

Here my master, interposing, said it was a pity, that creatures endowed with such prodigious abilities of mind as these lawyers, by the description I gave of them, must certainly be, were not rather encouraged to be instructors of others in wisdom and knowledge. In answer to which, I assured his Honour, that in all points out of their own trade they were usually the most ignorant and stupid generation amongst us, the most despicable in common conversation, avowed enemies to all knowledge and learning, and equally disposed to pervert the general reason of mankind in every other subject of discourse, as in that of their own profession.[128]

The English law, Gulliver's 'master' replies, is clearly fashioned by 'our gross defects in Reason'.[129] As has been suggested, there is much in the *Travels* which might be said to be as pertinent now as it was two centuries ago.[130]

SOME CONCLUSIONS

The first conclusion, and perhaps the most important, is that children's literature, in particular, addresses different audiences. It thus offers itself as a genre of literature which necessarily establishes what law and literature scholars term 'communities of language', and which in turn requires literary critics to employ interpretive 'double vision'. These characteristics make children's literature one of the most appropriate and potentially also one of the most interesting subjects of jurisprudential investigation. It becomes an exemplary exercise in the method of law and literature, and perhaps of any interpretive legal discipline. With regard to a children's audience in particular, the overriding conclusion is not surprising. Children's literature, in its portrayal of legal and jurisprudential issues, broadly follows the lines established by Piaget and Tucker. The pre-adolescent literature presents these issues in black and white terms. The good and the bad are clearly determined, the order–anarchy contrast is always sharp and there is an immanent justice present in every text. The pre-adolescent child can learn much from the literature, but, left with very little to add to the text, is called upon to make few ethical or jurisprudential judgements or decisions. As the child develops psychologically and intellectually, the literature changes. Narratives now reflect the child's distancing from the parental bond and increasing engagement with a wider society. There is a gradual awareness of social pressures and the conformity which a community constructs as rational. A children's community becomes firmly delineated from the adult, and the child becomes gradually aware of living amidst a number of potential communities. Immanent justice is replaced by an indeterminate jurisprudence which demands that the reader make decisions. Children must choose between concepts of law and justice which are more familiar to jurists as positivist, natural, Kantian or political. In other words, children must use their literary and social experience to formulate their own conceptions of law and justice. The more the text requires the self-assertion of the child, the more that child is empowered. However, the reader is of course empowered by the author, and so any empowerment is constrained by the text and the language which that text employs, because the child is placed within a community constituted by the text. This empowerment, and its constraints, must remain one of the most important conclusions to be drawn from a study of children's literature as jurisprudence. It is a literature which, like any literature, at once guides and educates, constrains and liberates.

With regard to the adult audience, the most immediate conclusion is that children's literature offers itself as a potentially rich source of jurisprudential debate. Many of the issues raised in children's literature, political and ethical, are as pertinent for an adult audience as they are for a children's. Philosophers of law can learn from *Huckleberry Finn* just as legal historians can from *Gulliver's Travels*. The texts might be unfamiliar, but the legal scholar can learn from them just as he or she can from any 'recognised' jurisprudence or legal history text. It is not the nature of the text that differs, it is the recognition. This, of course, is not a new discovery; it is very much the established law and literature position. It is, however, perhaps time to redefine and to widen this position. If the critical method demands interpretive space and identification of the text–reader relationship, this is nowhere greater than in the use of children's literature. If Kafka's *The Trial* or Camus's *The Outsider* are now established as jurisprudential texts, so should be the *Jungle Books*, *Huckleberry Finn* and *The Lord of the Flies*. As a final, and perhaps rather sobering conclusion for anyone engaged in legal education, it might be observed that before a student ever reaches law school, he or she may well have added further to their knowledge of Kipling, Twain and Golding, and encountered Shakespeare, Austen and Dickens. All three are revered figures in law and literature studies, and equally revered amongst teachers of literature in schools. Students may thus already know what Shakespeare thought of the constitution, what Dickens had to say about justice and the legal process, and what Austen thought about the position of women in a masculine legal order. In other words, long before arriving at law school to be belaboured by various worthy but impenetrable jurisprudential tomes, the student will already have learned from literature, and of course from life, what the essential questions are, and have already decided what the answers should be. Moreover, for the overwhelming majority who never engage in an immediate study of law, these early encounters with legal literature may well be the only occasion when these issues are ever seriously considered and when decisions might be reached. Only a tiny minority of the community will ever study law after the ages of around 18 or 19, but the vast majority who encounter a reasonably wide spectrum of children's literature will already have engaged in the jurisprudential debate. If legal language is, to use Foucault's phrase, a 'specialized knowledge', then literature, and especially children's literature, can serve to de-specialise it, and for that it should be treasured.

CHAPTER 6

Law, literature and feminism

We lived in the gaps between the stories.[1]

FEMINIST LITERARY CRITICISM: AN OVERVIEW

Feminist literary criticism, like law and literature, is not new, but it has in recent years emerged as one of the most active and vigorous areas of literary scholarship. Moreover, not only does it share with law and literature this same contemporary vigour, but feminist literary criticism also enjoys essentially the same ambitions: to educate and then to reveal the politics of literature. The two are inherently complementary. Over the last two decades, feminist literary criticism has taken two principal directions, first towards what is commonly referred to as the 'Anglo-American' position, which has emphasised the socio-political nature of literature, and secondly towards the 'French' position, which has concentrated on the construction of feminist texts as texts, or *écriture féminine*. According to Mary Eagleton, Anglo-American feminists perceive the socially and politically situated woman, whilst the French feminists perceive the woman as a form of writing. Thus, whilst the latter want feminist writing to unsettle, the former want women in the public arena and in the constitutional courts.[2] To some extent there is, once more, a certain congruence with law and literature. One direction has pursued the nature of language and language use, whilst another has sought to highlight the politics of language within texts. One of the most important differences, however, is that the two trends in feminist literary criticism have often appeared to vie with one another rather than to work as complementary forces. There is no essential reason for this, and indeed some of the most recent feminist literary scholarship has suggested that the immediate ambition must be to ally the two.

The majority of reviews of feminist literary criticism in recent years have tended to favour the 'French' approach, and to suggest that it appears to be in the ascendant, at least in academic circles.[3] Despite this, virtually all feminist literary critics acknowledge that the origins of the present 'renaissance' in feminist literary criticism can be identified in Kate Millett's hugely influential *Sexual Politics*, which must itself be situated at the foundation of the Anglo-American position.[4] Cora Kaplan's remains the most famous rebuttal of Millett's book, emphasising its one-dimensional approach to feminism.[5] According to Kaplan, feminist literary criticism must realise that there are a multiplicity of feminisms, and thus a multiplicity of political approaches to feminism. In making this statement Kaplan is joining a chorus of commentators who have suggested the suffocating effects of early feminism's alignment with left politics. This 'pluralist' approach was also advocated by Toril Moi. What both Moi and Kaplan suggest is that feminist literary criticism must move further towards the psychoanalytical and textual position of French feminist thinkers such as Julia Kristeva, Luce Irigaray and Hélène Cixous. Kaplan, in particular, has repeatedly attempted to direct feminism along a Lacanian road, suggesting that psychoanalysis is the medium which can link the political, the social and the literary. The exclusion of the feminist voice in literature is not just the result of history or politics, but is also the result of the psychology of sexuality. So the literature which Kaplan suggests should be specifically addressed by feminist literary critics is that which explores the suppression and potential liberation of female sexuality. Female sexuality, she suggests, is now 'centre-stage' in all feminist critical theories, literary or otherwise.[6] While Kaplan has concentrated perhaps most intensely on the incorporation of psychoanalysis and feminist theory, and most particularly Lacanian analysis, Moi has concentrated her attention on French linguistics, and has aligned herself very firmly with the semiotics of Julia Kristeva. This semiotics is itself derived from a desire to subvert the metaphysics of the Freudian analytic. Kristeva's ambition is to break through the metaphysics which she perceives as harbouring gender distinctions, in all disciplines, and in doing so to liberate the consciousness.[7] According to Moi, this ambition, which should be the ambition of all contemporary feminisms, is the ultimate 'deconstruction of sexual identity'.

At the same time as Millett was publishing her *Sexual Politics*, Maud Ellman was publishing *Thinking About Women*. According to Moi, Ellman's text represented the first deconstructionist critique of literature. Whereas Millett used a 'political anger', Ellman, better appreciating the true power of literature, used literary 'laughter'. The male text was critiqued as a political text, and not just as a political expression.[8] It is this deconstructive method which has been refined in French feminist criticism which, as Moi admits, in its strictest sense is more linguistic than literary.[9] This evolved and evolving textual and political pluralism, as advocated by Kristeva, owes its intellectual obeisance to Michel Foucault and Jacques Derrida. The realisation that metaphysical unity preserves the male order, and that any true feminism must seek to subvert this unity, was first pronounced by Foucault, and then developed in linguistics by Derrida. It is their inspiration which has convinced Luce Irigaray to present a feminist Derridean theory of textual criticism. In making this presentation Irigaray has consciously developed the initial attempts to develop a feminist poetics undertaken by Hélène Cixous, one which it was hoped would be an 'enactment of liberation' rather than a mere 'vehicle' of it.[10] The evolutionary mantle of *écriture feminine* has now passed to Julia Kristeva, who has sought to retreat further from the text to the reader. In making this move, Kristeva has not only followed Foucault and Derrida, but more immediately has followed Barthes's 'assassination of the author' in removing any semblance of authority in the text. It is this movement which, of course, subverts the particular 'value' of feminist literature as championed by the Anglo-Americans, and which is thus perceived as the most dangerous challenge to socio-political feminism. An excess of linguistic theory threatens the very ambition of critical literary praxis. It is the radical contingency of discourse, everywhere different, from text to text rather than from gender to gender, which represents the logical evolution of pluralist literary criticism. According to Kristeva, who harbours at all times the deepest distrust of textual identity, if there is to be a feminist literary identity it must be presented at the margins of theory, and must remain receptive to its own contingency.[11] To use Barthes's own metaphor, a feminist discourse must come into being between the lines, heard as a 'rustle of language'.[12]

Whilst the 'French' approach might appear, arguably, to be in the ascendant in contemporary feminist literary criticism, it is the

'Anglo-American' approach which, as will be suggested in the next section of this chapter, has perhaps the most immediate relevance to feminist critical legal scholarship. Certainly to the extent that feminist lawyers have approached law and literature it is to comment on the use of literary texts to reveal the political nature of law. It must not, however, be supposed that the Anglo-American approach is somehow exclusive of the nature of language, even if its immediate agenda has been to reveal the politics of literature. The essential difference is practical. Whereas Kristeva shies away from a strong and assertive feminist literary identity, Anglo-Americans such as Elaine Showalter are quick to emphasise the nature of an identifiably feminist literature. This literature, Showalter suggests, is always an experiential expression, and thus always an expression of politics and of history. It is this essential fact which distinguishes the Anglo-American approach to critical feminism, literary or otherwise. Where critics like Kristeva emphasise the text and deny the context, Showalter directs the critic to the context and away from the text as text.[13] In this sense the Anglo-Americans are the true inheritors of Millett's *Sexual Politics* and her uncompromising rejection of Freud. However, many Anglo-Americans have been quick to criticise Millett, most particularly Showalter, who was fiercely critical of Millett's perceived failure to present an identifiable female literature. It is the engendered binary opposition, which she thought was missing from Millett's book, and which Kristeva and Moi wish to suppress, that Showalter wants to underline.[14]

Showalter's position, or variants of it, has enjoyed considerable support amongst Anglo-American feminist critics. One of the more contentious issues is whether feminists should consider only texts written by women. Thus Myra Jehlen, whilst advocating a contextual approach, has also stressed the importance of using texts written by men.[15] Annette Kolodny, whilst agreeing that there may be an identifiable feminist literature, has similarly stressed that this identity must be made with continual comparative reference to male texts.[16] In her later work Kolodny has again acknowledged the ultimate value of a feminist literature, but, at the same time, has moved increasingly towards a pluralist position, recognising the possibility of many feminist literatures, and many varieties of feminist politics.[17] Kolodny's variant has proved increasingly popular amongst a number of Anglo-American feminists, including

Rosalind Coward and Lillian Robinson.[18] Another who has criticised the French position, whilst approving of the pluralist nature of feminist literary theory, is Gayatri Spivak. Spivak's is one of the most vigorous critiques of the excessive intellectualism of the 'French' approach to literary criticism. For Anglo-Americans, such as Showalter and Spivak, the immediate situation of the late twentieth century demands active politics, not unsettling literature. In other words, Anglo-American criticism remains aligned with the socialist feminism which was dominant during the 1970s.[19] As Spivak suggests, feminism, as its most pressing urge, must move 'outside the classroom'. Literary criticism is only the first, educative, step.[20]

As suggested earlier, the attempt to bridge the divide between the alternative political and textual approaches to feminist literary criticism has become the immediate ambition for a number of feminist critics. For Kaplan and Moi who are, as we have seen, sympathetic to the textual approach, it is the 'French' feminists who seem less inclined to perceive an irreducible difference of approach, and more inclined to suggest a common interest. Thus Kaplan has suggested, as have so many Anglo-American feminists, that feminism must guard against elitism and over-intellectualism, against the dangers of presenting itself as a reified or alien discourse and above all must present itself as a political force. Having said this, Kaplan is equally quick to assert that feminism needs literary theory, and in doing so has invoked Terry Eagleton, for example, as an authority for the necessity of an association between literary and political programmes. For the feminist, she suggests, 'the literary is always/already political in very obvious and common sense ways'. Interestingly, whilst generally approving of Eagleton's position, Kaplan's one criticism was that it was precisely the association between literature and politics which could serve to intellectualise feminism, and serve to reduce it as an educative mechanism. Concentration on the text as a text and as politics, as opposed to the politics alone, according to Kaplan, is the most effective way of making feminism 'matter'.[21] What feminism must do, according to another influential French feminist, Annie Leclerc, is to discover a new voice. This voice must be found apart from established progressive, in other words, male, politics. As Leclerc succinctly observes: 'The world is man's word. Man is the word of the world.'[22] Using an interesting, and in the context of this chapter, a particularly

pertinent metaphor, Luce Irigaray has suggested that the male voice
has 'raped' the female, violated it and taken possession of it. Thus
the linguistic critique must be merely the precursor to a multiplicity
of social and political critiques.[23] Like Kaplan, Leclerc suggests that
an authentic female voice must be accessed by a discourse of sexuality. Women, as the immediate ambition, must recapture the language of their own bodies. Again in the particular context of this
chapter, which in the second part will concentrate on rape, this is a
particularly pertinent observation. Language can be used, then, as
Leclerc vividly suggests, as a weapon against male suppression.[24]
Thus, in the final analysis, what unites both the contemporary
'French', and most 'Anglo-American' feminist positions is the realisation that the immediate role for progressive feminist politics is to
find a voice which can describe an identity. According to Kaplan,
literature has always provided the space in which a new politics can
evolve, and so it is within literature that a new feminist identity can
be nurtured.[25] Thus the two approaches are complementary, constituent components of the same essential ambitions. The extent to
which the two ambitions might be driven together has been suggested by the 'French' critic Catherine Clement. Revealing the considerable influence of Foucault's attempts to use language as a prerequisite for political action and awareness, Clement has suggested
that a feminist discourse will be 'more demonstrative and discursive,
following the most traditional method of rhetorical demonstration'.
According to Clement, the root of 'a truly democratic transmission
of knowledge' lies with 'teachers', because theirs is the first communication. Communication, and text use, is thus at the beginning of
the political process. It feeds the 'political register' with its ideas and
conceptualisations. So, she adds, '[c]lass struggle does not stop.
There is imagination, desire, creation, production of writing ... and
then somewhere else, on another level of reality, there is class struggle, and within it, women's struggle. There are missing links in all
that, which we should try to think in order to succeed in joining our
two languages.'[26]

LITERARY THEORY AND CRITICAL LEGAL FEMINISM

Despite this coincidence of interests, the approach of critical feminist lawyers to literature has proved to be somewhat less than
committed. There is certainly an awareness of the possibilities, but

as yet few feminist legal scholars have really embraced them with what might be termed real enthusiasm. One fine example is Susan Mann, whose very negative assessment of James Boyd White and his use of Jane Austen's *Emma* was geared to specifically limiting the appropriateness or use of literature in legal study. Although she is prepared to admit the value of literature as revealing the power of rhetoric, and the indeterminacy of reasoning, ultimately her praise for law and literature, by her own admission, goes little further than Richard Posner's notoriously backhanded compliments which we noted in chapter 1. This, it is submitted, is unfortunate. A number of non-legal commentators have used Jane Austen's novels to illustrate the nature of property and trust law in the eighteenth century, and most particularly the restricted rights of women.[27] However, according to Mann what White does in his analysis of Austen's novels is to present a rationally structured normative order, with which he can then compare the behaviour of various of Austen's heroines. What White also does, according to Mann, is to establish a wholly sexist normative basis, which totally ignores the 'social and economic reality' of the woman's position in eighteenth-century England.[28] White may have indeed ignored this particular reality, but that should not be a reflection on the validity of using Austen's novels to present jurisprudential statements. Another to have specifically critiqued White's work is Emily Hartigan, for whom the failure of either White or Richard Weisberg to communicate with feminist texts makes their enterprise essentially 'futile'. Moreover, as is perhaps inevitably the case for a critical legal feminist, Hartigan is also unsettled by precisely the same foundationalism which prompted Mann's critique. However, unlike Mann, Hartigan is prepared to embrace the potential of law and literature, even if she does not proceed to actually exploit it herself.[29] Another to have recognised the potential of law and literature, but who chose to present only a negative approach to text use, is Carol Sanger, whose review of two novels, *Presumed Innocent* and *The Good Mother*, recognised, at least implicitly, their potential as examples of sexist literature, but made no real effort to suggest any literature which could present a more positive feminist message.[30] The same is perhaps true of Judith Koffler, who, once again, while noting the power of language and its potential as a vehicle for feminist politics, tends to concentrate instead, rather sorrowfully, on the 'noxious vice[s]' of law and economics and legal nihilism, both of which appeared to have captured language. The fact that this capture might be reversed is held out more in blind optimism than as a genuine belief.[31]

The primary reason for this somewhat intermittent approach of critical legal feminism to law and literature is undoubtedly that the potential of the literary text is clouded by a North American feminist reaction against anything which appears to be too textual, and which does not appear at first blush to be obviously political. Precisely the same reaction as felt by 'Anglo-American' feminist literary critics. Thus Mann's critique of White is based on his overemphasis on the 'textual' as opposed to the 'social and cultural'.[32] North American critical legal feminism is very much of the active rather than the textual variety. This socio-historical, experiential approach to legal feminism has been re-emphasised recently by Jeanne Schroeder, who has suggested that the advance of literary studies, instead of emphasising the historicity of law, has masked the cultural origins of women's oppression.[33] This Critical Legal Studies type of assertion of the politics of law has been very much · the dominant force in critical legal feminism during the 1980s, perhaps encapsulated best in the uncompromisingly political writings of Catherine MacKinnon (whose specific comments on the nature of rape will be considered in the next section).[34] Critical legal feminism thus fits most comfortably with the wider political, rather than textual, movements in feminist critical theory, including, of course, 'Anglo-American' feminist literary criticism. This is perhaps to be expected. Both critical legal feminism and 'Anglo-American' feminist literary criticism share the same cultural and theoretical origins. This political nature of critical legal feminism is represented in the work of Robin West, perhaps the one scholar who has so far been able to claim a prominent position in both critical legal feminism and in law and literature. However, as we noted earlier, for West the political ambition remains the essential one, and it is not to be compromised by dwelling too long on literature as literature. It is the context of the text, not the text of the text, that must retain its privileged political interest.[35] Unsurprisingly, West's feminism emerges as distinctively political. In her influential 'Jurisprudence as Gender' West uncompromisingly championed radical political feminism over the type of 'cultural' feminism represented in the writings of Lyn Brown and Carol Gilligan, for example.[36] The reason for West's complementary and very obvious wariness of the literary text in 'Jurisprudence as Gender', as in her critiques of Posner and White, was undoubtedly the fear that the text might somehow take over the politics of critical feminism. Like so many 'Anglo-American' feminist literary critics, it is the pluralism of feminism which West is keen to assert and to strengthen in a specifically legal scenario. Pluralism will most effectively reveal the 'patriarchal hierarchies' in contemporary jurisprudence, and then provide the means by which to 'engage' in a 'reconstructive jurisprudence'.[37] In her critique of White, West stressed that we must remember 'to understand our laws not only as "texts" that embody our traditions and our cultural ideals, but also as interactive instruments of violence, violation, compassion or respect'. Literary texts have their place, but what matters is 'the production of narratives about the impact of legal norms and institutions upon the subjective lives of those whom the legal textual community excludes'.[38]

Thus, despite these efforts, or probably because of them, in a relatively recent appraisal of feminist approaches to law and literature Carolyn Heilbrun and Judith Resnik felt compelled to express their 'dismay' at the exclusion of the female voice from precisely the discipline which potentially at least offered critical legal feminism its most obvious possibilities.[39] Obviously this exclusion need not be solely the fault of legal feminists – as feminist literary critics have so often pointed out, literature for the most part is male literature. But Heilbrun and Resnik suspected that it was their fault. Two of the texts which they suggested might be used positively by legal feminists are Alice Walker's *The Color Purple*, which will be considered below, and Thomas Hardy's *Jude the Obscure*. Hardy's portrayal of the woman's position in nineteenth-century England with regard to adultery and divorce laws has already been explored by non-lawyers.[40] In perhaps the most vigorous application of literature by a feminist scholar, Linda Hirshman has made similar use of Nathaniel Hawthorne's portrayal of the unfairness of the adultery laws in seventeenth-century Boston in his *The Scarlet Letter*.[41] So as yet, despite the tentative approaches of West and Koffler, and as Carolyn Heilbrun comments, literature has not been tapped as the 'source by which readers may come to understand the sufferings of women'. Whatever the potential drawbacks of the literary approach to the female situation and to feminist politics, and no matter how deep the suspicions of intertextual analysis, as both

Heilbrun and Resnick comment, the alliance of feminism and literature is an essential one: 'We who work with feminist theory have long known of the need for a new language representing women's experiences.' The time, they suggest, has now come to seize the opportunities that literature presents.[42]

THE RAPE DISCOURSE

Rape is a universal crime. The rape discourse is a universal discourse. But once again the voices which in recent years have demanded critical attention are North American, and two in particular are essential to any attempt to develop an understanding of both the political and textual nature of rape. The first of these is Catherine MacKinnon's. The keystone of MacKinnon's critique is that the law of rape is constructed from a male standpoint. It thus, and this is of utmost importance, concentrates on the 'event' rather than the 'experience' of rape. Although MacKinnon acknowledges that the root of the present failings in rape law lies in the 'meaning' of sex, and the discourse of sexuality, MacKinnon concentrates her energies instead on the politics, rather than the language, of rape. Rape is, of course, more than just the experience of intercourse. It is defined as an event conducted with violence. It is an invasion of the body, as indeed is every sexual act. Rape is a pervasive social, rather than merely isolated individual, crime. In her opening comments on rape in her hugely influential *Towards a Feminist Theory of the State*, MacKinnon states: 'If sexuality is central to women's definition and forced sex is central to sexuality, rape is indigenous, not exceptional, to women's social condition.'[43] Thus the female 'experience' of rape is not restricted to the male-determined presence of violence. The female experience of rape is no more determined as the event of penetration than it is as the act of violence. However, given the male determinant of violent penetration as rape, the event of rape is determined solely by the vexed problem of consent, which as a legal standard of behaviour is again defined solely by men. Though 'supposed to be the women's form of control over intercourse' consent is not an effective defence due to the relative inequality of the parties. This is not only physical inequality, but also economic and social. Moreover, even if the woman tries to assert a refusal to consent to intercourse, and even if then, by definition, the man uses violence, such is the law's concentration on the male rather than the female experience of rape that 'in conceiving a cognisable injury from the viewpoint of the reasonable rapist, the rape law affirmatively rewards men with acquittals for not comprehending the woman's point of view on sexual encounters'.[44] The assumption of consent is established by men for men. Apart from the issue of consent, and the nature of the female experience of rape, the third problem which MacKinnon points up is the situation of the rape trial, which, she suggests, rather than correcting the sense of injustice merely serves to formally and impersonally reinvade the woman's privacy.[45] Whereas the more textually and pluralistically inclined feminists want women to reclaim the language of sexuality, MacKinnon wants women to reclaim the politics of the female body.

MacKinnon's concentration on the politics of rape has won many admirers. It has, however, also attracted its critics, particularly from those who are more inclined towards a textual determination of rape. One of the most vigorous of these critics is Robin West. MacKinnon's concentration on the one overriding issue, the determination of sexuality as everywhere and always the invasion of the female body, though not conceptually challenged by West led her to suggest that such a radical political position (one which she perceives MacKinnon sharing with other radical political feminists such as Andrea Dworkin) develops an essentially blinkered feminism that is unaware of the many alternative feminisms, linguistic or otherwise. MacKinnon's critical legal feminism, West stresses, is flawed in precisely the same way as the male-dominated CLS, determined purely by short-term political ambition, and should not be taken to represent the numbers of potential legal feminisms. For West, the problem of rape does not simply lie with sex or sexuality *per se*, but with the whole contingent discourse of sex.[46] Sex is not, as Patricia Williams has observed, a bad thing. It is how sex is 'done' that can be problematic.[47]

The second prominent voice in rape scholarship is Susan Estrich's. The force of her influential article 'Rape', published in 1986, and then developed in the book *Real Rape*, was compounded by Estrich's ability to speak from experience.[48] It is the particular urgency of her message which has elevated Estrich's article to a place in feminist legal theory which even MacKinnon has never occupied. Estrich's thesis is in accordance with all of MacKinnon's broad statements on the experiential politics of rape, the invasion of the female body and the inadequacy of a crime determined solely by force and consent. Power, she affirms, is about so much more than physical aggression.[49] The practice of courts in applying the standard of consent has repeatedly shown that the mere articulation of a denied consent is never enough. Because the language of consent is never enough, there must also be an event or action which evidences a denied consent. Thus at the very top of the feminist agenda must be the alteration of the law so as to give authority to the language of consent, not the action alone.[50] It is here in the area of intertextual and political reform that the essential virtue of Estrich's writings lies – in moving beyond politics alone and emphasising the intertextuality of rape and, like West, with the desire to approach sexuality from a pluralist perspective. The reforms which Estrich advocates present real theory and real practice. In Estrich's opinion the most immediate aim is to redefine the language of sexual assault. It is only with a new language that there can be a new experience. This does not, however, mean the abandonment of consent, as has been suggested in the Michigan Reform Statute. But it does mean an acknowledgement of the semiotics of rape. Rape must be redefined as a sexual act not of violence alone, but as a sexual act effected by power. Thus whilst Estrich is in sympathy with the move to 'staircase' sexual assaults effected by power, there must not be a clouding of the essential experiences of different sexual assaults. In other words sexual assault is a plural, not a unitary, experience.[51] A redefinition of rape will nurture a new understanding of the nature of rape, and thus in practice lead to a better understanding of how the law and the legal process should react to the invasive nature of any sexual assault.[52]

The virtue of Estrich's approach, as opposed to the purely sociopolitical analysis of MacKinnon, is that rather than simply describing the dynamics of rape Estrich questions the very language of rape. History and politics can set the scene, but only language can change the rules. The experiential issue is translated into a linguistic issue, and as always the controllers of language are the controllers of power.[53] The fact that the actual crime of rape, indeed the very word rape, was defined by men has emerged as one of the keystones of feminist discourse. It remains, as Schroeder has reminded us, derived as it was from the Roman *raptus*, one of the very oldest early English legal terms still in regular legal usage. In early medieval Europe 'rape' became determined as an abduction without consent of a marriageable woman. The consent was not that of the woman herself, but of the family, and given the nature of early medieval European domestic relations, this invariably meant the consent of the male head of the household. Thus in its orginal sense rape was a crime of theft, not of sexual conduct. Neither was it always a crime of violence, as MacKinnon suggests. A woman could gladly disappear with a lover, and still the family would have been raped. The violence issue has been added in more recent times, but not with either the hope or the effect of alleviating the female position. Violence was added simply as an evidential qualification. The fact that the origins of the very definition of rape lay in a crime of theft against a man has remained to cast a considerable shadow across the discourse and the reality of rape. Popular reporting of rape continues to stress the male experience of loss.[54] Contemporary rape continues to lean on the concept of violence, both substantively and evidentially. The need to address the language of rape, rather than just the political reality of the law of rape, has been appreciated by Carol Smart who stresses that rape is a 'discourse' with a very 'specific history and culture', an 'experience' which is 'already constructed in language – a language which is part of the formation of the subjectivity of womanhood'. Language defines women, and legal language defines the legal personality of the woman. That language has been defined by men.[55] It is at this point, in the strong demand for a redefinition of sexual offences, rape included, that contemporary critical legal feminism is making the same claims as feminist literary critics like Annie Leclerc, who advocates a recapture of language by women which starts with a redetermination of the language of sexuality. As Schroeder has re-emphasised, if rape was once ill-defined, then it can be redefined. Language is not the threat to feminist legal theory. It is the potential saviour.[56]

LITERATURE AND THE DISCOURSE OF RAPE

The purpose of this final section is to suggest how the use of literary texts may be able to contribute to a better understanding of the various stances on rape considered above. In other words, it is to suggest the extent to which literature can assist in the educative needs of critical legal feminism. In particular it will concentrate on the two essential positions common to feminist critiques of rape: the 'experience' as opposed to the 'event' of rape, and the nature of consent. Even if literature cannot, or perhaps should not, replace the learned text, at least it can complement and illustrate. If these two issues can be brought to popular consciousness, and it is here that the educative potential of law and literature is surely a strength rather than a threat, then the larger political ambition to redetermine the definition and the experience of rape can be effected.

The female voice: 'The Handmaid's Tale'

First published in 1985, *The Handmaid's Tale* quickly established itself as one of the most critically acclaimed feminist texts of the last two decades. It has already attracted the attention of critical legal feminists, and has been invoked as a text which can be used as a supplement to the legal and ethical arguments surrounding another of the perennially vexed feminist issues, abortion.[57] The purpose of this section is to suggest that *The Handmaid's Tale* is equally valuable as a text which can illustrate the essential feminist positions with regard to rape. The basic storyline of *The Handmaid's Tale* is set in the not-too-distant future in an America renamed Gilead and governed by male fundamentalists, the Commanders of the Faithful. The position of women in this regime is one of total subjugation, deprived of any form of social or economic power. The means by which they have been deprived is the law.[58] Even their identities are taken away, and the women simply assume the first name of their Commander, as a possessory patronymic. Thus the main female character of the book is called Offred, composed as 'Of' and 'Fred'. They are, as Hirshman suggests, merely 'Society's incubators'. Their sole purpose in life is to breed children, most particularly male warriors. As breeders with no other identity, the women wear a distinctive red muu-muu. The removal of identity, and its replacement by a formalised male-determined sexuality is the immediate, and one of the most powerful, metaphors in the book.

Atwood repeatedly returns to two themes in particular; first, the juxtaposition of rape and law, and thus implicitly the inadequacy of the semiotics of rape, and secondly, the female experience of rape as an invasion of the body, and thus as a struggle with, and then overpowering of, something possessed. These two themes are precisely those worked by MacKinnon and by Estrich. The actual occasions of intercourse, between the Commander and Offred, are very much events rather than experiences. The description of the first of these 'Ceremonies', in which the Commander's wife symbolically holds Offred, provides a vivid description of a coerced sexual act, which Offred recognises cannot be rape, or at least not rape according to the laws of Gilead (or of course, any laws she has known, which by implication means, any contemporary laws of rape). The account also emphasises the invasion of the body of Offred, very much as an event rather than an experience, and leaves the reader wondering, critically, whether it is the fact that it is an event rather than an experience which finally negates it as rape:

> My arms are raised; she holds my hands, each of mine in each of hers. This is supposed to signify that we are one flesh, one being. What it really means is that she is in control, of the process and the product... My red skirt is hitched up to my waist, though no higher. Below it the Commander is fucking. What he is fucking is the lower part of my body. I do not say making love, because this is not what he's doing. Copulating too would be inaccurate, because it would imply two people and only one is involved. Nor does rape cover it. Nothing is going on here that I haven't signed up for. There wasn't a lot of choice but there was some, and this is what I chose.[59]

The essential question that Atwood is posing is whether there is ever any choice for the woman, and if not whether every sexual event is rape or, of course, that no sexual event is ever rape. Language offers itself as a partial and tantalising escape for Offred: 'One detaches onself. One describes.'[60] This is a common theme in feminist descriptions of rape. Thus, in the same vein, by refusing to engage the event, these descriptions attempt to preserve some possession of the body. On another occasion, Offred describes herself as sinking 'down into my body as into a swamp'.[61] However, even the language has been raped. Women can never fully describe the experience, because the language makes it into an event. Offred's experience is geared by the language which is made available to her. So there can never be a total liberation of the female sexual experience. In one of Offred's recollections of her early pre-Gilead life, she realises that even then there was no such thing as freedom, textual or experiential. Even then, she remembers, '[w]e lived in the gaps between the stories'.[62] Similarly, as she lies awake at night

attempting to describe her feelings, Offred finds herself thwarted
by language: 'The difference between lie and lay. Lay is always
passive. Even men used to say, I'd like to get laid. Though sometimes they said, I'd like to lay her. All this is pure speculation. I
don't really know what men used to say. I had only their words for
it.' As her mind wanders on this theme, Offred recalls a conversation with an old friend Moira, on the subject of an essay Moira had
written on date rape: 'Date rape, I said. You're so trendy. It sounds
like some kind of dessert. Date rape.'[63] Offred had been no more
liberated before than now. Language entrapped her. Her immediate recollections of pornography, written by men for men, serve as
a metaphor to enforce this entrapment of the female body in a
male discourse.

The second Ceremony presents an interesting juxtaposition
because, following her growing personal relationship with the
Commander, Offred's description of the occasion is more experiential. To a certain extent this seems to suggest a form of consent,
even if once again it is not a liberated consent. But of course on
this occasion the very sentiment makes the event unlawful, outside
the limits of sexuality permitted by the laws of Gilead, and thus
strikingly outside the limits permitted by Offred's description. As
Offred comments, it was an event for which there was 'no name'.
Paradoxically, Offred now describes the event of the Ceremony in
the language of rape, as an invasion of privacy: 'This act of copula-
tion, fertilization perhaps, which should have been no more to me
than a bee is to a flower, had become for me indecorous, an
embarrassing breach of propriety, which it hadn't been before ...
But I also felt guilty for her [the Commander's wife]. I felt I was an
intruder, in a territory that ought to have been hers.'[64] Thus, she is
raped by the Commander, and she is raping the Commander's
wife. Both perspectives make Offred feel 'guilt'. It is, of course,
precisely as she has been educated by the 'Aunts', the female
instructors of breeders like Offred. Sex is not to be a personal
thing, or an experience. Sex is an event. The laws of Gilead
enforce the language and the ethics of male-determined sexuality.
Aunt Lydia's advice that 'to be seen' is 'to be penetrated' and that
the 'girls' must be 'impenetrable', vividly describes the use of a
language which determines rape penetration, but the experience of
rape as something else. What Aunt Lydia is describing is the look
of men, as penetration and as rape. However, in Aunt Lydia's

language the responsibility for such a penetration lies not with the men, but with the 'girls' themselves.[65] When the Commander looks into Offred's room, it is an invasion of her body, a penetration of something that was still hers.[66] During 'Testifying', Janine recounts being gang-raped at 14. In response, the audience, the 'girls', 'chant in unison', 'Her fault, her fault, her fault'.[67] Gilead is a theocracy, with a theological ethics and a theological language. Atwood reinforces this impression by empowering Gilead through its possession and use of the 'scriptures' of the Bible.[68] Gilead is governed by a transcendental theology, and women are oppressed by the same theocratic forces which oppress them in twentieth-century North America. In the Bible, rape was the possession of male property, as it was in Roman law, in early medieval English law and as it remains, conceptually, in contemporary legal texts. In Gilead, the only unlawful sex is that enjoyed with somebody who does not own a woman by right. Offred, as she acknowledges, is owned by the Commander.[69] Thus Offred's intercourse with the driver is rape, and the Guardian is torn to pieces by the women because he is alleged to have raped a woman who belonged to the state, and thereby to have committed not just an invasion of woman's propriety, but an act of supreme treason.[70]

The juxtapositioning of sexual events which are determined by the language, and not by the experience, of rape, are repeated throughout the book. The examination of Offred by the doctors is described in the language of rape, because it is an invasion of the body for which Offred was not empowered to offer a liberated consent. The doctor subjugates Offred with language. Offred is his 'honey', just as she is the Commander's and Gilead's 'incubator'. What the doctor has, and it is this which is most vigorously described, is the power to invade Offred's body, explicitly as a doctor, and implicitly as someone who may be able to make her pregnant. Offred must be proved to be fertile, otherwise she could become an 'Unwoman'. Again there is a choice, but again Offred's consent is not freely enjoyed. Circumstances, like language, dictate Offred's sexuality, not Offred.[71] Most importantly, Offred looks back to her 'sexual' experiences before Gilead, and in acknowledging the male control of both the experience and language of sexuality then realises that Gilead and contemporary North America are, conceptually at least, little different.[72] The film of a doctor's examination of a woman, pre-Gilead, is shown to the girls by Aunt

Lydia in an effort to impress it as an act of penetration.[73] Read in juxtaposition with the Doctor's penetration of Offred, it provides the same unsettling paradox as the films, which Aunt Lydia also shows, of pre-Gilead pornography; women being mutilated, raped and killed.[74] When the Commander attempts to access Offred's sentiments, the ultimate act of invasion, by bribing her with gifts, it is described as precisely the date-rape which in her earlier, supposedly liberated existence, she had not really been able to comprehend. For Offred the event, with whomsoever, is always the same, regardless of whether it is legal or not, whether it is 'rape' or not.[75] Is Gilead different from contemporary North America? Certainly the discourse of sexuality is no different, and neither, therefore, is the discourse of rape.

A selection of texts

There are many other texts which could be used to supplement jurisprudential approaches to rape; *The Handmaid's Tale* is only one example. The texts which will be considered briefly here are thus not only purely subjective but only a selection of those which could be used. However, it is suggested that they do offer a sample of the possibilities available to the legal scholar who is prepared to embrace the opportunities which literature presents.

One of the most powerful examples must be Andrea Dworkin's *Mercy*. Dworkin has repeatedly approached the issue of rape from an overtly political position, and her most recent novel presents a vigorous and uncompromising demand for overt political action against men.[76] *Mercy* describes the life of a young woman repeatedly raped, and who relates the rapes as a series of political events which are indistinguishable from the fascism of contemporary American culture and politics. Women, according to Dworkin, are politically excluded, marginalised like children, Jews and negroes, and frustrated, not only by this politics, but also by their resultant failure to access an audience.[77] At the heart of this exclusion and this frustration is the inability of the male-dominated legal order to execute justice for women.[78] Much of the book is also a running commentary against theology, Judaic and Christian; a theme which Dworkin obviously shares with Atwood.[79] Indeed, many of the themes of *Mercy* are those which can be found in *The Handmaid's Tale*, including the three most important: the definition of rape, the issue of consent and the limitations of a male-determined language. In Dworkin's opinion every sexual act is ultimately a rape and, moreover, male presence is a continual threat of rape. The former assertion is repeatedly described in the book, as each potentially enjoyable sexual act becomes an issue of power and subjugation, invasion and pain. Only with another woman can the central character, Andrea, enjoy sex based on equality. The idea that the male presence is a continual threat of rape, as a potential invasion of the body, is portrayed in the first chapters of the book when Andrea is still a very young girl, and though 'only' touched by men, still experiences rape. Indeed, rape can be just as threatening as a visual event as a sensile one.[80] Rape is not, then, for Dworkin, simply penile–vaginal penetration, and as the book progresses more and more examples of sexual coercion present non-vaginal penetration. Because every sexual act is always an assertion of power between unequal 'partners', then every sexual act is coerced, and thus consent becomes in fact a non-issue.[81]

Ultimately, and it this which really elevates Dworkin's text from the purely political and which places it alongside Atwood's in textual ambition, the problem of rape is a problem of language. Sexuality is the language of rape.[82] Language oppresses women. Words are power, and women are excluded from words.[83] Dworkin's thesis is both very much Atwood's and very much that presented by the textual feminist literary critics considered earlier. Ultimately the essential problem with rape is the word itself. It is a semiotic problem. Rape, it is repeatedly asserted, is 'just some awful word'. A word which is noteworthy only in its utter inadequacy. A word which, above all, was determined by men, for men.[84] Repeatedly Andrea tells herself that rape does not 'exist', and increasingly she realises that what the word 'rape' signs itself serves to preclude female existence in the full existential Sartrian sense: 'such things do not happen and such things cannot occur, any more than the rape so-called can happen or occur or the being beaten so bad can happen or occur and there are no words for what cannot happen or occur and if you think something happened or occurred and there are not words for it you are at a dead end'.[85] The male existence is the negation of the female, and sexual and linguistic oppression is the immediate expression of this relationship.[86] Feminism is then an existential 'responsibility', textual as well as political. Dworkin recognises that women somehow will have to learn how to describe the experience before they can present a politics which can address it.[87] In the Prologue to *Mercy* she suggests that the responsibility of feminism is to present, through texts, a constructive feminist agenda. In the Epilogue, she further defines this agenda, as drawn from the text. It is above all a discourse. The current discourse of rape must be replaced by a 'discourse of triumph'. This discourse will be created by literature which can serve to outflank the dangers of excessive intellectualism. Clearly Dworkin's own intellectual sympathies lie with the Anglo-American as opposed to the French schools of literary and political criticism, but ultimately her agenda is complementary. Feminism, she concludes, must develop an awareness of the power of 'signs', a new semiotics, at the same time as it stresses the true nature of rape, as power not sexuality.[88] Dworkin repeatedly stresses that *Mercy* is not autobiographical, and yet equally acknowledges that such a text can only be written from experience.

A similarly harrowing but more openly autobiographical text is Elly Danica's *Don't*. Like Dworkin, Danica emphasises the enduring effects of rape, and the intense loneliness which accompanies it. Marginalisation is both physical and emotional. Elly is raped by society, literally and metaphorically, by its businessmen and by its judges. The forces of law and order are directed against her. What Danica's book also re-emphasises is again the inadequacy of the received masculine definition of rape, both as a political and as a linguistic constraint. Ultimately Danica's liberation comes through literature, and the possibilities of a new means of expression. As both Atwood and Dworkin emphasise, literature effects freedom.[89] Another text which famously described the experiences of incest and rape is Alice Walker's *The Color Purple*, a text which also combines the double exclusion of the main character: being a woman and being black. The very first scene in the book is of Celie being raped by her father, and again the experience endures throughout the remainder of her life. The forces of society repeatedly serve to suppress Celie, and sexual suppression symbolises that oppression just as it does for Atwood, Dworkin and Danica. What is perhaps most vividly portrayed in *The Color Purple* is not only the inadequacy of society and its order, but also the utter irrelevance. Rape is a continual threat, and a continual expression of power. Above all, just as it is for Dworkin, sexuality geared to power represents the suppression of the female identity.[90] One final example of a feminist text which can be of use in illustrating the limitations of contemporary jurisprudential approaches to rape is Julia Voznesenskaya's *The Women's Decameron*, wherein ten women each describe an experience of coerced sexual intercourse, only four of which could be legally described as rape, and only one of which could ever hope to be prosecuted in an American or English court of law, let alone prosecuted successfully. The statistics of these stories present the raw political effects of the textual inadequacies of the present discourse of rape.[91]

The extent to which texts written by men should be considered as appropriate for illustrating the problems of rape is of course contentious. Feminist literary critics line up on either side. However, a number of male literary critics have staked a claim to relevance in feminist literary criticism, and it is suggested that there are examples of literature written by men which can be of use in describing the experiences of rape, just as there are, indeed, examples which are useful in their inadequacy.[92] Carol Sanger has already castigated some recent male literature for its inability to describe the female sexual experience, particularly literature aimed at the commercial as opposed to the critical market.[93] This inability of the male author is not only limiting textually, but it also serves to continue the stereotypes around which it is constructed. One pertinent example of a piece of commercially directed literature which falls into this category is the recent 'best-seller' *Degree of Guilt* by Richard North Patterson, which is replete with all the usual characterisations: the hard-nosed rape victim who abandons her child, puts herself in danger and who perpetually casts 'icy' stares to all and sundry, and the softer, more acceptable career woman, who puts her family first, and is also raped, but without any culpability. The former victim is really quite unpleasant, but the latter is very much a character with whom we can sympathise. She certainly did not deserve to be raped, and at the end of the novel at least finishes up on a yacht with the lawyer-hero. Politically the portrayal of rape in the novel is at times sympathetic, but textually it is wholly destructive.[94]

At the same time, however, there are certain texts written by men which have already attracted critical acclaim as accounts of rape. One of the most famous is, of course, Shakespeare's *The Rape of Lucrece*. Another is Samuel Richardson's *Clarissa*, with its enigmatic non-account of the rape of Clarissa, which according to

Terry Eagleton represents the textual inadequacies of male sexual discourse. According to Eagleton, Lovelace's rape of Clarissa is also a rape of female language: 'Clarissa's body is itself the discourse of the text.' Yet, just as the rape is an assertion of male textuality, so it is also, as a source of intense frustration for Lovelace, a symbol of the inaccessibility of female textuality. For Eagleton, the rape is itself a symbol of the historical and political position of the woman, for whom the only existential assertion is death. Eagleton has repeatedly asserted that literature always presents a political potential, and thus Richardson's *Clarissa* represents an 'indispensable moment' in the as-yet unfulfilled 'emancipatory movement' of women. [95] Another eighteenth-century text, which like *Clarissa* caused an immediate sensation, is Choderlos de Laclos's *Les Liaisons dangereuses*. The language with which Laclos describes the rape of Cecile and the seduction of Madame de Tourvel is a language of possession, conquest and subjugation. According to the two chief protagonists, Valmont and the Marquise de Merteuil, men 'conquer', whilst women 'surrender' and are 'subjugated'. The remarkable subtlety of these descriptions, however, really lies in the contrasts between the language used by the rapist Valmont and his victims. The most pertinent example of this is probably in the alternative accounts of the rape of Cecile. Cecile's account makes it quite clear that the intercourse was non-consensual, forced and an experience of invasion. She simply blames herself for not having put up a successful 'defence'. Valmont's description makes it equally clear that to him there was ultimately consent, even if not at first, and that that is sufficient to justify the 'conquering' of 'his charming enemy'. This conquering is very much an event. Valmont never approaches describing an experience of sexuality, just of possession and subjugation.[96]

A final example, if only to show that masculine appreciation of the experience of rape, and the inadequacies of the discourse of rape, both political and textual, did not die with the close of the eighteenth century, is Mordechai Richler's *St Urbain's Horseman*. The story of *St Urbain's Horseman* is founded upon a false accusation of rape and various other sexual practices, and is then developed as a satire of various social groupings: the British middle classes, North American Jews and above all the English legal order. At times the satire, as represented in the trial scene towards the end of the novel, is Dickensian in style. But the satires are

hardened by a textual edge which comes closer to Camus than to
Dickens. The trial is conducted by a series of caricatured lawyers,
chiefly for their own benefit and only marginally for the benefit of
either the alleged victim or the alleged perpetrators of the crimes.
The alleged victim of the sexual assaults was 'normally' a 'well
brought-up' and 'comely young girl', who unfortunately had
become an au pair, thereby leaving herself wide open to being sex-
ually assaulted on a regular basis, and especially so as the court
heard that on four occasions during the previous three months she
had stayed out all night. When Jake is found guilty of indecent
assault, the judge castigates him not for committing the assault, but
for consorting with the sort of people who did. Jake, party to various 'disgusting acts', is warned about how damaging such behaviour can be to his family, is given a second 'chance' and fined
£500. His co-defendant, impoverished disgusting little Harry, with
his skin peeling off, gets seven years. No one mentions the alleged
victim.[97]

CHAPTER 7

Law and justice in the modern novel: the concept of responsibility

There is no doubt that modern literature has been more extensively used by law and literature scholars than any other literary source. It does not, then, represent a particularly new perspective. There are, of course, certain contemporary 'modern' texts which are fresh, and I will look at a couple of these in the final two chapters of this book. However, in this chapter I want briefly to provide an example of how modern literature can be used as a means of accessing certain key concepts in contemporary critical theory and critical legal scholarship. The concept which I shall consider in this chapter is responsibility.

RESPONSIBILITY IN MODERN LITERATURE

Two texts which have proved to be particularly popular in law and literature scholarship are Kafka's *The Trial* and Camus's *The Outsider*. The specific concept of responsibility, however, has not received any especial notice. Richard Weisberg used Camus's novels as representative of Nietzschean *ressentiment*.[1] While admitting the force of the argument that the novels of both Camus and Kafka do present the nihilism of despair, I would suggest that they also reveal the possibilities of responsibility and self-assertion. Most importantly, these texts are not significant for what they might or might not tell us about the specifically legal situation: Austro-Hungarian or French civil procedure. What *The Trial* and *The Outsider* actually do is to use the legal situation, and its peculiarly intense concern with motivation of the individual, as a medium for describing the human condition. This is why Weisberg, in particular, has concentrated on the interaction between the Examining Magistrates, representing the 'ethics' of the community and the individual 'hero' of the novels. This approach places the reader in the position of juror, or participant in the actual events – the reader contributes to the narrative. Camus has no interest in any particular situation, but he is aware that this intensity, intrinsic to any legal situation, furnishes a particularly powerful parable that can be used to describe the human condition. This is why the drama of such narratives is reduced to a minimum, so that the reader, as he or she adds more and more of his or herself to the story, becomes ever more aware of his or her own guilt and despair. This, in turn, leads not only to an awareness of despair, however, but also to an awareness of the responsibility for this despair and thus, ultimately, to hope. The guilt that Camus isolates is the guilt of abrogating the responsibility of self-assertion. Thus in the trial scene in *The Outsider*, as Mersault tries to come to terms with his own guilt, it is not guilt for the murder of the Arab, but guilt at having submitted to the alienation of the human condition and the abandonment of hope that Mersault comes to understand. With the trial, Mersault, for the first time, becomes 'involved' in life, and for the first time has to justify his existence, not so much to the court as to himself. In his final outburst before his execution, Mersault finally acknowledges his guilt and cries out for a hatred compatible with it. The most important statement that Camus made with regard to *The Outsider* is in the 'Afterword', written thirteen years after publication:

So for me Mersault is not a reject, but a poor and naked man, in love with a sun which leaves no shadow. Far from lacking all sensibility, he is driven by a tenacious and therefore profound passion, the passion for an absolute and for truth. This truth is as yet a negative one, a truth born of living a feeling, but without which no triumph over the self or over the world will ever be possible.[2]

Mersault was 'an outsider to the society', but that is a constituent of the human condition. It is not, however, determinative of it. Weisberg sees Mersault as irreducibly alienated, and the fact that he is 'innocent' only adds to the tragedy. But for Camus it is not a question of innocence or otherwise. What is important is that Mersault is true to himself, and it is that which makes *The Outsider* not a story which can tell a lawyer much about criminal procedure in North Africa in the 1940s, but a story which can portray human existence as a condition of hope. Richard Weisberg, who wishes to portray Mersault as a figure of irreducible pessimism, would respond that it is not what the writer intended that matters, but what he wrote. Weisberg believes that in modern society, the lawyer is uniquely positioned to use words in order to disguise the truth and to cause harm.[3] To some extent this is indeed what Camus suggests, but Camus is also suggesting that what matters is not only what the lawyer or the magistrate does, but also what the individual chooses to do.[4] Camus's interpretation of his own work is at least as valid as anyone else's, and better reflects the cultural atmosphere in which the novel was created because it appreciates that *ressentiment* is only the catalyst for the twentieth century and not its definition. Moreover, if the most immediate context for literature is the writer's context, then there is much to be gained from ascertaining precisely the cultural context that Camus perceived. If *The Outsider* is not ultimately a literary manifesto of hope, then Camus presented a narrative fundamentally at odds with his own philosophy. In *The Myth of Sisyphus*, he suggested that the 'absurdity' of the human condition, as an ultimately finite condition, was not a factor in determining that condition as either hopeful or desperate, but instead as a matter of self-determination or responsibility. Nothing intrinsic to the human condition precludes happiness and, indeed, in Camus's opinion, literature was a prime means of describing and enhancing this possibility. For the modern man, the 'work of art' is the 'the sole chance of keeping his consciousness and of fixing its adventures'. The only sure way of self-assertion is creation, and art is the only authentic means of creation. Camus himself uses his interpretation of the actual 'myth' of Sisyphus to describe his own ultimate philosophical position: 'Sisyphus teaches the higher fidelity that negates the gods and raises rocks. He, too, concludes that all is well. This universe henceforth without a master seems to him neither sterile nor futile ... The struggle towards the heights is enough to fill a man's heart. One must imagine Sisyphus happy.'[5]

Kafka's *The Trial* has perhaps attracted more attention from law and literature writers than any other novel. Kafka's world appears to be uncompromisingly bleak, and it is not easy to dispel this image. However, one famous section, the parable of the doorkeeper in chapter nine, is Kakfa's attempt to make the same point as Camus. In this chapter, the priest tells Joseph K. a parable, where a man comes 'before the Law', described as a door guarded by a doorkeeper. At the man's enquiry the doorkeeper refuses entry, simply suggesting that future entry might be 'possible'. The door to the law 'stands open', and the man is clearly tempted to enter, but the doorkeeper warns him that there are many more doors and each is guarded. Kafka implies that admittance to the law is a never-ending process. The man, who had expected permission to enter through the door, is taken aback and takes a seat offered to him outside the door. There he waits, in occasional conversation with the doorkeeper, until he finally asks: 'Everyone strives to attain the law ... how does it come about, that in all these years no one has come seeking admittance but me?' This is the man's final question, so the doorkeeper 'bellows in his ear': 'No one but you could gain admittance through this door, since this door was intended only for you. I am now going to shut it.' The law is the man's, and the decision to access it was also the man's. His failure to do so was a failure to take responsibility, and his ultimate demise, to waste his life in futile 'hope', was also his responsibility – and possibly ours. The parable serves as a parable of the entire novel. K. himself consistently fails to take responsibility. On the priest finishing the parable, K. immediately comments: 'So the doorkeeper deluded the man.' In making this statement K. betrays his own condition of continuing delusion. The manner of K.'s death, in the final chapter, at the hands of others and 'like a dog', affirms that K.'s ultimate fate, like that of us all, is futile, devoid of self-assertion. However, it can equally well be seen as making the same statement as Mersault's final exclamation; an ultimate recognition both of his own failings of responsibility and of the appropriateness of his death. Either way, for many, including Maurice Blanchot and Jacques Derrida, the parable is chiefly about one thing – taking responsibility.[6] Camus certainly thought that both he and Kafka were describing essentially the same thing, for 'the more tragic the condition described by Kafka, the firmer and more aggressive that hope becomes'. As Camus and subsequently Erich Fromm have suggested, the degree of guilt in *The Trial* is dependent upon the nature of the duality of the human condition, internal and external, as represented by the moral and civil law. Guilt does not define the condition, and does not preclude hope. As far as Camus is concerned, both he and Kafka are writing to describe the human condition as one of hope determined by the possibility of self-assertion and the recognition of the responsibility to do so.[7]

RESPONSIBILITY IN HEIDEGGER'S POLITICAL THOUGHT

What Camus and Kafka were describing, the responsibility of self-assertion, was not only mirrored in contemporary philosophical writings, but was done so in a way which again used both the concept and the word of law as a metaphorical catalyst. Martin Heidegger only rarely made statements about political or legal issues. However, during his brief flirtation with Nazism in early 1933, he made a series of statements about the nature of a National Socialist 'law', the most famous of which was presented in the *Rektorat*, given to the students of Freiburg University on 27 May 1933. In this address, 'The Self-Assertion of the German University', Heidegger states that, '[t]o give the law to oneself is the highest freedom'.[8] Before considering the meaning of this statement, it is important to establish a context. In 'Facts and Thoughts', composed shortly after the war, Heidegger emphasised the importance with which he had perceived his position at Freiburg. Heidegger wanted to be nothing less than the spiritual Führer of National Socialism. He wanted to revolutionise the German university, and German society with it. Heidegger's rectorship thus represented, albeit perhaps briefly, a determination to define the nature of the National Socialist ideal in the real political situation.[9] The entire *Rektorat* has generated considerable controversy. For a time a number of Heideggerian apologists, going directly against Heidegger's own wishes, tried to dismiss the address as 'inauthentic' Heidegger, or as some sort of political aberration. However, as the 'Heidegger debate' has returned to prominence during the last few years, the consensus of opinion has been that Heidegger's statements during 1933 cannot be ignored or dismissed, and indeed for many, including Derrida and Habermas, they represent the purest application of Heidegger's philosophy.[10]

Heidegger advocates a reawakened awareness of the power of self-assertion and the possibilities that the acceptance of responsibility can generate. This self-assertion can only be if 'we know who we ourselves are'. In his 1935 Nietzsche lectures, he admitted that the correlation between the essential determination of man and the essence of truth 'was the impulse for the treatise *Being and Time*', continuing, '[t]hrough Being itself the essence of man is determined from the essentializing of the truth of Being'.[11] This was also the 'impulse' behind the *Rektorat*; the 'self-assertion of the

German University', he emphasised, 'is the primordial will to its essence'. 'Essence' represents a central Heideggerian construct, something 'authentic', and above all, for the Heidegger of 1933, something potentially determinative. Throughout the address Heidegger continually compares the truly 'essential' with the complacency of a contemporary scientised *Wissenschaft*. The new 'constitution' which he presented to the students represents a rejection of its metaphysical structures. *Dasein*, the there-ness of being, was presented in *Being and Time* as a temporally determinative construct designed to overcome this metaphysics.[12] This determination or 'presencing', in the *Lichtung*, representing truth and unconcealment, expresses 'self-assertion', and necessitates the taking of responsibility. German students, and indeed the German people, were to 'assert' themselves, and to come to 'presence', as a cultural and historical people, so that they could 'give' the law to themselves; this would be an ultimate act of responsibility. In this sense, the 'self-assertion' would be at once the first step towards 'presencing', and its culmination, or to use the phrase which Heidegger took from Kierkegaard, its 're-trieval'; what Derrida describes as 'the entry on stage of spirit itself ... again'.[13] The early Heidegger was still able to cling to the ambition of 're-trieving' an 'authentic' law, which he urged the German people to do. In political terms he was advocating an abandonment of the liberal *Wissenschaft* of rights or *Recht*, and putting in its stead the self-assertion of National Socialist *Geist*. The idea that this 'self-assertion' would represent the 'highest freedom' refers, in part, back to the *Lichtung* metaphor, because only in this 'space' or 'lightness' of 'essential' Being could freedom be located. But it also refers Heidegger back to his first and enduring encounter with Kant, and the third antinomy of freedom, around which Kant constructed his critical philosophy.[14]

Towards the end of the address, Heidegger consciously and uncompromisingly dismisses the classical metaphysical idea of freedom, 'for this freedom was not genuine, since it was only negative'. In its place Heidegger presented a 'freedom' that was a freedom to accept responsibility, and to embrace the 'spiritual mission' of self-determination.[15] Heidegger made a series of similar collateral statements with regard to law in the abstract sense during this period of political flirtation. During the summer of 1933, in his course 'The Fundamental Questions of Philosophy', he commented that 'the fundamental Question' was 'the Question of law and the structure of Being'.[16] As Derrida has noted, the isolation of the Question as one of law and Being represented the political–philosophical development of Heidegger's thought during this period. Increasingly the two were being regarded as one, and the need for the people to reassert their own 'law', in other words the responsibility for their existence within a community or *Volk*, became a central theme in Heidegger's writings during this period. To use Heidegger's own favourite metaphor, if 'essence' was to be found in the 'space', or *Lichtung*, then its 're-trieval' would be done by following the 'pathways' or *Holzwege* to this 'space'. The guides for this journey would be the Questions of Being and of law. If the 'essence' of individual Being was properly appreciated, and the relationship between the individual and the 'authentic' community redefined, then, for the Heidegger of 1933, the political ideal of National Socialism could be attained.[17] Even after his encounter with Nietzsche, Heidegger still refused to abandon altogether this ideal, and despite various pleas from disciples such as Marcuse he consistently refused to make an act of 'recantation', instead suggesting that his was the 'authentic' National Socialism, and that the reality of National Socialism had been nothing but a metaphysical sham. According to Phillippe Lacoue-Labarthe, Heidegger devoted the rest of his life to 're-trieving' his own National Socialism.[18] As Blanchot has noted, in Heidegger's opinion, Hitler had abandoned National Socialism when he had abandoned the politics of 'responsibility'.[19]

RESPONSIBILITY IN CRITICAL THEORY

The extent of literature on the various influences of the Heideggerian project is vast, and well beyond the scope of this chapter. Our necessarily limited purpose is to simply explore the extent to which contemporary critical legal thought has developed as part of the Heideggerian project, most particularly from this concept of responsibility. The concerns common to Heidegger, Kafka and Camus are concerns which lie at the very heart of critical legal thought. These concerns, with 'technicity' and the demise of the 'human condition', in many ways have become the totem for Heideggerian critical theory. Heidegger's own insistence that 'philosophy' was 'dead', and that the future of thought lay in exploring the intersection between disciplines such as politics, psychology and most especially language, has also become something of a keystone in twentieth-century critical theory. It is of course the belief that guides such interdisciplinary work as law and literature. Heidegger and Heideggerians such as Derrida, Arendt or Marcuse have advocated precisely the 'cross-disciplinary' study, or 'Ciceronian unity', which law and literature scholars such as James Boyd White have advocated.

Before considering critical legal scholarship, it is useful to briefly trace one or two of the more pertinent lines of these 'cross-disciplinary' studies. Associating themselves with Heidegger's impulse, a number of these writers have concentrated on the breaking down of disciplinary structures, most particularly exploring the intersections between philosophy, psychoanalysis, literature and politics, in precisely the same way as Kafka and Camus. Jean-Paul Sartre produced a series of novels in a bid to explore the possibilities of an alternative discourse. He also investigated the relationship between philosophy and psychoanalysis in *The Psychology of Imagination*, in an attempt to develop the central problem of freedom in the human condition which had dominated *Being and Nothingness*. Arendt, Foucault and Marcuse all continued this particular interest in the relationship between philosophy and psychoanalysis, and its impact on the politics of the human condition. Foucault's attempts to break down structures and disciplines were used to full effect in his own studies on the nature and historical treatment of mental illness.[20] According to David Couzens Hoy, Foucault stands at the end of a 'history of consciousness' which has stretched from Kant and Hegel, through Husserl and Heidegger, to Derrida and Foucault himself. The 'history of consciousness' for these writers, he suggests, has become 'the privileged subject-matter'.[21] Certainly Derrida, in his discussion of Kafka's parable 'Before the Law', suggests that he came to the parable, via Freud and Heidegger, in a bid to write something about Kant's 'moral law'.[22] It is this immanent historicity which situates Foucault within the tradition, and which determines all who write about the human condition. Any such writing, whether 'fictional' or not, according to Foucault is part of the same literary tradition, because all such writers struggle with the desire to internalise language. According to Foucault, literature has taken over as the postmodern medium, because it makes a claim to historicise psychology and consciousness. In suggesting that 'consciousness' must be released from its own essentially reflective language, Foucault implicitly attacks Freud and the 'culture' of psychoanalysis. Foucault's own essay on Blanchot's use of fictional narratives contemplates the thesis that if language can be truly internalised, it can become an expression of self-assertion.[23]

Herbert Marcuse took his investigations of the relationship between philosophy and psychoanalysis further than Foucault, most strikingly in *Eros and Civilization*, where he suggested that the dominant Freudian thesis of repression and performance as the gears of the mind was merely a symptom of historical contingency. As Foucault noted, Freud's placing of the 'reality principle' over the 'pleasure principle' was historically contingent. In place of a scientised approach to psychoanalysis, as represented by this earlier Freud, Marcuse asserted the later political–sociological Freud. In common with Kafka, Heidegger and a host of other writers of the early and mid- twentieth century, Marcuse portrayed a 'repressive society' as typified by the totalitarian state, founded on the 'alienated performance' of the individual, subjected to the dominance of the community. It was, he suggested, the loss of '[r]esponsibility for the organization of his life' which had crushed man. Freud asserted that this subjection was the product of 'self-repression'. Although Marcuse shared this premise, by stressing the political and thus historically contingent nature of psychoanalysis he presented, instead, an 'unrepressive society' based on the 'liberating potentialities' of 'imagination', on art and on poetry. An unrepressive literature could lead to an unrepressive society. Like Heidegger, Gadamer, Arendt and Foucault, Marcuse drew his original inspiration from Kant's third *Critique* and the assertion of subjectivity, and, like Foucault again, with a 'liberating' literature, rather than 'consciousness philosophy', Marcuse proposed to release a 'new' psychology.[24] In his later *One-Dimensional Man*, Marcuse repeated his same critique of the scientised and repressively technological twentieth century: if man was to reassert his 'responsibility' he could do so only by reasserting 'art' over 'technics', as advocated by the Greeks and the later Kant.[25]

If Marcuse did most to explore the intersections between philosophy and psychoanalysis and did so, ultimately, to effect an improvement in the politics of the human condition, Hannah Arendt investigated the nature of this condition and its demise the furthest. Moreover she did so by using the work of Marcuse,

Sartre, Heidegger and Kant, both on the human mind and on the conception of freedom. Like Marcuse, in *The Life of the Mind* she tried to reorientate the study of consciousness, from the ability to think to the method of thinking, from a scientific or metaphysical philosophy of the mind to a socio-historical critical theory of the 'act of thinking'. Politically, in her particular study of the Jew, or 'pariah', Arendt stressed the need, not only to preserve privacy, but to act in the public situation, and to bridge the peculiarly modern distinction between the 'social' and the 'political'. It was, after Heidegger, a responsibility not just to exist in/outside a community, but to create or 'work' in that community, for the community. In doing so, she took Heidegger and the problem of the alienation of the individual and from it presented a theory of inter-subjective participatory democracy, based on fundamental human rights and liberties. This is not a Natural Law or, as she perceived it, a democratic-republican conception of fundamental rights, but a consciously Kantian community-articulated conception of rights.[26]

RESPONSIBILITY IN CRITICAL LEGAL THOUGHT

The themes that are common to critical theory, particularly alienation and responsibility, are those which lie at the conceptual core of much – though not all – contemporary critical legal scholarship. Some critical legal scholars would not share Arendt's faith in reconstructed rights. The concentration on communities and community consciousness, however, is very much the rhetoric of Critical Legal Studies. Moreoever, what can be presented as a totem of such scholarship is precisely the interdisciplinary approach to legal problems which Arendt and Marcuse adopted for wider political issues and which contemporary law and literature writers forcefully advocate. Any critical theory, though it might present various visions of political, economic or legal justice, is primarily a theory of method. This interdisciplinary methodology defines all critical theories. The most committed interdisciplinary approach to remodel legal method among recognised CLS has been Roberto Unger's. Unger's political 'vision' was presented as early as 1975 in *Knowledge and Politics*, where he recognised the essential tension between the individual and society, but also suggested that an acceptance of the responsibility of the individual in the civil situation was the only possible justification for law.

Acceptance of this premise, he asserted, can lead to responsibility and freedom. Though critical of the structuralism of modern philosophy, Unger is not only concerned with social deconstruction, but also with social reconstruction, which can be realised only through acceptance of a purposive theory of adjudication which reintroduces and is validated by an idea of substantive justice. The pretence of universality is denied, and in its place is a recognition of law as the reflection of immediate community ethics. This system will, Unger suggested, demand individual contribution, and will thus evolve as a self-affirmation of the individual as representative of the community.[27] Although the 'vision' has been modified during the previous two decades, it has remained in essence the same.

In his more recent *Passion: An Essay on Personality*, Unger urges us to 'execute our social vision', so that we must 'enact this vision and a better project, or else fail in the self-affirmation'. At the same time, *Passion* emphasises Unger's increasing concentration on the problem of method, and particularly the virtues of interdisciplinary 'method'. In *Passion* the essential problem or 'predicament' remains that of 'contextuality and solidarity'. More than in some of his earlier work, Unger suggests that this is a problem of discourse and language. Like Richard Rorty and Paul Ricoeur, he advocates the possibilities of 'storytelling' instead of social theory as a 'method' of advancing social 'solidarity'. Like Arendt, he refers to the alienation of the individual, and like Richard Weisberg suggests that it was Nietzsche's *ressentiment* which first defined the problem of the human condition in the modern era, and isolated the potential affinity between theology, politics and literature. The modernist literature of Proust and Kafka, he suggests, describes this condition, and complements Heidegger's existential angst. The failure of Kafka and Heidegger, Unger suggests, lies in not presenting a 'vision of a reconstructed society' and liberating the potentialities of 'personality'. But he recognises that their great success lay in identifying the essential problem of metaphysics as one of method. Like Arendt, Unger is determined to present a normative ethics. His will be a Kantian, rather than a Heideggerian, 'self-affirmation'. If there is to be a new 'vision' it will be guided by a communicative ethics and represented by a 'psychology of empowerment'. For Unger, the key to solving the problem of the human condition lies in the association of politics, ethics and literature with pyschology. In making this statement, he places himself within the same tradition as Heidegger, Arendt, Kafka and Camus. In emphasising the need to reorient the practice of psychology as a social rather than a biological science, he is saying very much the same as Marcuse. It is psychology, Unger suggests, which can banish 'alienation' and reassert 'the school of freedom' as a 'passionate', and thus radically subjective, idea, and the 'assertion', meaning 'self'-assertion, of these 'passions' will enable us to 'expand the scope of democratic politics'. A new de-objectified understanding of the human mind will facilitate a new de-objectified society.[28]

Unger is not alone in his approach to critical legal scholarship. The concepts of responsibility, self-affirmation, community consciousness, the dangers presented by modern society and its alienation of the individual have been the meat and drink of critical legal writing for the last two decades. Drawing expressly from Sartre, and thus implicitly from Heidegger, Peter Gabel and Duncan Kennedy in their seminal essay 'Roll Over Beethoven' accused us of fearing individuality and the responsibility which it brings. 'In the pain of isolation', they suggested, 'we become attached to the utopian content of legal imagery.'[29] According to Gabel, our 'perception of reality' is rendered impossible by a Sartrean 'false-consciousness'. The alienation of the human condition has particularly characterised Gabel's writings. In asserting that the only solution lies with participatory politics or 'the lived experience', and that 'individual growth and change occurs not through mere free will, but through affirmation by the other', he presents not only the most Heideggerian of statements, but also the most Kafkaesque.[30] Certainly no statement in contemporary critical legal scholarship has come closer to bottling the spirit of Kafka's parable, and then releasing it onto a page of 'legal' text. Pluralism has represented a particular idol for critical legal writers, but an awareness that the need to address the method of discourse as a prerequisite for the presentation of any such idol has gradually risen in the critical legal consciousness. Allan Hutchinson, for example, has recognised that both 'the method and medium must change', so that 'self-creation becomes the engine and energy of social change ... We can only fully grasp life by living. We cannot complete this task outside of language, but we cannot accomplish it entirely through language.'[31]

It is not surprising, or indeed particularly original to suggest that the political visions of thinkers such as Arendt and Marcuse, or indeed their inter-disciplinary approach to the problems of the human condition, bear a striking similarity to some of the theses presented by a number of critical legal thinkers during the previous decade. But it needs to be reaffirmed in the context of this particular chapter, because it provides a link in a chain tracing the origins of contemporary forms of critical legal scholarship with the narrative fictions of such writers as Kafka and Camus, and the political philosophies of such thinkers as Heidegger. To understand critical legal scholarship one must appreciate its association with literary theory and literary texts. The style, the rhetoric and the ambition of critical legal theory lies in the writings of Kafka, Camus and other such novelists as well as in thinkers like Heidegger or Marcuse. In a sense then, this can be termed a 'weak' defence of law and literature. The stronger defences seek to justify law and literature, and most particularly law *in* literature, by asserting its value as a form of jurisprudence in its own right. The strongest defence is that law is a part of life and plays an integral role in the determination of the human condition. This is not, however, a purely legal condition. Once this is understood, then political, social and philosophical texts will be admitted to jurisprudential discourse. At that point there is also no reason why narrative texts should not be included in the discourse. Once a narrative text is understood to be a piece of fiction, and once it is appreciated that Kafka never intended to instruct us with regard to the nature of Austro-Hungarian criminal procedure, then the narrative can be understood as contributing to the general debate on the nature of the human condition. At the same time by presenting itself as a fiction, and as subject to the vicissitudes of interpretation, there is no requirement that a narrative text should present a determination of any concept. It is for us to 'create' our interpretation, and in doing so to enjoin a participatory dialogue. As Joseph Singer suggested, 'indeterminacy' is not a monster that devours all possibility of a rational and fulfilled existence.[32] It is simply a fact of life which, when appreciated, can be used precisely to enhance our understanding of our own possibilities. This simple fact lies behind Kant's final unifying third *Critique*, the ambition of Heidegger's address to the students of Freiburg in 1933, and was that which drove Kafka to present Joseph K. with the parable 'Before the Law', and Camus to see Sisyphus 'happy'.

PART III

Two studies in contemporary literature

CHAPTER 8

Ivan Klima's 'Judge on Trial'

What unites all law and literature scholars is the belief that
literature impresses upon us a sense of textual contingency. Such
texts can be at once social, historical, political and ethical as well,
of course, as literary. In other words, literary texts offer legal scholars a contextual window, and it is the purpose of this chapter to
suggest that Ivan Klima's *Judge on Trial* presents precisely such a
window. Through this window Klima presents not merely a catalogue of twentieth-century jurisprudence – at various points in the
narrative, through his central character the lawyer Adam, Klima
considers the whole gamut of legal theories, natural law, positivism,
Kantianism and critical legal theory – but at the same time does
so in the particular context of the modern novel and its portrayal
of legal situations. The central themes of the novel, culminating in
that of the alienated individual, makes *Judge on Trial* a suitable
text for an investigation of many of the issues introduced in the
previous chapter. Alienation, or the 'politics of exclusion', is the
problem of the 'human condition', which Richard Weisberg
has placed at the root of the modern novel's treatment of the 'legal
protagonist', and which he suggests derives originally from
Nietzsche and Heidegger. It is, of course, the alienation which
George Steiner famously suggested had culminated in the 'long
and precise imagining' represented by the Holocaust.[1] The
Holocaust has proved to be, not surprisingly, something of a watershed in legal as well as in literary culture, and it comes as no
surprise that Adam's experiences of it provides one of the prime
dynamics of *Judge on Trial*.[2] The initially tepid jurisprudential
response to the Holocaust in the form of the Hart–Fuller debate
was itself one of the strongest impulses behind the call for a
new jurisprudence. The ultimate alienation of the individual
was perceived as requiring a fundamental reconstitution of the

community. The alienation works on two levels. First, there is alienation from the legal system of sections of society such as women, blacks, the poor and, in Klima's world, the political incorrect. On a second level there is the pervasive alienation of all individuals in the modern world and, again, in Klima's world, the Czechoslovakia of 1986, this is a particularly acute alienation. Although both levels of alienation are everywhere present, the perspective that Klima presents serves to intensify them. The particular position of the lawyer in modern society has proved to be an especially popular mechanism by which writers can present an intense sense of alienation as, of course, has the position of the individual in a 'totalitarian' political system. Moreover, it has been combined before in, for example, Kakfa's *The Trial*. The role of the judge in the continental tradition, as an examining magistrate, has served to further concentrate the idea of the individual judge as 'external' to the community. Kafka, Camus, Dostoevsky and now Klima have all been able to exploit this particular magistrate–individual–community relationship as a means of intensifying the sense of 'mutual alienation' which critical legal scholarship so vigorously seeks to emphasise.

One of the most interesting facets of Klima's narrative is the sense of reality which it presents. There is certainly a greater sense of 'reality' than in the metaphorical treatment provided by Kafka, or perhaps by Camus. So *Judge on Trial* seems more akin to *Crime and Punishment* than to *The Trial* or *The Outsider*. Indeed, the alleged crime that Adam must consider bears a striking resemblance to Raskolnikov's in *Crime and Punishment*. It is often suggested that the more 'real' the presentation, the more 'useful' is the narrative as a law and literature text.[3] The alienation of the individual, which remains at the heart of the novel, thus enjoys a perhaps greater sense of reality than it does in the portrayal of Joseph K. or Mersault. Adam is a more easily identifiable character, and what he feels as an individual and what he feels as a lawyer can be more readily accessed by the reader. Adam is very definitely presented as having two characters. He is at once an individual and also a lawyer. Adam is thus fully engaged in the 'politics of exclusion', both as an excluding force and one who is himself excluded. He is employed to exclude individuals not only from the legal system, but perhaps more importantly from the possibility of justice. At the same time he also feels himself to be excluded both from society as a whole and from the individuals around him, but also ultimately from the legal system which he represents and of which initially he thought himself a part. *Judge on Trial* thus presents two narratives, the story of Adam the individual and Adam the lawyer. These two narratives continue throughout the novel, but are structurally divided. There is the continuing narrative of Adam the individual wrestling with his own life and its problems, and the immediate demands placed upon him as a judge, and there is the sequence of flashbacks into Adam's own experiences and gradual association with the law. In presenting these narratives and thus constructing Adam's 'contemporary' approach to law from his own experience, Klima very skilfully emphasises the lawyer as the product of both the past and the present. This historicist analysis of the lawyer's mind is very much in line with that presented by critical legal scholars as a counterpoint to the image of the ahistorical and apolitical lawyer which has been perceived until now as lying at the heart of the established liberal tradition.

THE JURISPRUDENCE OF THE TEXT: CREATING THE LAWYER

Adam's earliest flashbacks recall his experiences during the Second World War.[4] It was his 'first encounter with punitive justice, or rather with an all-powerful police'.[5] The pervasive atmosphere of these recollections is one of isolation and desperation. Adam is a displaced person subsisting in a community of displaced persons. There is a constant sense of betrayal: individuals betraying individuals, and a reflective betrayal of the state and its people. In other words, Adam's experiences during the war, shunted around from one camp to another, are of his own alienation and the alienation of the human condition. These wartime experiences present themselves as a metaphor for the entire novel. Adam loses a number of friends and family, and the effect of these losses, gradually decreasing as the number increases, serves to intensify Adam's sense of loneliness. Moreover, the losses also contribute to his earliest impressions of legal justice. Two of his uncles were arrested: 'The court, which ever delivered one verdict and hence lost all right to be called a court pronounced the inevitable sentence and shortly afterwards they were executed.'[6] Adam recognises that these are memories which he will 'always' carry 'within' him, and which will colour the rest of his life.[7] The real bitterness of these early experiences is encapsulated in the final sentence of the first recollections, when Adam, with hindsight, stresses their centrality to the fate of the human condition. The Nazi occupation could not be categorised as the exception:

Convinced I had to do something to ensure that people would never again lose their freedom, so that they should never again find themselves in hermetically sealed surroundings with no chance of escape, ruled solely by butcher's knives, I prepared to become a foot-soldier of the revolution, a hobby-horse for a new generation of butchers to mount, and wielding their cleavers drive the scattered human herd into rebuilt enclosures, and set to with their knives to carve out the splendid future.[8]

The second set of recollections develops the sense of naivety which, with hindsight, Adam can attribute to his earliest behaviour, and to the effects of his wartime experiences. At school he first encounters what he perceives to be a dichotomy between philosophy and politics. This dichotomy serves to determine Adam's attitude to jurisprudential issues for most of the rest of the novel. Adam's experiences led to a virulently pragmatic political approach:

I saw little sense in contemplating the meaning of concepts such as beauty, happiness, justice, well-being or even truth. Far more important, it seemed to me, was to reflect on how to make sure that people had access to beauty and an opportunity to hear, proclaim and discover the truth ... I did believe, however, that in most of our arguments I had truth on my side, because, after all, I had behind me an unrepeatable experience of life.[9]

Even at this early stage, Adam is convinced by a raw Marxist vision of· justice. 'The basis of all crimes' was 'inequality, and material inequality above all'.[10] His friend Mirek suggests that such a system of 'rules' is rather easy to formulate, and tends to ignore the 'various contradictions' that life presents. Precisely the criticism that critical legal scholarship has levelled on numerous occasions against a rule formalist approach to law; the rigid application of rules on the basis that the greatest virtue of any legal order is its consistency, regardless of any possible concerns for natural justice. Mirek is another friend who is lost to Adam. He abandons Adam or, more precisely, what Adam represents, and escapes to Germany. During his last year at school Adam was 'appointed' chairman of the class committee of the youth organisation.

Adam became a judge of his peers, and immediately took the responsibility to be their political overlord: 'my experiences and convictions fitted me for just such a role'.[11] Aware that he was 'hemmed in by opponents', he decided to establish a committee to investigate his fellow pupils, and to judge them; he 'yearned to sit in judgement'. The role that Adam assumed had the immediate effect of isolating him from the rest of the class; he excluded them from justice, and they excluded him from their society.[12] One of the most powerful scenes in the entire novel is Adam's investigation of three of his fellow pupils. When he informed one of them, the disease-ridden Zora, that her 'attitude' to the state was 'largely hostile', he was met by a total silence. When he tried to destroy the ambition of another to become a teacher, because she was too clever, and dangerously so, the silence is shattered by her hysterical screaming, but is then restored when Adam leaves the room: 'I was expecting someone to come up to me (after all, we had been indulgent towards so many of them) with a word of thanks or perhaps criticism, but they walked out past me as if I had the plague, or more accurately, as if I didn't exist.'[13]

The next two sets of recollections, whilst Adam is at university and at the law faculty, portray a gradual realisation of disillusionment. Initially Adam is still very much the idealist, and perhaps inevitably determines to study political 'science'. He is, 'at first' convinced by the Marxists whom he encounters. He 'spoke their language', and 'lived in the deep shadows of the idols of social revolution'.[14] Adam is enrolled by the Party to visit a factory to explain 'the meaning' of the political show trials which had been going on. At the time he was unaware that political justice was 'simply a terrifying play in whose last act the reluctant actors were hung on a real gallows by a real executioner.'[15] At this time also Adam has his first experience of sex, with Eva, the leader of his youth party. It proves to be a metaphor for his subsequent realisation of the distance between himself and the state. Adam finds the experience to be one of acute isolation. This sense of confused and dawning disillusionment is sharply crystallised by the seizure of his father which immediately follows. In an account strongly reminiscent of the fate of Joseph K. in *The Trial*, Adam's father is taken away without any information as to why or where he is to go. Adam can ascribe his father's fate only to some 'appalling miscarriage of justice'. His Uncle Gustav could suggest only that they put their 'trust in the Party', but at the same time warned the family against making any contact with anybody else in the community. The family had to isolate themselves from everyone. Ironically, in reading the Criminal Law and Penal Code from cover to cover, in an attempt to better understand why his father had been seized, Adam became convinced of a desire to be a lawyer. Of course, reading the Code did not make the law any more understandable or accessible for Adam, or for his father. But Adam was captivated by the law as a symbol, and as an instrument for social and political justice: 'Like most people I viewed the law more as a device for obscuring true justice. All of a sudden, to my surprise, I had encountered a code. Its perfection, adequacy or absurdity compared to other codes of the same kind of course were issues I could not possibly judge, but the very attempt to encompass the whole of life and organise it into a system enthralled me.'[16]

Having enrolled in the law faculty, Adam's first experience of the law is one of complete alienation. As he enters the law faculty building, which extolled the role of socialist law as 'an auxiliary in the construction of the socialist homeland', Adam felt himself to be back in his 'old situation', as 'the only non-initiate amongst the initiated'. His new colleagues appeared to be a world apart from the rest of the community which Adam had experienced: better dressed, more socially involved, and correspondingly, less politically aware.[17] When he first comes into immediate contact with jurisprudence, Adam experiences a myriad of different intellectual responses to the theories which are presented to him. His initial response is one of contempt for theories of justice. The natural and rational philosophies of law presented by such as Weyr and Kant seem to be hopelessly abstract: 'Who could possibly have any need for reflections on pure law or the supreme legal norm?' The question, of course, represents the most acute of ironies.[18] Ultimately, Adam will come to advocate a rational or Kantian philosophy of law as the only way of overcoming the horrors of alienation which he has experienced. Thankfully for Adam, his own research dissertation was not expected to foster any original ideas. The research for this dissertation, on seventeenth-century Czech justice proves, however, to be something of a watershed in Adam's intellectual development. Reading about law in action, and its potential power to inflict misery, suddenly makes the theory of law matter. Also for the first time, Adam realised what the authority of law and of the lawyer meant:

They had spilled so much blood that no one will ever measure it, but none, apart from rare exceptions, were ever called to account, because unlike the rest they had been able to cloak their craving for violence in the right kind of authority. And for the first time I realised that I too would be one of that band some day, although so far I had not had the faintest inkling of its actual nature.[19]

Adam's reading leads him to see the Enlightenment as banishing the inadequacies of medieval justice:

Throughout history, the class struggle had assumed the character of a battle between reason and unreason. Bit by bit, reason was displacing unreason – which always promoted belief and blind obedience, and disparaged thoughtfulness, the spirit of conciliation and the opinions of others.

It is, however a particular reason which Adam perceives, and then requisitions for his socialist ideal:

Hence reason would always find a way out of the darkness; it would only emerge from silence and rise from the dead. Only now was I approaching the purpose of my essay. What else was reason's supreme achievement but my Model State: a society carefully run so as to leave no scope for unreason? What else as the apogee of reason but the idea of socialism?[20]

The contingency of reason, and the impossibility of accessing a universal metaphysics of reason, is the keystone of critical legal thought. At best, in a Rawlsian analysis, a community can 'construct' a rationality, by which it can then live.[21] This disillusion with the possibilities of a universal rationalist conception of justice, first sensed by Kant, and then forcefully and irrevocably established by Hegel and Heidegger, has been the root of critical legal thought's impatience with universalism. It is very much the motif of twentieth-century jurisprudence. In his interview with Professor Lyon, Adam gives voice to this disillusion:

Yes, of course, that was how it always started. Everyone yearned for perfection and purity. As if there existed some collective creative spirit that soared higher and higher. However, it soon found itself far above the earth and got lost in the clouds, whereupon it forgot why it had set out in the first place and where it was bound. At that point it could only see itself and became fascinated by its own image. It actually became bewitched by its own face, its own proceedings, its own words, its own form, its own perfect logical judgement. That was when concepts of pure reason and justice emerged, along with theories about the absolute norm in art, philosophy and jurisprudence ... There was nothing wrong with my striving for absolute justice if it tickled me to, but I should never delude myself that it was attainable. Unless I wanted to assist a further decline, I had always to remember that in reality there was no such thing as justice or law. What was there then? All there was was compromise with the rulers as they decreed a greater or lesser degree of injustice.

Law and philosophy, the Professor assured Adam, were mutually exclusive, and the 'practice of law led either to cynicism or madness'. An example was Kafka: Adam, who had never heard of Kafka, said nothing.[22] The recollection of Adam's student experiences ends with the relation of his father's trial and sentence. The nature of the proceedings, the secrecy of the trial and the reading of the verdict 'as if it were a report about shoe production, or the potato harvest', stressed once again the alienation of the accused, his exclusion from justice, and also Adam's increasing awareness of it. If he had heard about Kafka, of course, it might have been less of a surprise.[23]

Adam's first experiences as a lawyer are to be in a place he calls 'the Hole' in the distant north-east of the country, and a place where he feels completely isolated and alone. The presiding judge is a drunkard, Adam's only colleague long ago gave up thinking anything 'but what he was supposed to think' and the clerk whom Adam befriends is discovered to be corrupt. It is here also that Adam first encounters the corruption of the legal system of which he had become a part. He is obligated by the presiding judge and prosecutor to find a man guilty, because he was one of the 'enemies'. There is a very tangible sense of a 'them and us' attitude in the language that the prosecutor uses. Despite recognising that the defendant had only done what he thought was 'right', and that Adam knew that the sentence was 'unjust', he gave the man three and a half years: 'I convicted a victim. The only thing that I can say in my defence is that I lived in a vacuum and lacked courage.' Adam's growing self-doubts were articulated by Magdalena, with whom he embarks upon an affair. She said that she 'hated' him, because of his being part of a system that excluded: 'Why? Because of what I had done with her, what I was doing to people, to the whole of this country. And what was I doing? I was pushing it deeper and deeper into the void, casting it into darkness.'[24] Eventually Adam leaves Magdalena, the only woman he thought that he had ever loved. The more experienced Adam becomes, and the more disillusioned, the more he realises how little he knows, and how complicated things really are. On his return to Prague, from Magdalena and from the Hole, he returns to his jurisprudential studies, only to reel from the weight of his ignorance. It is in this confused state that Adam meets his wife, and encounters her confused family. His conversations with Alena graphically convey the extent of Adam's disillusionment with his own existence as a person and as a lawyer. Of all his recollections this confusing period, when Adam feels completely alienated from the system to which he had committed his own faith, is the most blurred.[25] Adam's visit to England only serves to intensify the sense of disillusionment at his own naivety. In conversation with Anglo-American jurists, Adam becomes aware that he has no understanding of fundamental justice, merely of a political justice.[26] The extent of this disillusionment leads Adam to produce an article against the death penalty, and in so doing to rebel against the political norm. In an ironic twist of fate Adam is then himself put on 'trial' by a Party Committee who seek to investigate the motivation behind the article, and is interrogated with a particular earnest by one of his former classmates, over whom he had exercised his authority so many years ago.[27] The final series of recollections, of a visit to Michigan, and a return to Prague at the time of the 1969 uprising reveal Adam finally, if hesitatingly, discovering a new philosophy by which to live, and it is to this philosophy that I want, now, to turn.

THE JURISPRUDENCE OF THE TEXT: DESTROYING THE INDIVIDUAL

The flashbacks considered above reveal the construction and then destruction of Adam as a lawyer. At the same time, the 'contemporary' narrative mirrors the destruction of Adam as an individual; a destruction brought about in large part because of his very acutely felt sense of isolation. This narrative is underpinned by the saga of Adam's role as investigating judge in the case of a young man who he is obligated to find guilty of murder, regardless or not of his innocence. Although the jurisprudence, and the philosophy–politics clash which dominates Adam's conception of it, is not as explicit in much of the 'contemporary' narrative, there are again a number of scenes which serve to underscore the central themes of the novel. Without the portrayal of its evolution, the sense of disillusionment is, if anything, even more oppressive in the 'contemporary' narrative. Listening to a friend, Petr, read out his paper on law and government, Adam concentrates most sharply on the seemingly unavoidable misery of the human condition:

They had elected parliaments and taken pains over their choice of representatives, but again and again the parliaments would declare a war and leave people no less desperate or hopeless than before. Therefore they had tried getting rid of parliaments and establishing leaders enthusiastically in their place. And what had been the upshot? Even greater disaster.[28]

The history of the human condition, as critical legal theorists repeatedly emphasise, is a history of the failure to take responsibility. The failure of the human condition is, at the same time, juxtaposed by Adam with his own failings as an individual and a lawyer. Prompted by Petr, he muses upon the possibilities of doing something to break out of the system, but is able to convince himself that it would be futile. Reflecting on his own experiences at the end of the war, he bitterly recalls his naive optimism that things might change as 'the greatest mistake of his life'. Whereas his friends are fired by an optimism for change, the only thing that Adam wanted 'to know above all was how one should live in the knowledge that destiny is irreversible'. His friends stay to discuss the recreation of an ethical community. Adam decides to leave.[29] As Adam comes to grips with the dilemma that he faces, he becomes ever more aware of the similarities of his own position with those of the defendant, Karel. The letter that Adam writes to his brother is potentially more subversive than Karel's correspondence.[30] The guilt in the novel is Adam's.

One of the most powerful scenes is Adam's interrogation of Karel. The interrogation is conducted whilst Adam himself is betraying his own wife, colleagues and friends, shirking responsibility for his own existence, and losing his own identity and becoming ever more aware of the fact. Even his own lover, in the scene immediately preceding the interrogation, berates Adam for 'helping' to 'sustain their disgusting system'. At the beginning of the interrogation, Klima immediately emphasises Adam's own isolation, cut off 'from the world he had so far inhabited'. Both Adam and Karel are alienated, from one another and from everyone else. What is particularly striking about the interrogation dialogue is the extent to which the onus is placed upon Karel to exonerate himself. It is for Karel to prove his innocence, not for Adam to prove Karel's guilt. The system excludes the defendant as a matter of course. By interweaving narrative accounts of Adam's affair with Alex with the interrogation dialogue, Klima is able to further stress the fact that both Adam and Karel are guilty of essentially the same actions, only that the sense of betrayal is Adam's alone. Whilst Karel expresses his innocence and the truth of this statement, for Adam there was instead 'a sudden devastating intuition: right now everything that had seemed significant to him in his life was disintegrating. But what was disintegrating in fact: his life or, on the contrary, his delusions about his life ...?' Adam realises that his life to date had indeed been a story of the failure to take responsibility himself. But now, faced with the acute ethical dilemma posed by Karel's case, Adam could no longer hide: 'Now there was no skirting the traps, too many had been laid. He would either have to decide on what action to take, or become bogged down. But he was not accustomed to taking any decisive action; not on his own behalf, anyway. Even the thing that had just happened had not been of his doing.'[31]

One of the most intriguing passages, a conversation between Adam and his lover, reveals a double confusion: Adam's own confusion, brought about by the dilemmas which he has been forced to experience, and a paradox inherent in any legal system, whether or not judges should take political responsibility.

'You're just like the rest! How can you be a judge then?'
'I judge people according to the law.'
'How can you judge people when you don't know how we ought to
    live ?'
'I don't like people who think they know the right way to live.'
'Why don't you like them?'
'Most of them force others to live their way.'
'But they don't know anything: the ones that force others to do things.
They're just as grotesque as the ones who judge according to the law.'[32]

In other words, why should judges not take political decisions? Is there any reason why politicians should be any more capable? Perhaps the most important jurisprudential question lies between the lines. Is this not what happens anyway? As Adam drifts from one lover to another his sense of alienation intensifies, as of course does his disillusionment with even the possibility that justice can 'exist'. Marx, he comes to realise, shared the same doubts, but they had not bothered him.[33] Increasingly Adam comes to question his right to sit in judgement over others. His wife resents him judging her. According to Adam, he does it because she is a 'stranger' to him. In other words, any act of judgement is only possible if the person judged is externalised. Adam also does it because it enables him to avoid judging himself. It is a mechanism for escaping the responsibility of life. Adam realises that he has spent his entire life running away from responsibility.[34] His return to Czechoslovakia at the close of the novel represents a final act of self-assertion. The reasons for this final act, which develop from Adam's realisation that the root of his demise lay with his evading responsibility, are established by the evolution of a different philosophy of law and of life.

TOWARDS A 'POETHICS' OF THE TEXT

In a sense the purpose of this final section is to suggest the possible subversion of the basic premise of the first three sections: the portrayal of two alienated characters, Adam as the lawyer and Adam as the individual. It is moreover a subversion which Klima himself gradually integrates into the novel, and which is finally produced explicitly in the final chapters. What Klima presents in the last chapters is precisely the 'poethics' which Richard Weisberg suggests is the ultimate ambition of law and literature scholarship; the use of literary texts to discover an ethical basis which can transcend the alienated condition. As I suggested in chapter I, according to Weisberg the use of literature enables lawyers to 'see the other'. It bridges the gap which analytical jurisprudence has established, and enables the reconstitution of a community ethics. The lawyer must become a judge of him or herself, as well as a judge of others. The legal situation cannot be distanced from the real world. Justice can only ever be a community justice. Above all justice can only ever be communicated. In the final analysis, legal theory is irreducibly a theory of language and language use. In short, for Weisberg, '[p]oethics, in its attention to legal communication and to the plight of those who are "other", seeks to revitalize the ethical component of law'.[35] Weisberg's work is in large part a result of a frustration at the immediate responses amongst Anglo-American legal theorists at the events of 1933–1945.

The only substantive response during the first three decades was the renowned Hart–Fuller debate, conducted between two of the leading positivist and natural law theorists.[36] Both were concerned purely with the nature of sovereignty in a legal order, and used National Socialist Germany as a metaphor for their argument. According to Hart, who presented the positivist position, National Socialist law was valid providing it was established in accordance with its own sovereign norms; in other words, without regard for any ethical component. Fuller, the natural lawyer, suggested that the Nazi legal order was only valid if it established laws which were in accordance with universal moral norms.

Having made its statement and reached its inevitable impasse, western jurisprudence moved on to pastures new, or rather to repeating again and again the same positions. In Germany, meanwhile, a number of jurists, particularly taking note of Hart and Fuller's misuse of Gustav Radbruch, a leading Kantian jurist in the 1930s, to whom they tried to ascribe positivist or natural law sympathies, noted with virtual bewilderment that the entire debate was founded upon a fundamental misunderstanding. If Hart or Fuller wanted to understand Radbruch, or indeed the continental jurisprudential tradition as a whole, they had to understand the dominant influence of Kant. If anyone wanted to advocate the re-establishment of a philosophy of ethics at the heart of a new legal order in central Europe, then they would have to look to Kant.[37] It was Kant who first and most influentially developed the idea of a constructive or communicative ethics in *The Metaphysics of Morals*. The theories which have since been produced by Arendt, Habermas, Gadamer, Rawls or Weinrib have paid universal homage to Kant's inspiration. It was Kant who suggested that the moral law lay within, not without, the individual. When Heidegger first advocated the self-assertion of the individual he did so by developing it from his own reading of Kant.[38] Kant empowered the individual to accommodate a conception of freedom within the demands of the community. The categorical imperative preserved at once the freedom of the individual and the freedom of the community, and thus geared the establishment of communicative ethics.[39] When Weisberg suggests that literature should be used as a means of re-establishing an essentially communicative legal (po)ethics, he, too, is advocating a return to Kant.

Although in the final chapters of *Judge on Trial* Adam is still racked by disillusionment and self-doubt, it is the increasing realisation in his own mind that a new philosophy, both for himself and for his country and its legal system, must be established around a conception of freedom and a re-established ethics. In other words there must be an ethically reconstituted community, developed through a communicative interaction between the individual and the community. This realisation is crystallised by Adam's experiences in Michigan and on his return to Prague. In Michigan Adam is immediately impressed by the academic freedom and the possibilities presented by so much and varied literature. Klima concentrates on the nature of freedom and its interaction with individual development. This development must be recognised as a development within a community context: 'It was there that I realised for the first time that lack of freedom harms people not only by blocking their path to knowledge and curtailing what they can say and where they can go, but also by damaging the very core of their being and enslaving them by switching their attention to themselves alone.'[40] When Adam returns to the Prague of 1969, he finds the freedom which can regenerate both the community and himself.[41] The arrival of the Russians serves to intensify Adam's sense of freedom. His own freedom is threatened just as is the freedom of his community. Adam now abandons the legal order which had finally abandoned him and in doing so finally excludes himself, as opposed to excluding others and being excluded by them. It is a gesture at once of acute disillusionment and also acute hope. It is the kind of gesture which made Camus see 'Sisyphus happy'.[42] Adam becomes reconciled to the inevitability of his own fate and, at the same moment, master of it:

He was overcome with a forgotten exaltation: he caught the sound of an organ from the depths below him – someone had started to play the same old melody. With amazement he realised the coincidence, even though he had discovered long ago that one could not escape one's fate, that there was no way of climbing out of one's own life ... The most that one could hope for was to stand on the summit – if one managed to reach it – and view the landscape one had passed through on one's travels and try to descry within it what had so far eluded one's gaze; one could also raise one's eyes to the heavens which one had forgotten ... He also knew by now that one would never find freedom in this world – however perfect were the laws and however great one's control over the world and people – unless one found it in oneself. And nobody could endow one with moral grandeur if it was not born in one's soul, just as nobody could release one from one's bonds if one did not cast off the shackles of one's own making ... He was running away from no one, renouncing no one, not intending to abandon anyone or bind anyone to him, and least of all did he want to judge anyone.[43]

Klima presents the critical philosophy of ethics which finally can serve to collapse the distinction between Adam the lawyer and Adam the individual. It is, in the final analysis, a Kantian philosophy of ethics. Moreover, it is the communicative ethics which White demands, and the poethics which Richard Weisberg suggests can be found in literature. A study of Klima's *Judge on Trial* is a study of the origins and of the fate of critical legal thought. It is also, and perhaps this is most important of all, a novel which presents not merely the possibilities for a reconstituted legal ethics but the necessity for one.[44]

CHAPTER 9

Umberto Eco's 'The Name of the Rose'

Umberto Eco's *The Name of the Rose* represents a particularly fruitful text for jurisprudential investigation, first because of its author. Umberto Eco is Professor of Semiotics at the University of Bologna and a renowned leader in the field of semiotics and the philosophy of language. If anybody knows about literary theory and its uses, it is Eco. More precisely, as we discussed in chapter 2, Eco has advanced the idea of the 'model reader' as a means of determining the use of a text. More than anyone, perhaps, he has urged upon us the importance of the author in establishing the audience, if not the audience's interpretation. So in writing *The Name of the Rose*, Eco is writing with his model audience in mind. The novel is particularly fruitful, secondly, because Eco chooses to present a series of quasi-legal scenes, complemented by a constant discussion of philosophical and jurisprudential issues. Eco has consciously presented a particularly legal narrative. If we want to use it, and we feel that we can trust it, *The Name of the Rose* offers itself as a window into medieval jurisprudence, just as it does into contemporary theories of semiotics and language. If we, as a legal audience, learn nothing from Eco's novel, we can learn nothing from the study of literature.[1] In the first part of this chapter I will provide a necessarily brief introduction to the intellectual context within which the chapter works, and then in the second part I apply Eco's modelling in a reading of the text of *The Name of the Rose*. This reading will seek to show the extent to which the text constrains the reader by its presentation of a semiotics, a philosophy and a jurisprudence of its own. Ultimately, in the final part of the chapter, I suggest that Eco's novel presents a particular jurisprudential position, and one that is characteristic of modern literature.

THE INTELLECTUAL CONTEXT

Set in the fourteenth century, *The Name of the Rose* is thus sited in a period of acute intellectual unrest. Eco utilises fully these possibilities, exploring in considerable depth the extent to which the various theoretical positions played against one another. At its very basic level, the struggle in late medieval intellectualism was an essentially three-cornered one between the Socratics, the Thomists and the nominalists, between reason, revelation and individualism. The towering figure of St Thomas Aquinas, whose 'accommodation' of reason and revelation dominated late medieval theology and philosophy, and whose intellectual presence dominates in Eco's novel, will be considered shortly. But first it is important to widen the context. Medieval learning was ruled by texts and text use, far more so than is the case in the twentieth century. Rather than restricting the advancement of learning it was thought that these texts, and particularly the 'Commentaries' on them provided the 'vehicle[s] for original thought'.[2] Moreover, it was on the scriptural texts, most particularly the Bible, and the commentaries on them, that the principles were centred. In the great universities of the thirteenth and fourteenth centuries, such as those of Paris and Oxford, the concentration was upon the method of 'reading' texts in order to extract their meaning, and then upon the open 'disputation' of this meaning. The great 'textbooks' of the period were constructed around this system, using *quaestiones* or *summae* in order to construct internalised 'disputations'. These constructions were geared deliberately in an effort to resolve or accommodate the contradictions inherent in so many scriptural texts. Aquinas' *Summa Theologiae* and *Summa contra Gentiles* represented the epitome of the method.[3] The actual interpretive methods of reading were dominated, like so much else, by the enduring influence of Aristotle. It is impossible to overestimate the extent of Aristotle's influence on medieval philosophy. The rigour of the syllogism remained a dominant force in the medieval art of reading. It is repeatedly used in *The Name of the Rose* by Brother William, whose continual reference to Aristotelian authority rightly reflects the extent of its influence on the medieval mind. The syllogism was also extensively used by William of Ockham who emerges, of course, as the mentor for Brother William's scepticism. As the interest in interpretive method gathered pace during the thirteenth and fourteenth centuries, it was still the rigour of Aristotelian logic, as presented in the *Posterior Analytics*, *De Interpretatione* and *De Sophisticis Elenchis*, which reigned supreme.[4]

The rationalism which was so influential in medieval theories of reading, presented an equal potential threat to the philosophy of medieval theology. In the words of one contemporary commentator, 'the encounter between biblical revelation and Greek philosophy' geared the entire intellectual development of medieval Europe.[5] Much has been made of the early resistance to Aristotle's natural philosophy as contained in the *Metaphysics* and *Libri Naturales*, particularly of Robert de Courçon's famous edict which banned their use at the University of Paris in 1215.[6] This edict immediately assumed a symbolic importance, and its echoes resound throughout the narrative of *The Name of the Rose*. The determination of the abbey to secrete the 'dangerous' books, including the second book of Aristotle's *Poetics*, is a metaphor for the fears which inspired de Courçon's instructions. By the late thirteenth century, however, the edict was losing its force. Not only were Aristotle's texts reaching an increasing circulation, they were coming through an interpretive filter provided by prominent Islamic and Jewish philosophers, most importantly Avicenna, Averroes and Maimonides. The presentation of a supreme cognitive reason, the *kalaam*, was very much the centrepiece of contemporary thirteenth-century Islamic philosophy, and both Avicenna and Averroes, whose 'Commentary' on Aristotle enjoyed a virtually universal reverence in the west, impressed the apparent incompatibility of reason and revelation. By the late thirteenth century, Averroes' doctrine of the primacy of a human reason, expressed in the unity of a potential and creative intellect, was being articulated in Paris by both Siger and Boethius. So much so that in 1270, and again in 1277, both were to be condemned as heretical by Pope John XXI. Indeed, although Aquinas openly challenged Siger's extreme position, such was the reaction against any accommodation of reason that Aquinas' writings were also implicitly condemned. In the words of one contemporary commentator, medieval theology was being increasingly destabilised, 'challenged by views, supported by argument, which were plainly incompatible with faith'. Moreover, being arguments which were presented as logic, they were arguments which could not be explained away by allegory. In the end it was to the Jewish philosopher Maimonides that Aquinas sought recourse for the seeds of an accommodation.[7]

But before examining Aquinas' accommodation, and his use of Maimonides, there is one final perspective that needs to be noted. Throughout *The Name of the Rose* Brother William repeatedly acknowledges the influence of nominalist scepticism in the person of William of Ockham. No sooner had Aquinas presented his accommodation than a number of scholars began to doubt the very essentiality of even this accommodated universalism, amongst whom the nominalists and the Ockhamites were perhaps the most influential. Ockham was an original thinker in a very real sense, and explicitly rejected the substance of received wisdom, Aquinas' included. Whereas Aquinas presented a mediation of what seemed to be logically incompatible, Ockham felt no compunction in triumphing the power of the individual intellect. His ultimate position on speculative knowledge was, in the final analysis, perhaps closer to that of Averroes than any contemporary Christian theologian. However, whereas Averroes championed rationalism, Ockham championed contingency, and did so by an uncompromising rejection of Aristotelian metaphysics.[8] In his study of medieval aesthetics, Eco reveals a particular awareness of the existential potentialities in Ockham's writings, and his unavoidably nominalist influences. For Ockham, he suggests, 'created things' were 'absolutely contingent', and conformed to 'no stable cosmic order'. Any order or unity in the world was relative to things themselves. The individual existence was radically contingent. As Eco acknowledges, Ockham was a man well ahead of his time and by aligning his central character with Ockham Eco was exploiting the most radically sceptical position in medieval philosophy, and the position nearest to that in contemporary critical theory which, as we shall see, Eco ultimately wishes to assume.[9]

With the benefit of hindsight, it might be easy to align Ockham with a kind of theological existentialism now familiarly associated with, for example, Karl Jaspers. However, in thirteenth-century Europe, it became increasingly difficult for the papal authorities to make any sort of ascription except one of heresy. Concentration on the role of the individual, and moreover the equality of all individuals, which gained support not only from a number of heretical sects, but also from some of the most influential of the established orders, such as the Franciscans, emerged as a very real threat to the authority of Rome. As well as their association with an egalitarian politics, it was the Franciscans' devotion to poverty which took the Order ever nearer to the more unacceptable heretical positions. Ockham himself, a Franciscan like Brother William in the novel, was eventually condemned by the Pope and famously forced to flee Avignon along with Michael of Cesena, Minister General of the Franciscan Order, in 1328. Michael plays a fleeting part in *The Name of the Rose* and through Adso, Eco provides a brief account of his attendance for disputation at Avignon, and his subsequent flight. These philosophical–theological disputes are the intellectual and indeed political backdrop to the novel, and in constructing the model reader from the very first pages, Eco immediately provides contextualising descriptions of theological politics.[10]

It was Aquinas who most successfully presented an accommodation of the apparently rival demands of reason and revelation. This apparent incompatibility was directed towards two essential problems; the nature of the Creation, and the limits of intellectual speculation. Both problems were rooted in the Aristotelian reason. In order to maintain the authority of the Christian faith it was essential that Aquinas, or any other Christian theologian, should assert, first, the reality of the Creation, and thus dismiss the notion of an eternal world without beginning or end, and second, the supreme unquestionability of revelation, as a recognitive as opposed to a cognitive force, beyond the powers of reason. This was of course the received wisdom, as pronounced by St Augustine, which had ruled relatively unchallenged over early medieval theology. The purpose of philosophy for Aquinas was a means of accessing truth and blessedness. He thus rejected, of course, any of the scepticism which was to emerge in later medieval philosophy. Furthermore, although he used an Aristotelian *telos* at the heart of his philosophy, he uncompromisingly placed it in a position of subservience to God's power of divine revelation. This position was established in Augustine's hugely influential Doctrine of Divine Illumination, wherein God was presented as the source of all reason, and thus of all proofs. God's existence was always a matter of belief rather than thought, summed up perhaps most famously in the dictum: 'Therefore do not seek to understand in order to believe, but believe that thou mayst understand; since, "Except ye believe, ye shall not understand."'[11] Aquinas's early education, received from his teacher Albert the Great, was hugely influenced by Augustine, and indeed in the final analysis Aquinas remained essentially faithful to the basic Augustinian framework. However, by the mid-thirteenth century the challenge of reason had been vigorously renewed and reinforced, and the difficulties with which Albert tried to reconcile his respect for both Augustine and Aristotle had been inherited by Aquinas.

Aquinas' accommodation centred on the subjecting of all powers of human reason to the divine authority by an eternal law. To this extent he maintained the same position as Augustine. However, the manner in which he reached this position was philosophically quite different. Most importantly, he maintained reason and revelation to be governed by wholly discrete principles. In this way reason was 'used' as a means of complementing revelation, not challenging it. In Aquinas' opinion Aristotle had provided a unique 'instrument' for the furthering of God's work. The accommodation was to be in no sense a reconciliation, because there was no conceptual contradiction. The key to understanding this lay in realising the conceptual determination of the two. As one commentator has observed, Aquinas saw Aristotle's 'teleological ethics' as a 'substructure for Christian ethics'.[12] Reason possessed its own truths or *quidditas*, just as theology did. It was of course here, in his treatment of complementary truths, that Aquinas moved furthest away from established Augustinian doctrine, and it is much, much further along this way that one finds Ockham's nominalism. By establishing the complementary nature of the human intellect, Aquinas had established an active, creative intellect in the same way as Averroes and Ockham. As a number of commentators have observed, this movement took Aquinas closer to Aristotle than any previous Christian theologian had been, and most particularly to the famous passage in the *Nichomachean Ethics* where Aristotle had asserted the nature of discrete proofs.[13] Ultimately, and it was here that the Aristotelian influence shone through, revelation and reason would complement each other as a 'harmonic whole'. Because no truly correct reasoning could be contrary to revelation, revelation could thus correct reason by illustration. The frame was still in place, but the picture was quite different.[14]

Aquinas' jurisprudence was situated at the heart of this accommodation, which was effected most completely in the construction of his legal and political order in Questions 90–108 of the *Summa Theologiae*.[15] Eco's account of Day Five in *The Name of the Rose* and the jurisprudential issues that it raises are geared around these

Questions. The influence of Aristotle is perhaps most explicit in Aquinas' political theory. However, before considering this theory, it is first necessary to examine the considerable influence of the Jewish philosopher and jurist Maimonides, whose treatment of Aristotle was to gear Aquinas'. Recent scholarship has re-emphasised the extent of Maimonides' influence on Aquinas, most particularly on his jurisprudence.[16] It was Maimonides who first explored the nature of a complementary relationship between reason and revelation, as opposed to a purely subservient one, in his *Guide to the Perplexed*.[17] Maimonides constructed two 'planes' of 'cognition'; the first plane was the 'recognition' of revelation, and the second was the 'cognition' of reason. Maimonides' *Codes* were geared to this theoretical complement.[18] The existence of the two planes was rooted in Maimonides' description of the Creation, in the second chapter of Book One, wherein Adam was deprived of his 'intellectual apprehension' and instead, because of his sin, cast into a state of cognition. With his philosophy in place, centred on the complementary two planes of cognition in Books Two and Three of the *Guide*, Maimonides described the role of reason in the governing of man's affairs. The law he presents is thus natural because it is rational, and is in no way a challenge to divine revelatory law. It has the appearance of being natural: 'therefore I say that the law, although it is not natural, enters into to what is natural'.[19] In other words the law is not the product of reason, but of revelation, but it is accessed by reason. It is accessed because of the divine law: 'law that takes pains to inculcate correct opinions with regard to God ... you must know that this guidance comes from him, may he be exalted, and that this law is divine'.[20] Law is not questioned by reason, but cognised; it can be determined as good or bad, but not as true or false.[21]

Aquinas adopted the same two planes of cognition in the construction of his accommodation of reason and revelation. Moreover, like Maimonides and, of course, a whole tradition of Christian scholars, Aquinas used the Creation as his biblical authority.[22] These planes of cognition reflect, first the ability to apply reason to certain issues of morality and virtue, and secondly, the superior and unquestionable validity of those laws given us by divine law, which must be perceived without recourse to a questioning reason. As with Maimonides, the philosophical quest is at once a jurisprudential quest. In the very first part of the *Summa*

Theologiae, which is given over to establishing the existence of God, Aquinas is drawn into speculation about the natural order of government.[23] He is drawn into this speculation because of Aristotle's positing of the state as 'ideal'. For Aquinas, God is 'ideal', yet at the same time the demands of Aristotle, together with the dictates of medieval polity, require the positing of the state as an ideal of sorts.[24] Aquinas's immediate solution was to suggest that the state was the product of God's revelation, and so it and its laws were perfect in so far as God created them perfect. Whether or not they were good or bad was a subject for cognition, and not, of course, for political disobedience. This, as has been noted, can give rise to an almost 'positivist' expression of Aquinas' much-vaunted Natural Law.[25] Aquinas' political writings reveal the degree to which he was aware that philosophy and jurisprudence were, at once, political disciplines: a fact which is very definitely stressed in *The Name of the Rose*. Aquinas' concern with asserting the authority of the state, both secular and spiritual, was presented as a theory of obligations. Man, he asserted, taking his cue from Aristotle, is a political animal, subject to the *triplex ordo*, Divine Law, reason and political obligation; three parts of a harmonic whole. Man must take part in the political if he is to obtain the virtues, and so he must be subject to the constitution and its laws. Following Maimonides, Aquinas could thus state that politics was the 'natural' condition of man; a condition into which he must 'enter'. The whole became idealised in the *respublicana Christiana*, the unity of the single Christian society, so that with Plato and Aristotle Aquinas could assert that the individual good was congruent with the common good.[26]

Questions 90–97 of the *Summa* presented the nexus between the juridical and the philosophical in Aquinas' theology. This is made clear from the premise of Question 90, where Aquinas asserts that 'the essence of law ... [is] nothing else than an ordinance of reason for the common good, made by Him who has care of the community and promulgated.' It is a common good comprehended by reason, but promulgated by divine authority, to be used to address the rational efficacy of the perceived law as a discrete concept; 'the natural law is promulgated by the very fact that God instilled it into man's mind so as to be known by him naturally'.[27] In Question 91 Aquinas established his four kinds of law, by which he could interweave his philosophy and political theory: eternal law, which is the realisation that our reason is the product of divine guidance; natural law, which is the 'participation in the eternal law by rational creatures'; human law, which is the rational comprehension of eternal law; and the necessity of divine law, necessary because man is 'destined to an end of eternal blessedness'. The 'destiny' is that established by Augustine. The divine law is the keystone of the structure, not only because it prescribes the 'destiny', but because it regulates and orders the other three, which are then developed in Questions 93–97. It is, however, the eternal law developed in Question 93, which binds the philosophy with the politics, because it establishes the two planes of cognition as discrete concepts. All law, including the intensely Aristotelian human or civil law presented in Questions 95–97, derives from eternal law. It was the eternal law which, thus, gave unquestioning authority to the Roman church, spiritually, intellectually and, in the eyes of many politically.[28] Aquinas' jurisprudence, presented in the *Prima Secundae* of the *Summa*, presents not only Aquinas' juridical order, but also provides the critical link between the political and the philosophical. In essence, Questions 90–97 established the late medieval Christian constitution, and it was this constitution which was being challenged intellectually and politically in *The Name of the Rose*.[29]

READING THE TEXT

Dissecting a text in order to facilitate analysis seems particularly perverse when performed on a text which is being used primarily to reveal the inadequacies of traditional analytical method. Yet at the same time, as suggested in chapter 2, the pragmatics of text use can, to some extent at least, justify such an exercise. *The Name of the Rose* is sectioned by seven days, and this analysis of the text will follow this sectioning. Such a chronological analysis has the added advantage of playing Eco's game by allowing the text to develop itself and to exercise its own constraints. In theory it should allow the reader of this chapter to read in the same way as the model reader of the actual text.

Day One

As Eco subsequently commented, the long account of Day One sets the essential intellectual frame of the novel. Brother William himself is riddled by the pervasive intellectual doubts which we have just considered. According to Adso, on 'occasions' William spoke 'with great scepticism about universal ideas and with great respect about particular things', something which Adso ascribes to his being 'both a Briton and a Franciscan'.[30] Certainly, throughout the novel, William is presented as generally sceptical of the rigours of established theology. The contrast between the questioning and the unquestioning position is sharply brought out in William's first meeting with Abo, when William stresses doubts with regard to the infallibility of reason. Abo's unquestioning belief in the role of the Devil and the purity of the inquisitor is challenged by William's belief that even those who judge might be possessed of the Devil. Abo is 'bewildered' by William's position. Yet William himself is similarly confused, though perhaps in a more informed way. His interest in science and progress and his affinity with Ockhamite teaching strain his underlying belief in the Thomist synthesis. William still adheres to this synthesis, though, and uses it as the authority for the inability of human judges to judge questions of evil.[31] But Aquinas, though effecting his accommodation, had, by suggesting the contingency of the human situation, made the first move towards the nominalism of Ockham, and it was in this direction that William found himself moving. William expresses himself to be a close friend of Ockham, as well as of Roger Bacon. In a long discourse with Ubertino in the middle of the first day, William reveals the extent to which he is prepared to reconcile condemned heretical sects. In Ubertino's opinion it is William's 'intellectual pride' in preparing to do disputational battle with the papal representatives over the questions of heresy which represent the greatest danger, both to theology itself and to William and his fellow Franciscans in general.[32] The position of knowledge, and its challenge to established theology, is not only the fulcrum of the novel, but is also, of course, the battlefield of medieval theological politics.

Symptomatic of the struggle was the advance of science. William is fascinated by these advances. At the same time, however, he is also wary of them. Science is a potential source of evil, as well as of advancement. The same is, of course, true of knowledge. In his discourse with Nicholas about the possibilities of science, William emphasises that, as with all things, science is a matter of words. The words themselves are not dangerous, but they can disguise things that can be. This does not mean that 'secrets must not be revealed', but it does mean that the 'learned must decide when and how' they should be revealed.[33] Learning, then, is of paramount importance. However, if William is cautious with regard to the use of science, Abo's fears are less ambivalent. For Abo science, like knowledge, represents the 'abyss' of sin. Knowledge, of course, was sin. The library, then, which is of enormous symbolic importance in the novel, is a potential house of sin. For William the library opens up untold intellectual possibilities. But Abo keeps it locked and secret. The library, as befits a house of language, is constructed as a 'labyrinth', through which only the librarian can pass:

[O]nly the librarian knows, from the collocation of the volume, from its degree of inaccessibility, what secrets, what truths or falsehoods, the volume contains. Only he decides how, when, and whether to give it to the monk who requests it; sometimes he first consults me. Because not all truths are for all ears, not all falsehoods can be recognized as such by a pious soul ... It was the firm and holy conviction of those who founded the abbey and sustained it over the centuries that even in books of falsehood, to the eyes of the sage reader, a pale reflection of the divine wisdom can shine.[34]

The received wisdom was that wisdom was a dangerous thing.

Already in the first pages of the book Eco is using the two essential themes of the novel, language and philosophy, to stress that any theoretical investigation is at once a semiotic investigation, and that the critical model reader of *The Name of the Rose* will be created through both. 'The world', according to Brother William, 'speaks to us like a great book', because God 'speaks to us' through 'an endless array of symbols'. The very first thing that Eco does in his novel is to impress upon the reader the importance of the art of reading and decoding symbols. Reading is a life experience. It is not a matter of reading, but of knowing how to read.[35] The account of the first day is saturated with symbolism, and the impression that the exercise of reading holds the key to understanding the wider issues of the human condition and experience are unavoidably directed towards the critical model reader. Therefore William's eyeglasses, the use of which he vigorously articulates to Nicholas at the end of the first day, become something of an enduring symbol in the novel. When he has his glasses, William can not only read more effectively, he can understand more effectively.[36] Along with the eyeglasses and the library, Eco presents three more striking semiotic metaphors in the account of the first day. First, there is the symbolism of the church door, which so impressed Adso that he was 'plunged ... into a vision that even today my tongue can hardly describe'. The horrors of human existence, of Divine Judgement and condemnation which it portrayed were symbolic of life, both inside and outside the abbey:

I realized the vision was speaking precisely of what was happening in the abbey, of what we had learned from the abbot's reticent lips – and how many times in the following days did I return to contemplate the doorway, convinced I was experiencing the very events that it narrated. And I knew we had made our way up there in order to witness a great and celestial massacre.[37]

Eco's own researches into medieval symbolism of course emphasised the enormous impact that such a portrayal would have on the medieval mind.

Second, there is the encounter with Salvatore, an unfamiliar and frightening figure who speaks an unfamiliar and frightening language. In fact, as Adso comes to realise, Salvatore speaks 'all languages, and no language'. Salvatore speaks for the horror of the human condition, and for the damning inability to communicate which lies at the heart of this condition. Yet, because he can speak no language which can be understood he is cast out of society, heretical both in his theology and his existence, and is destined to suffer for it. Even William, steeped in the rigours of scientific rationalism, or perhaps because of it, treats Salvatore as alien and dangerous.[38] It is Salvatore's character which represents the most pessimistic philosophy of life. Finally, there is Adelmo, representing the sharpest constrast with Salvatore. Adelmo is an illuminator, one of what Eco termed the 'heroic' artists of the Middle Ages, and thus also one of the most potent threats to the established church.[39] Looking at Adelmo's illuminations, Adso was 'torn between silent admiration and laughter'. Brother Jorge's immediate condemnation of laughter, and his discourse with William on the subject, serves to underline once more the perceived threat that poetics and knowledge represent. William's invocation of Aristotle's work on poetics only serves to further subvert the Thomist synthesis. Adelmo was 'seduced' by laughter and by poetics, by intellectual vanity and finally by a fellow monk, and he suffered for it: 'Adelmo ... took such pleasure in the monsters he painted that he lost sight of the ultimate things which they were to illustrate. And he followed all, I say all ... the paths of monstrosity. Which God knows how to punish.'⁴⁰ The account of the first day closes with Jorge repeating the subversive evils of laughter in his reading of the chapter of the Rule at dinner, and with William employing the powers of logic in order to work out a way into the library.⁴¹

Day Two

Once again, the same two increasingly related issues dominate the account of Day Two; philosophy and the language of philosophy. William's first actions as a detective are semiotic, looking for signs in the snow and on Adelmo's body.⁴² The final events of the day see William and Adso lost in the labyrinth of the library, looking for 'signs' that will enable them to find their way out. Eco describes the library, like the abbey itself, as a symbol of the impenetrability of language and of texts, and the resultant indeterminacy of the human condition. The abbey has spread an 'atmosphere' of confusion across its surrounding country. In an interesting passage William suggests that the abbey may not be a '*speculum mundi*' because it does not have a form of its own, and, in doing so, reveals the extent of his own scepticism. The implication is that either the abbey cannot be reflective of the world because it is confused and not immanently rational: the Thomist position. On the other hand, there is the alternative suggestion that the abbey is reflective of the indeterminacy of the human condition: the nominalist position. Adso, like the model reader, is left to muse upon the ambiguity.⁴³ The metaphor of the labyrinthine library is developed as it continues to reflect the uncertain late medieval attitude to knowledge. In William's opinion the intransigence of the Roman position leads to knowledge being used to spread this confusion, rather than to enlighten.⁴⁴ Knowledge is concealed by images and reflections, by secret signs that defy decoding. The library is protected in precisely the same way.⁴⁵

Again, through William, Eco emphasises the liberating possibilities of a creative, more active, language, which can improve the communicative possibilities of the communicants. The discussion between William and Benno and then William and Jorge with regard to Adelmo's metaphors reveals the disputants fighting over Aquinas' approach to the use of metaphors in scriptural texts, where metaphors can be used in that particular context alone to convey the truths of the text. Jorge adopts the more rigorously

Thomist position: 'Our Lord Jesus never told comedies or fables, but only clear parables which allegorically instruct us on how to win paradise.' William, following Aquinas, invokes an Aristotelian authority for his attitude towards metaphoric use, and suggests that this use can simplify understanding and be an aid to reading a text. Laughter, he suggests, is a 'sign' of man's 'rationality'. So, replies Jorge, is speech, and that is always capable of creating evil. As the dispute progresses, William reveals still further his scepticism, suggesting that sometimes it is right to 'doubt' what is given as a truth. Human reason is empowered to doubt. Jorge refuses to accept this, countering that doubt must be dispelled by seeking authoritative statements.[46] The essential difference is again, of course, the one at the heart of medieval theology; whether or not the individual is empowered to reason by God, and whether this reason is in any way a challenge to the authority of revelation. Jorge presents the most conservative Roman position, whilst William's reply presents the most progressive nominalist counter, at the very end of the Thomist spectrum:

Of us God demands that we apply our reason to many obscure things about which Scripture has left us free to decide. And when someone suggests you believe in a proposition, you must first examine it to see whether it is acceptable, because our reason was created by God, and whatever pleases our reason can but please divine reason, of which, for that matter, we know only what we infer from the processes of our reason by analogy and often by negation.[47]

The second day also restates and develops the impact of these philosophical disputes on the theological politics. The immense wealth of the abbey 'dazzles' Adso, just as it disturbs William. The abbot is both proud and protective of it. For him it is the 'heritage of centuries of piety and devotion, testimony to the power and holiness of this abbey'.[48] As a commentary on the discussion between William and the abbot, Abo, Eco, through Adso, further reveals the nature of the dispute between the Franciscans and the papacy, emphasising that the core of it lay in the nature of poverty. The Benedictines, the Order of the monks at the abbey, are mediating the dispute in an effort to avoid schism, but there is little doubt where Abo's sympathies in the dispute lie. Abo stresses the position of the church as a sovereign authority in society, just as he seeks to preserve his sovereignty within his abbey. The Roman church must maintain this position at all costs. The position would be quite untenable if it were to support the kind of social and economic levelling advocated by the Franciscans. The greatest threat to the established church lies with heretical sects; civil disturbance 'jeopardize[s] the very order of the civilized world' and leads inexorably to the extremes of human misery. When William speaks eloquently on the extent of existing misery in the world, and implicitly suggests that the church has played an instrumental role in shaping it, Abo challenges him as to where the truth then really lies, if not in the established church. William's necessarily brief response speaks volumes: 'Nowhere, at times.'[49] The response is of course little short of heretical itself, and Abo says as much.

Day Three

The philosophical and semiotic issues deepen further in the account of Day Three. Whereas on the second day William's attitude towards the abbey as a possible microcosm of the world seemed somewhat abstruse, on Day Three William is unequivocal in the appropriateness of the metaphor. The symbolism is compounded by the fact that William's certainty is complemented by his forging fresh eyeglasses.[50] Just as science can aid William's eyesight, so too can it help in defeating the complexities of the labyrinth.[51] The whole issue of the challenge of science is intensified on Day Three. Just as William uses the eyeglasses so that he can look closer at the texts in the library, so he feels the need to look 'more closely' at the nature of 'universal truths'. In one of the key passages of the book, William explains to Adso precisely this challenge of science, and his own interest in the works of Bacon and Ockham. In doing so, he ties in both the philosophical dispute and its political ramifications. The new 'natural philosophy' which is advocated, associated as it is with the emerging humanist movement, will inevitably challenge the sovereign theological and political authority of the church. Agreeing with Bacon's demands for a realignment in the medieval polity, William comments: 'So I think that, since I and my friends today believe that in the management of human affairs it is not the church that should legislate but the assembly of the people, then in the future the community of the learned will have to propose this new and human theology which is natural philosophy and positive magic.' Equally explicit is his acknowledgement of Ockham's influences. Ockham's concentration on the discretion of the 'individual', has 'sown doubts' in William's mind about the possibility of science being able to 'recompose the universal laws':

[I]f only the sense of the individual is just, the proposition that identical causes have identical effects is difficult to prove ... How can I discover the universal bond that orders all things if I cannot lift a finger without creating an infinity of new entities ? For with such a movement all the relations of position between my finger and all other objects change.[52]

The problem did not of course originate with Ockham or with Bacon. The march of science and naturalism served merely to intensify the challenge. As William articulated:

You understand, Adso, I must believe that my proposition works, because I learned it by experience; but to believe it I must assume there are universal laws. Yet I cannot speak of them, because the very concept that universal laws and an established order exist would imply that God is their prisoner, whereas God is something absolutely free, so that if He wanted, with a single act of His will He could make the world different.[53]

The 'new learning' that William speaks of, as Adso muses, has already seeped irreversibly into the abbey in the person of Adelmo. The irony is not lost on Adso; the church built its power on learning, now it is going to lose it because of learning. As Eco stressed in his account of medieval intellectualism, by the later Middle Ages the preserve of learning was being wrested away from the church. When Adso considers the nature of learning he analogises its essentially active nature and the need for it not to stagnate with the leaves of books that lose their vigour when too often turned.[54] It is this process of dissolution which William fears. Just as he wants to somehow maintain the presence of philosophical universals, so he is desperate to somehow maintain the wholeness of communities. It is this which leads him to seek, if not a reconciliation with the heretical sects themselves, certainly a reconciliation with those who have been marginalised by the church, and who have mistakenly been tempted into heretical sin. This was the fourteenth-century politics of exclusion. Heresy, according to William, is essentially an 'illusion':

The recovery of the outcasts demanded reduction of the privileges of the powerful, so the excluded who became aware of their exclusion had to be branded as heretics, whatever their doctrine. And for their part, blinded by their exclusion, they were not really interested in any doctrine. This is the illusion of heresy. Everyone is heretical, everyone is orthodox. The faith a movement proclaims doesn't count: what counts is the hope it offers. All heresies are the banner of a reality, an exclusion. Scratch the heresy and you will find a leper.[55]

Heresy must still be destroyed. As William stresses, heresy leads to anarchy and the abandonment of 'reason' and 'justice'.[56] But destroying the heretic will not destroy the cause of heresy. The final event of Day Three, the seduction of Adso, provides a sharp juxtaposition with the sin of heresy. To Adso, the girl appears like Eve before Adam, and in succumbing to temptation Adso too becomes a leper from the church, if not from mankind. Just as Abo had perceived knowledge to represent an 'abyss' of sin, so does Adso see sex as precisely the same 'abyss'. In recounting the event, Adso recognises that he is using the same language to describe his act of sin as he used in describing earlier acts of heresy. Language precludes any distinction, even if there was one to be made. The metaphor of the shooting flame which consumed the heretic Michael and with which Adso describes his orgasm stands as a necessary metaphor, better equipping Adso to relate a situation which requires the envisaged and creative contribution of the reader. In Adso's opinion this is 'the teaching left us' by Aquinas, and is, furthermore, the destiny of any metaphorical usage: 'the more openly it remains a figure of speech, the more it is a dissimilar similitude, and not literal, the more a metaphor reveals its truth'. The key word, of course, being 'its'.[57]

Day Four

The symbolism of the girl is continued in Day Four. Indeed, she becomes an image in Adso's mind of something far greater: 'just as the whole universe is surely like a book written by the finger of God, in which everything speaks to us of the immense goodness of its Creator ... that morning the whole world spoke to me of the girl'.[58] Increasingly Eco identifies the girl with nature. Adso sees himself torn between the 'appetites' of nature and the dictates of reason, and seeks recourse to Aquinas' accommodation for an explanation.[59] The intensification of an immanent symbolism in the novel becomes increasingly apparent as each day is accounted. The investigation of the library towards the end of the day reveals that the key to the labyrinth lies in decoding a series of letters.[60] The discussion of papal politics in the middle of Day Four concentrates on the symbolism of the papacy, which Ubertino suggests is 'pagan' and 'worthy of the Persian kings'. In making this aspersion Ubertino is cutting at the very heart of papal authority. Moreover, Berengar suggests that Pope John is 'planning some mad if not perverse propositions that would change the very substance of doctrine'; plans that would be effected by reinterpreting the semiotics of the Apocalypse. In other words the Pope is going to declare a new scriptural truth. As William comments: 'It's a test he allows himself, an act of pride. He wants to be truly the one who decides for heaven and earth.' Brother Michael sees it as the thin end of a very dangerous wedge: 'Worse, still worse ... On one side a mad pope, on the other the people of God, who, even if through the words of His theologians, will soon claim to interpret Scripture freely.'[61]

Adso is Eco's primary textual mechanism for creating the model reader, and it is in Day Four that Adso's uncertainties become correspondingly more unsettling. When discussing the possible reasons for Berengar's blackened fingers, William ridicules Adso's blind faith in the Aristotelian syllogism. Adso confesses that he 'had always believed logic was a universal weapon, and now I realized how its validity depended on the way it was employed. Further, since I had been with my master I had become aware, and was to become ever more aware in the days that followed, that logic could be especially useful when you entered it but then left it.'[62] Later when William discusses the contingent nature of rational deduction, Adso comes to realise the extent to which William symbolises the challenge to the established teachings: 'I understood at that moment my master's method of reasoning, and it seemed to me quite alien to that of the philosopher, who reasons by first principles, so that his intellect almost assumes the ways of the divine intellect. I understood that, when he didn't have an answer, William proposed many to himself, very different one from another. I remained puzzled.' For a moment, Adso 'despaired' of his master, and was relieved to know of the imminent arrival of Gui, the Inquisitor, for he was still 'on the side of the thirst for truth' that inspired Bernardo Gui.[63] When Gui is first presented in the narrative he immediately discovers the truth of the girl as witch, condemned by the symbols of the cat and the cock, and Adso is very quickly disabused of his faith in Gui's 'thirst for truth'.[64] As the symbolism increasingly 'envisages' the reader of the text, Eco reflects more and more on the contingencies of language in the act of reading and establishing truth. Day Four is very much a semiotics of language theory. William's decoding of Venantius' parchment is itself a metaphor for the relationship between texts and knowledge. In discussion with William about the nature of reading texts, Adso

realized that not infrequently books speak of books: it is as if they spoke among themselves. In the light of this reflection, the library seemed all the more disturbing to me. It was then the place of a centuries long murmuring, an imperceptible dialogue between one parchment and another, a living thing, a receptacle of powers not to be ruled by a human mind, a treasure of secrets emanated by many minds, surviving the death of those who had produced them or had been their conveyors.[65]

A rustle of language indeed. No other passage in the book better describes the power of the text as a living creating organism. Later in the library, William further impresses upon Adso the contingent nature of language, and the idea that the written word can create many truths: 'Books are not made to be believed, but to be subjected to inquiry. When we consider a book, we musn't ask ourselves what it says but what it means, a precept that the commentators of the holy books had very clearly in mind.'[66]

Day Five

Day Five is potentially the most interesting for any law and literature study because it includes the disputation and trial scenes. The reality of the action in the account of Day Five presents something of a contrast with the more reflective tones of Days Four and Six. That, of course, does not suggest any decrease in the intensification of textual semiotics. Indeed, the account opens with Adso's commentary on the sculptures of the tympanum, which, in their brightness, offer a sharp contrast with the sculptures which had so unnerved Adso on Day One; an 'augury', Adso hopes, of success in the impending disputation.[67] The disputation opens with a long account of recent papal history, and then gradually crystallises around the issues of property, and the poverty of Christ. The first major contribution is from Ubertino who presents the Franciscan case. Ubertino immediately concentrates on the jurisprudence of the claim to property as he interprets it from the scriptural texts.

From these texts, Ubertino suggests that there were two ways in which Christ and the Apostles could possess goods. First, there is the 'civil and worldly' way, and secondly there is the 'holding' of things in nature:

> Whereby it is one thing to defend in a civil and worldly sense one's possession against him who would take it, appealing to the imperial judge ... but in the other way temporal things can yet be held, for the purpose of common fraternal charity, and in this way Christ and his disciples possessed some goods by natural right, which right by some is called *ius poli*, that is to say the law of heaven, to sustain nature, which without human intervention is consonant with proper reason, whereas *ius fori* is power that derives from human covenant. Before the first division of things, as far as ownership was concerned, they were like those things today which are not among anyone's possessions and are granted to him who takes them; things were in a certain sense common to all men, whereas it was only after original sin that our progenitors began to divide up ownership of things, and thus began worldly dominion as we know it.[68]

The papal response vigorously resisted the idea that there was a division in the holding of property which validated a common ownership of property which could lie beyond the jurisdiction of Rome. The poverty of Christ was, in fact, a representation of the fact that, as the son of God, Christ owned everything. Civil authority thus has jurisdiction over everything, and moreover, with regard to disputations like these, drawn from the scriptures 'the Roman Pontiff, in everything concerning faith and morals, can revoke the decisions of his predecessors and can even make contrary assertions'.

From there the disputation rapidly dissolves into various accusations and counter-accusations of heresy, and finally into a brawl between the disputing parties, although, as William points out to Adso, in essence, both disputants' parties are arguing within the parameters that Aquinas tried to set; the relative jurisdictions of divine and civil authority.[69] William's discourse operates precisely within these parameters. At the very beginning he stresses that, 'the Lord had given to Adam and to his descendents power over the things of this earth, provided they obeyed his divine laws, [from which] we might infer that the Lord also was not averse to the idea that in earthly things the people should be legislator and effective first cause of the law'. However, from this point William begins to reveal his own progressive brand of politics by divorcing the ecclesiastical authority from the civil. According to William, it was

clear that legislation over the things of this earth, and therefore over the things of the cities and kingdoms, has nothing to do with the custody and administration of the divine word, an unalienable privilege of the ecclesiastical hierarchy ... his deductions seemed to him supported by the very example of Christ, who did not come into this world to command, but to be subject to the conditions he found in the world, at least as far as the laws of Caesar were concerned. He did not want the apostles to have command and dominion, and therefore it seemed a wise thing that the successors of the apostles should be relieved of any worldly or coercive power.[70]

Encouraged in no small way by his advocacy of the emperor's case against that of the papacy, William then added more pointedly still, '[i]f the pope, the bishops, and the priests were not subject to the worldly and coercive power of the prince, the authority of the prince would be challenged, and thus, with it, an order would be challenged that, as had been demonstrated previously, had been decreed by God'. Furthermore, with regard to the vexed issue of heresy, the church can warn the heretic that he is removing himself from the 'community of the faithful', just as the prince can condemn the heretic if his action 'harms the community', but only God can judge the heretic. If the church tried to usurp this role, then 'Christianity would no longer be a law of freedom, but one of intolerable slavery'. William's discourse, as it progressed from stage to stage, had cut to the very heart of medieval political and philosophical dispute, and revealed the depth of the challenge to the established papal position, both in political and doctrinal matters.[71]

The disputation is followed by the trial scene in which, in direct contrast with William's submissions with regard to the judgement of heretics and sinners, the Inquisitor, Gui, condemns Remigio, Salvatore and the girl. The account opens with a description of the 'courtroom', the chapter house. Gui takes his place at the 'centre' of the hall, and proceeds to dominate the proceedings, opening with 'some ritual formulas' about his role as Inquisitor. Gui's role is that of an interrogator. This role places Gui in precisely the same position as the examining magistrate in the novels of Dostoevsky, Kafka and Camus. He will enjoin the defendants in a game of words in a bid to discover 'signs' of their guilt. Trials are always a matter of words. Eco emphasised this point in the first pages of the book. William gave up being an inquisitor precisely to avoid building 'a castle of suspicions on one word'.[72] Remigio's easy submission to Gui's judgement surprises Adso who thought that his long training would better equip him to answer 'ritual questions with equally ritual words'. In fact, as Gui exasperatedly declares, Remigio using 'with grim obstinacy the formula' which was taught in his 'sect', is quite capable of playing the word game.[73] The 'language' which Gui uses with Remigio contrasts sharply with that which he uses with the ill-educated and less skilful Salvatore, the man who 'knew all languages and no language'. Whereas with Remigio Gui had employed the rituals of the advocate, with Salvatore he enjoins a conversation, easing from Salvatore his own confession and with it the condemnation of Remigio. Salvatore, aware that success would depend solely on his ability to marshal his language, makes no effort to defend himself. Remigio, of course, is aware that neither of them can access a language which can save them from condemnation. Theirs is the language of heresy. Remigio finally traps himself when he moves outside the ritual discourse, and attempts to present the truth of his actions.[74] The process of being an inquisitor, the exercise of trying to discover the truth of anything, is constrained by language and Gui, the consummate Inquisitor, changes discourse from one defendant to another. The actual murderer, Malachi, of course lies about his actions, but because he takes a symbolic oath, and follows the rituals of the court, he preserves his freedom. Yet when Remigio tries to 'swear' to the truth of his statements, Gui reveals the paradox of such symbolism: 'You swear, hoping to be absolved, but I tell you this: a single oath is not enough for me! I can require one, two, three, a hundred, as many as I choose. I know very well that you Pseudo Apostles grant dispensations to those who swear false oaths rather than betray the sect. And so every oath will be further proof of your guilt!' Remigio, as Gui triumphantly points out to him, has lost a trial of strength by words; a trial he could have never hoped to win: 'You must only confess. And you will be damned and condemned if you do confess, and damned and condemned if you do not confess, because you will be punished as a perjurer!'[75]

The interrogation of Remigio provides Gui with the opportunity to widen the scope of the trial, and to 'retry' the Franciscan challenge to the civil authority of the papacy.[76] The abbot too appeared to realise that Gui was going to try 'all the evils of the century' in his church. Remigio cut himself loose from the restraints of language with which he had attempted to preserve himself, and acknowledged his past in 'words' and 'images'. The root of his heresy, he admitted, indeed lay in the exercise of civil disobedience. According to Gui, at the centre of this disobedience was the belief that laymen were not bounded to pay tithes to 'priests who do not practice a condition of absolute perfection and poverty as the first apostles practiced', but should be paid to their sect. It was the ultimate heresy, and the most immediate challenge to the church, founded, as Remigio admitted, on a fundamental belief in the 'universal law' of 'poverty'.[77] Remigio is then handed over to the secular authorities so that a full confession can be extracted from him, so that he can 'purify' himself. Both Gui, and indeed William, perceive the word as the only effective means of purification, although in William's eyes Remigio, in advocating his belief in the universal law of poverty, has already purified himself. This is a timeless truth, and neither believe that it can be hastened by human intent.[78] Thus destroyed by the failures of language, Remigio is left like one robbed of the power of speech, 'mumbling' like a drunkard. Transformed, he then expresses a long and entirely fictitious confession in a manner which Gui finds entirely suited and thus believable, which he ends by invoking the symbolism of the Devil. Finally, in his deceit, Remigio is speaking the right language. Right because it is the language which Gui can understand, and right because it is the language which he expects Remigio to articulate.[79]

In his closing speech, Gui reminds his audience that Remigio is himself only a symbol of heresy, and moreover that heresy itself can be assuredly rooted out by detecting the six 'indicators' or signs of its presence. The sixth sign, he stresses, lies in the misuse of language and of rationalism, both of which, invariably found in the written word, are the essential tools of heresy.[80] An ironic closure, given that the abbey is secreting the largest library in Christendom, and that the librarian is murdering his colleagues in an effort to maintain its secrecy. The triumph of Gui has borne out William's warnings about the roles of Inquisitors and trial. As he comments to Ubertino, in such a situation 'every word' can be 'distorted'.[81] In William's opinion, a 'lust' for justice is potentially as dangerous and as sinful as any other lust, because such a lust will be fed by and will feed upon a lust for power. Justice does not need to be possessed, but a 'distorted lust' for it can lead to a distorted conception, and a distorted reality of it. It is precisely the same indeed as a distorted lust for books, which William suspects has led to their being incarcerated in the library tower. A book that is not read is a sin, and a distortion of a book: 'The good of a book lies in its being read. A book is made up of signs that speak of other signs, which in turn speak of things. Without an eye to read them, a book contains signs that produce no concepts; therefore it is dumb.'[82] Just as it hordes its wealth, so the church tries to hoard the liberating potential of knowledge. For, as Jorge indeed stresses, the most important possession is knowledge; knowledge is always power. In Jorge's opinion the role of the church is to protect a knowledge which God has entrusted to its protection. The role of the church is to suppress any attempts to create knowledge. Knowledge is not a matter for creation; merely for recognition. Jorge's reassertion of the traditional theological approach to the postion of knowledge, as an emanation of sin, is a fitting way to end the momentous events of Day Five, a day which William describes as 'nasty ... Full of blood and ruination.'[83] The ultimate victim of Day Five was not Remigio, or Salvatore, but knowledge itself.

Days Six and Seven

In a sense the events of Day Five, without doubt the centrepiece of the novel, represent also its zenith, and following these cataclysmic events Day Six seems rather shorn of events or semiotic commentary that speak to an identifiably legal audience.[84] Day Six does, however, present a series of symbols which reflect the events of the previous day. There are the relics which Nicholas uses in an effort to dispel his own doubts about the condition of the abbey, in an effort to invoke the certainties of the past to counter the uncertainties of the present and which William suggests represents an 'epitome' of the debates on poverty, if not the cause of them.[85] More pertinent perhaps is the abbot's comments on the design of the abbey, which was indeed contructed as an architectural symbol of the faith and of life, and on his ring of authority, which is a symbol of the sovereignty of the church of its own affairs, and the affairs of man. According to Abo, the ring is a 'marvelous language': 'The symbol of my authority, but also of my burden. It is not an ornament: it is a splendid syllogy of the divine word whose guardian I am.' The ring, like the abbot himself, and of course the library, are all symbols of the church's perceived role in the protection of knowledge against outsiders. The ring protects against the 'lures' of the Devil. Indeed the abbot is keen to force Adso to take an oath on the symbolism of the ring to seal his lips with regard to what he has heard and learned during the previous five days. It is only the interjection of William that prevents the ring silencing Adso. The abbot retaliates by dismissing William, whom he describes as a recalcitrant 'mendicant' and an 'outsider'.[86]

It is at the end of Day Six that William finally manages to crack the code for entrance into the *'finis Africae'* and thereby gains entry to the inner reaches of the labyrinth and the forbidden knowledge that it protected. Day Seven, the final day, thus represents the final denouement of the novel. Much more than just the account of the final events, it represents the final schism, which, symbolised in William, reflects the irreducible schism in the human condition. The entry to the *'finis Africae'* provides the answer to the immediate puzzle. It does not provide the answers to any bigger questions. In the room he finds Jorge, who reveals to him the secrets which the library and the abbey hide. William thus succeeded in solving the mysterious deaths in the abbey, but by his own admission, he did so largely by chance, by following a 'false pattern'. William was, in the end, simply lucky.[87] Reason did not provide him with the answers, any more than revelation. That is why solving the mystery does not lead to any solutions to the bigger mysteries which trouble him. Having followed his fortune, William had realised in advance that the particular knowledge which the abbey sought to hide referred to laughter and the 'misuse' of scriptural symbolism, as represented by Aristotle's second book of *Poetics*, a book of such rarity that its secretion in the library was an especial suppression of knowledge. It is, of course, no coincidence that Eco uses a book which sought to develop the possibilities of communication as symbolic of the fears which led the abbey to suppress its particular knowledge. As William knows, the second book of *Poetics* was used by Aristotle to facilitate the creative and questioning power of the writer and reader of texts. For Jorge this represented the most acute of threats to the intellectual primacy of the church. In his opinion, '[e]very book' written by Aristotle, had 'destroyed a part of the learning that Christianity had accumulated over the centuries'. Aristotle's writings had led men to question the 'power of the Word'. Most dangerous of all, it had led men to question the literal truth of the Creation and the inevitability of the Apocalypse. It was the ultimate misuse of metaphor. Now everybody sought earthly proof for all the events described in the Scriptures. Only the image of God was left unquestioned, and in Jorge's opinion the semiotic potentials contained in the second book of *Poetics* would, in making the image 'become an object for interpretation ... have crossed the last boundary'.[88] In questioning why Jorge so feared to make the book accessible, observing that, 'You cannot eliminate laughter by eliminating the book', William is asking the essential question of textual use – does the Reader exist independently of the text? The answer of course is yes, but when the reader engages the text, then the isolation is unavoidably compromised, as indeed Jorge suggests. The book can envisage its reader and create its audience. If the civil authorities are ridiculed in the text, they might be ridiculed by the audience.

Of all social structures, the legal order has suffered from the rigours of satire more than most, and so the model legal reader is perhaps more capable than most of understanding the veracity of Jorge's statements. It is of course an uncomfortable truth, and it does not necessarily mean that knowledge must be suppressed. All truths are uncomfortable, and as William is well aware the requirements of the human condition demand that they must be compromised at times. Laughter, Jorge suggests, 'distracts the villein from fear' and the 'law is imposed by fear'. The law must at all costs be respected. This jurisprudence remains as valid as an idea as it was in the fourteenth century, championed by various legal thinkers from Hobbes to Bentham to Hart: uncomfortable, but true. Aristotle's teaching would lead to the 'absence of law' by turning the world upside down and leaving it without order. It is the essential jurisprudential tension between control and freedom, between, as Plato recognised, the state and the individual.[89] William responds uncompromisingly. What Jorge has advocated represents the Devil's work, because it makes a claim to an ultimate truth which is beyond human cognition. Jorge has been trapped by his own intellectual pride. Sovereign authority, not mediated by the demands of Aristotelian equity, is likewise condemned. It too is the work of the Devil.[90]

The destruction of the library might be said to represent the end of the abbey's attempts to secrete knowledge. Yet at the same time, of course, the destruction of its contents might be said to represent its final success. William, in 'an explosion of ire', assaults Jorge in an attempt to save the *Poetics*, but it was '[t]oo late. The Aristotle, or what had remained of it after the old man's meal, was already burning.' Adso 'realized that the whole labyrinth was nothing but an immense sacrificial pyre, all prepared for the first spark'.[91] The atmosphere of destruction and chaos is continued to the final pages of the account. The reader is envisaged, even constructed, but he or she is not provided with any answers, save perhaps the suggestion that there are none. In Adso's mind the struggle between William and Jorge symbolised the struggle between good and evil. But the answer is not that simple. The dual death, of Jorge and of the library, leaves William devoid of resolution. His observations to Adso condemn such illusions: 'Perhaps the mission of those who love mankind is to make people laugh, because the only truth lies in learning to free ourselves from insane passion for the truth.' There is no 'truth', just as there was no 'plot'. The previous seven days had been spent searching for the unfindable.[92] Adso remains unnerved by such a 'self-contradictory' statement, and tries to access some discovered relation between the signs with which William stumbled across the truth. The final exchange between Adso and William reveals the extent of the essential uncertainty in William's condition, and, of course, in that of humankind: 'I have never doubted the truth of signs, Adso; they are the only things man has with which to orient himself in the world. What I did not understand was the relation among signs... I behaved stubbornly, pursuing a semblance of order, when I should have known well that there is no order in the universe.' It is not that there is no perceptible or cognisable order in the universe. There is simply no order at all. Signs are the only truths in life, as they are in texts. It is an unremittingly disturbing truth, at least for William, because it strikes at the very heart of the received Thomist wisdom: 'It's hard to accept the idea that there cannot be an order in the universe because it would offend the free will of God and His omnipotence. So the freedom of God is our condemnation, or at the least the condemnation of our pride.' Even worse is the ancillary, but seemingly unavoidable, conclusion which Adso articulates. That, if there was no truth, there would no longer be any 'possible and communicative learning'. The final words are William's: 'There is too much confusion here ... *Non in commotione, non in commotione Dominus.*'93 To the very last, Eco remains unswerving. The model reader may have been constructed, but the text of *The Name of the Rose* will do nothing more.

USING THE TEXT: ECO ON ECO

In response to the depth of critical and intellectual response to *The Name of the Rose*, three years after its publication Eco produced a collection entitled *Reflections on the Name of the Rose.*94 It was, he stresses, not intended in any way to present some sort of definitive interpretation of the text. Novels were written, he remarks, precisely to negate any such interpretation of any text. The extent of the various interpretations which his novel had engendered, Eco suggests, further inclined him to confidence in this belief. Extending some crumbs of comfort to interpretations such as this, he continues by suggesting that all the interpretations which he had encountered enjoyed their own validity, regardless of whether they coincided with his authorial intent.95 Having said this, in *Reflections* Eco takes the opportunity to emphasise certain of his positions with regard to writing and reading texts. First, he underscores the roles of the model author and model reader in creating and then accessing texts. Eco suggests that he chose to situate his text in the Middle Ages precisely because it was a period in which he enjoyed a deep academic knowledge, thus better enabling him to envisage and create his model audiences. To tell a story effectively, and man is naturally a 'storyteller', a creator of interpretations, it is above all necessary to 'construct a world' as detailed as possible. The author always frames the novel.96 Similarly, although he dodges any explicit statement with regard to whether or not the novel is an 'open' or a 'closed' text, Eco stresses that his purpose, particularly during the account of the first day in which there is so much description of fourteenth-century philosophy, semiotics and political history, is to better create his model reader. Eco's ambition, as his critics have noted, was certainly that of presenting an 'open' text which could try to 'produce' a reader, rather than one which simply fulfilled an already existing audience. There is, Eco hopes, throughout his novel, a continual 'dialogue' between the author and his audiences. The notion of a multiplicity of audiences, critical or uncritical, is further evidenced by Eco's assertion that he wanted to narrate the events through the mouth of Adso, who understood nothing, because then from the base of potential understanding the audience could define its own degree of 'sophistication'. Adso remained unsophisticatedly confused. William, on the other hand, was confused in a much more sophisticated way.[97]

The second continuing dialogue in the novel, according to Eco, is that between the text and earlier texts. Books are always about other books. According to Eco any book will always 'speak' of other books.[98] In other words every book is a semiotic of literature. This is certainly the conclusion of one recent critic of Eco's, who stresses that the novel is itself a 'semiotic', wherein the reader is educated, along with Adso, through the use of signs.[99] By his own admission Eco writes historically. That was his ambition. More precisely he writes as a historicist, presenting a text that is a mosaic of past and present.[100] Thus the sophisticated reader will read historically. As a number of critics have recognised, this requires a knowledge of medieval semiotics. Not just because Eco is interested in semiotics, but because of the centrality of semiotics in medieval philosophy and theology. As one recent commentator has observed, semiotics was a 'theological discipline ... inseperable from divine knowledge'.[101] More exactly it requires an appreciation of Eco's knowledge of medieval semiotics.[102] As with the siting of his novel, Eco's theoretical writings are always historical, and continual reference to the origins of his own theoretical positions is a characteristic of his work.

Eco's earliest researches were conducted in the field of medieval aesthetics. In his *Art and Beauty in the Middle Ages* Eco presents the thesis that the medieval approach to aesthetics gradually became less systematic and more pragmatic. The story of medieval aesthetics and symbolism was, like virtually everything, a story of accommodating the classical and the biblical, the rational and the revelatory. In Eco's words, there was the ever-present 'tension between the call of earthbound pleasure and striving after the supernatural'.[103] The Socratics emphasised that beauty was immanent, and an expression of harmony. The Scriptures, however, promoted a transcendental beauty. The essential accommodation, and the most influential, was achieved, according to Eco, by Aquinas. Aquinas asserted that material beauty reflected an ideal beauty, established by the 'hand of God'. The beauty which was thus disclosed to the knowing subject was an objectivised beauty. This objectivisation was effected by a medieval semiotics, the most influential exponent of which was of, course, Aquinas himself. Aquinas rationalised semiotics by suggesting that natural objects had no allegorical qualities. Thus the use of symbolism in the Scriptures was effected only by the texts themselves, and the model readers which they envisaged. His assertion that the Scriptures must thus be read literally rather than figuratively represented a major reversal on the received wisdom, and dealt a crushing blow to the 'mysticism' of early medieval metaphysics.[104] Aesthetics was thus founded upon a Socratic 'metaphysical certainty', as opposed to a poetics. Most importantly, Aquinas emphasised the utility of beauty. The 'perfection' of a thing lay in its usefulness. In making this assertion Aquinas was articulating the mood of the day, the 'tendency to identify the beautiful and the useful'.[105]

However, this accommodation was itself to be immediately challenged by a nominalism most famously associated with the Ockhamites. It was the desire to use this challenge, articulated through Brother William that, according to Eco, made him situate the text in the fourteenth rather than the thirteenth century. The importance of the accommodation in the novel should not then be underestimated. In Eco's opinion, the Ockhamites were the first to develop a coherent theory of semiotics, semiotics which could complement a philosophy, and which was centred on a system of signs which could be 'used to acquire knowledge of individuals'.[106] The immanent semiotics of the novel make the role of medieval, particularly Ockhamite, semiotics an essential ingredient. In one sense *The Name of the Rose* itself becomes a semiotic of semiotics. The Ockhamite assertion of the absolute contingency of created things reflected a gradual drift from universalism to particularism in the arts. This drift gained momentum from the increasing influence of Judaic and Islamic cultures, from the creativity of such as Maimonides and the poetics of Averroes. The 'rise of the artists' represented the decline of the Thomist accommodation, because it represented a splintering in Aquinas' hitherto universal system. Art was no longer perceived as a threat to religion, and was no longer subject to its own demands. Art was for its own sake, and the 'heroic' artist emerged as a privileged figure in the challenge cast against early medievalism.[107]

Eco's observations on the nature of medieval aesthetics and symbolism were repeated in his *Semiotics and the Philosophy of Language*, where he stressed again the constant 'ambiguity' in the 'medieval mind', trapped by the tensions engendered by the Socratic-Thomist synthesis and the emerging challenge of nominalism and poetics. Aquinas's destruction of the symbolic code and his privileging of the literal was then itself immediately challenged by the poetic influences of Judaism and the Ockhamites. The result of these challenges and accommodations was, in Eco's opinion, the championing of the text, rather than the author, as the source and control of codes and decoding. Symbols produce texts and texts were interpreted by using symbols. In other words, the upheavals of medieval semiotics and philosophy laid the foundations for the contemporary semiotics with which Eco and the rest of us work. It is moreover an essentially pragmatic semiotics.[108] The centrality of medieval semiotics and aesthetics in Eco's work cannot be overestimated. In Eco's opinion they hold the key to modern theories of reading and understanding. It is thus not surprising that he should use them as the essential context to both of his novels, *The Name of the Rose* and *Foucault's Pendulum*. In the conclusion to *Art and Beauty in the Middle Ages*, he stressed that an 'accurate reconstruction of medieval aesthetics' was not only important for 'its own sake', but was vital to any understanding of both medieval and contemporary society.[109] The envisaged critical model reader of Eco's novels is constructed precisely with this vitality in mind.

SITUATING THE AUTHOR AND THE TEXT

In assessing a series of overinterpretations of his novel in the third of his Tanner lectures, Eco was keen to do so by reasserting the constraining power of the text: 'Between the unattainable intention of the author and the arguable intention of the reader there is the transparent intention of the text, which disproves an untenable interpretation.'[110] So how can we be sure that any interpretation of the text is true? Of course, we can never make that assertion. But, as Eco himself suggests, any interpretation is an interpretation, and valid as that. For the critical model legal audience, the text has constrained the possible interpretations. The possibilities are no longer limitless. The above interpretation is, thus, one 'envisaged' by the text, and that is the most confidence that any interpretation can claim. In *Reflections* Eco suggested that he had constructed his plot as a detective novel, because the 'fundamental question of philosophy (like that of psychology) is the same as the question of the detective novel: who is guilty?' In an effort to discover an answer we try to discover some sort of rational order in the sequence of events.[111] This is certainly the tenor, it has already been suggested, of the final exchanges between Adso and William at the end of Day Seven. Ultimately philosophy is a detective novel, a searching not just for order, but a discourse about justice and guilt. This is, of course, what Aquinas asserted, and later Ockham: theology is philosophy. The statement is even more powerful in the final words of *Reflections*: 'Moral: there exist obsessive ideas, they are never personal; books talk among themselves, and any true detection should prove that we are the guilty party.'[112] If collateral evidence is permissible, it is perhaps instructive to look at Eco's more recent novel, *Foucault's Pendulum*. Unsurprisingly, the strongest themes which run through *Foucault's Pendulum* are similar to those in *The Name of the Rose*, in particular the investigation of books as signs, and the return to the medieval semiotic as a comparison and guide to the contemporary situation. The essential 'plot' in *Foucault's Pendulum* is precisely the absence of a plot, both in the narrative itself and perhaps in life itself. One of the sub-themes of the book is the Trial of the Templars. The contemporary investigation proceeds by way of various attempts to decode the sign-system of Templar writings. Yet the accounts of the Trials themselves seem to be as enigmatic and contingent as the sign-system. Eventually the bemused Casaubon realises:

A trial full of silences, contradictions, enigmas, and acts of stupidity. The acts of stupidity were the most obvious, and, because they were inexplicable, they generally coincided with the enigmas. In those halcyon days I believed that the source of enigma was stupidity. Then the other evening in the periscope I decided that the most terrible enigmas are those that mask themselves as madness. But now I have come to believe that the whole world is an enigma, a harmless enigma that is made terrible by our own mad attempt to interpret it as though it had an underlying truth.[113]

The 'underlying truth' that Casaubon and his friends seek is eventually ridiculed by Casaubon's wife, who discovers that the enigmatic Templar texts are in fact laundry accounts. The discovery of the 'truth' in *Foucault's Pendulum* is as contingent as was William's in *The Name of the Rose*. 'Not bad, not bad at all',

Diotallevi observes, echoing Brother William's final comments, 'To arrive at the truth through the painstaking reconstruction of a false text.'[114] Casaubon's final comments serve to reinforce the essential theme of the novel: 'I have understood. And the certainty that there is nothing to understand should be my peace, my triumph. But I am here, and They are looking for me, thinking I possess the revelation They sordidly desire. It isn't enough to have understood, if others refuse and continue to interrogate.'[115]

This, I would suggest, echoes Camus's conclusion in his commentary on the Myth of Sisyphus. Sisyphus' task is futile, but we can still leave Sisyphus 'happy'.[116] Yet Sisyphus has found a tranquillity that continues to evade Casaubon and, it is suggested, continues to evade Brother William. It is the same tranquillity which twentieth-century literature has continued to seek. In isolating this tranquillity and suggesting that it can be realised, Camus distinguished Kafka's Joseph K. and acknowledged that he alone was ploughing a lone furrow in modern literature. Existential angst is the common factor in so many of the texts used by law and literature scholars, and, as we have already noted, the alienation of the human condition, as recognised by Richard Weisberg, for example, has become the pervasive theme.[117] Lest we should labour under the illusion that the alienation of the human condition is purely a twentieth-century phenomenon, Brother William can dispel it for us. Looking back from the fourteenth century, history seemed to be merely the history of 'storms of intolerance, hope and despair'.[118] William's final comments at the end of Day Seven place him in exactly the same position as Camus's heroes Sisyphus and Clamence, Kafka's Joseph K. and Dostoevsky's Raskolnikov, condemned to live in a world without truth, left to decide, not between truth and falsehood, but between happiness and unhappiness. Eco presents to the model reader precisely this decision, the ultimate decision, just as did Camus, Kafka and Dostoevsky. The final confirmation of this interpretation is perhaps Adso's. In the Prologue to *The Name of the Rose* Adso comments, with hindsight, that he suspected that William had constantly sought the truth without ever having any confidence that it was recognisable. Even the wisest of men were beset by 'contradiction'.[119] This essential conclusion is repeated by Adso in his final commentary on the events that he has recorded:

The more I reread this list the more I am convinced it is the result of chance and contains no message ... the more I repeat to myself the story that has emerged from them, the less I manage to understand whether in it there is a design that goes beyond the natural sequence of the events and the times that connect them. And it is a hard thing for this old monk, on the threshold of death, not to know whether the letter he has written contains some hidden meaning, or more than one, or many, or none at all.[120]

Notes

I LAW AND LITERATURE: A CONTINUING DEBATE

1 J. White, 'Law as Language: Reading Law and Reading Literature', *Texas Law Review*, 60 (1982), 437.

2 See the recent essentially synoptic essays of Brook Thomas, 'Reflections on the Law and Literature Revival', *Critical Inquiry*, 17 (1991), 510–37, and C. Dunlop, 'Literature Studies in Law Schools', *Cardozo Studies in Law and Literature*, 3 (1991), 63–110. A slightly older synopsis is presented by Robert Weisberg, 'The Law–Literature Enterprise', *Yale Journal of Law and the Humanities*, 1 (1988) 1–67.

3 See Thomas, 'Reflections', 510–11, noting the emergence of an increasing number of interdisciplinary journals concerned not only with literature but with the humanities as a whole. He specifically cites the *Yale Journal of Law and the Humanities* and *Cardozo Studies in Law and Literature*. See also R. Posner, *Law and Literature: A Misunderstood Relation* (Cambridge, Mass.: Harvard University Press, 1988).

4 J. Allen Smith, 'The Coming Renaissance in Law and Literature', *Journal of Legal Education*, 30 (1979), 13–26. With hindsight it is now popular to suggest that the first impetus towards the renaissance was provided by James Boyd White's *The Legal Imagination* (Boston, Mass.: Little, Brown and Co., 1973). Currently, more North American law schools offer courses in law and literature than do not, a fact which has led Dunlop to observe that '[l]iterature study in law faculties is a growth industry'. See 'Literature Studies', 63.

5 See Posner, *Law and Literature*, chapter 6, particularly 271–81.

6 See Ricoeur, *The Rule of Metaphor* (London: Routledge and Kegan Paul, 1978), particularly studies 3, 4, 5 and 8. For the development of the historicity of the text, see P. Ricoeur, *Hermeneutics and the Human Sciences* (Cambridge University Press, 1981), particularly chapters 5 to 11. A good introduction to Ricoeur's later work, wherein he develops the idea of the 'story' to the full, is his essay 'On Interpretation' in *Philosophy in France Today*, ed. A. Montefiore (Cambridge University Press, 1983), 175–96.

7 Ricoeur, 'On Interpretation', 180–1.

8 See R. Rorty, *Contingency, Irony, and Solidarity* (Cambridge University Press, 1989), particularly chapter 1 for the discussion of language, and chapter 9 for solidarity.

9 See *The Rule of Metaphor*, study 1 and 'On Interpretation', 177–81.

10 For Aristotle's use of metaphor in discussing justice, see *Ethics* (Harmondsworth: Penguin, 1976), 171–202. For contemporary use of Aristotelian metaphor in 'formalist' scholarship, see for example E. Weinrib, 'Legal Formalism: on the Immanent Rationality of Law', *Yale Law Journal*, 97 (1988), 949–1016.

11 For his treatment of metaphor, see *Rhetoric* (Cambridge University Press, 1909), book 3, chapter 2. For Ricoeur's commentary on this position, see *The Rule of Metaphor*, study 1.

12 See Brook Thomas, 'Reflections', 525. For a commentary on the influence of the Enlightenment project on the nature of legal discourse, see P. Goodrich, *Languages of Law: from Logics of Memory to Nomadic Masks* (London: Weidenfeld, 1990), particularly chapters 2 and 7.

13 See generally K. Llewellyn and F. Hoebel, *The Cheyenne Way* (Norman: University of Oklahoma Press, 1941). For a particularly useful example of metaphor and symbolism in native peoples' jurisprudence, see Goodrich, *Languages of Law*, 179–86. See also F. Hoxie, 'Towards a "New" North American Indian Legal History', *American Journal of Legal History*, 30 (1986), 351–7.

14 See O. Leaman, *An Introduction to Medieval Islamic Philosophy* (Cambridge University Press, 1985), and H. Englard, 'Research in Jewish Law: Its Nature and Function', *Mishpatim*, 7 (1975–6), 34–65.

15 See I. Ward, 'Natural Law and Reason in the Philosophies of Maimonides and St Thomas Aquinas', *Durham University Journal*, 86 (1994), 21–32.

16 See Maimonides, *The Guide to the Perplexed*, trans. M. Friedlaender (London: Dover, 1956), book 1, chapter 2, 23–7, and Aquinas, *Summa Theologiae*, ed. T. McDermott (London: Methuen, 1991), Questions 90–108 and 276–307.

17 See Bacon's essays 'Of Truth' and 'Of Judicature' in *The Essays* (Harmondsworth: Penguin, 1985), 61–3 and 222–5, and also *The Advancement of Learning* (Oxford University Press, 1974), chapter 23, 170–299.

18 See J. Bonsignore, 'In Parables: Teaching Through Parables', *Legal Studies Forum*, 12 (1988), 191–210.

19 S. Fish, *Doing What Comes Naturally: Change, Rhetoric, and the Practice of Theory in Literary and Legal Studies* (Oxford University Press, 1990), 138. Unsurprisingly Fish has used metaphors and parables as a means of describing legal problems. Most obvious perhaps is his essay 'Dennis Martinez and the Uses of Theory', in *ibid.*, 372–98.

20 See *The Legal Imagination, When Words Lose Their Meaning: Constitutions and Reconstitutions of Language, Character and Community* (University of

Chicago Press, 1984), *Heracles' Bow: Essays on the Rhetoric and Poetics of the Law* (Madison: University of Wisconsin Press, 1985) and *Justice as Translation: An Essay in Cultural and Legal Criticism* (University of Chicago Press, 1990).

21 Some of the best examples of this can be found in James Boyd White, *When Words Lose Their Meaning*, particularly the Introduction, ix–x, 8–9, and 275–89.

22 An observation also made by Dunlop, 'Literature Studies', 63 and 70–1, and also by William Page, 'The Place of Law and Literature', *Vanderbilt Law Review*, 39 (1986), 408–15.

23 White, 'Law as Language', 430–1.

24 Dunlop, 'Literature Studies', 70.

25 See generally Richard Weisberg, *The Failure of the Word: The Lawyer as Protagonist in Modern Fiction* (New Haven: Yale University Press, 1984).

26 See *ibid.*, particularly 1–9, 19–20 and 181–2.

27 Richard Weisberg, 'Text Into Theory: A Literary Approach to the Constitution', *Georgia Law Review*, 20 (1986), 946–79.

28 G. Steiner, *In Bluebeard's Castle* (London: Faber, 1971) particularly 47–8 and 61.

29 Weisberg, 'Text Into Theory', 979–85.

30 The quotation is taken from 'Family Feud: A Response to Robert Weisberg on Law and Literature', *Yale Journal of Law and the Humanities*, 1 (1988), at 72.

31 Richard Weisberg, 'Coming of Age Some More: "Law and Literature" Beyond the Cradle', *Nova Law Review* 13 (1988), 121.

32 See *ibid.*, 123.

33 Richard Weisberg, *Poethics: And Other Strategies of Law and Literature* (Columbia University Press, 1992), 46.

34 R. West, 'Authority, Autonomy and Choice: The Role of Consent in the Moral and Political Visions of Franz Kafka and Richard Posner', *Harvard Law Review*, 99 (1985), 384–428.

35 *Ibid.*, 387.

36 West's most explicit attack on 'foundationalism' can be found in 'Authority, Autonomy and Choice', particularly 388–91.

37 R. West, 'Communities, Texts, and Law: Reflections on the Law and Literature Movement', *Yale Journal of Law and the Humanities*, 1 (1988), 138–40.

38 *Ibid.*, 146–56. 'Intersubjective zap' was presented by Gabel and Kennedy in 'Roll Over Beethoven', *Stanford Law Review*, 36 (1984), 1–52.

39 West, *ibid.*, 153–6.

40 *Ibid.*, 156.

41 See 'Adjudication is Not Interpretation', in West's *Narrative, Authority, and Law* (Ann Arbor: University of Michigan Press, 1993), 96 and 174–5.

42 West, 'Narrative, Responsibility, and Death', in *Narrative*, 421–6.

43 See P. Williams, 'Alchemical Notes: Reconstructing Rights from Deconstructed Ideals', *Harvard Civil Rights–Civil Liberties Review*, 22 (1987), 401–34.

44 See A. Hutchinson, *Dwelling on the Threshold* (Toronto: Carswell, 1988), particularly the essays, 'In Training', 'Indiana Dworkin and the Law's Empire' and 'And Law'. In another essay 'Doing Interpretive Numbers', he comments, at 126, that CLS, whilst saying much about alternative discourse, has failed to do much about it.

45 R. Posner, 'The Ethical Significance of Free Choice: A Reply to Professor West', *Harvard Law Review*, 99 (1985), 1433.

46 *Ibid.*, 1438.

47 *Ibid.*, 1439–48. For West's observations see 'Submission, Choice and Ethics: A Rejoinder to Judge Posner', *Harvard Law Review*, 99 (1985), 1456.

48 Posner, 'Law and Literature: A Relation Reargued', *Virginia Law Review*, 72 (1986), 1356.

49 *Ibid.*, 1358.

50 *Ibid.*, 1359–60. For the observation that Posner's dispute is essentially about method or 'technique', see Brook Thomas, 'Reflections', 515.

51 Posner, 'A Relation Reargued', 1367.

52 Posner, *Law and Literature*, chapters 2 and 3, particularly 75–131.

53 *Ibid.*, 87–90.

54 Posner displays varying confidence in his dismissals. He is sure that Kafka and Camus cannot instruct us with regard to civil procedure, but is prepared to admit that *Bleak House* is a more accurate description of the workings of the nineteenth-century English legal system, and that *Billy Budd* may be able to tell us something about courts-martial. See *ibid.*, 94–131.

55 *Ibid.*, 132–75.

56 For the critique directed primarily against West, see *ibid.*, 179–205. See 200–1 for the apparent dilemma of seriousness.

57 Robert Weisberg, 'Law–Literature Enterprise', 1–67.

58 R. Delgado and J. Stefancic, 'Norms and Narratives: Can Judges Avoid Serious Moral Error?', *Texas Law Review*, 69 (1991), 1929–83.

59 *Ibid.*, 1933.

60 *Ibid.*, 1957–60.

61 Rorty, *Contingency*, 60–1.

62 Posner, *Law and Literature*, 269–316.

63 D. Couzens Hoy, 'Interpreting the Law: Hermeneutical and Poststructuralist Perspectives', *Southern California Law Review*, 58 (1985), 135–76.

64 J. Balkin, 'Deconstructive Practice and Legal Theory', *Yale Law Journal*, 96 (1987), at 763 and 786.

65 J. Balkin, 'The Promise of Legal Semiotics', *Texas Law Review*, 69 (1991), 1831–52, stressing at 1837 the common purpose of the two

literary techniques. For a more substantive investigation of semiotics and its previous associations with legal writings, see Goodrich, *Languages of Law*.

66 Balkin, 'The Promise of Legal Semiotics', 1839–40.
67 S. Fish, *Is There a Text in This Class? The Authority of Interpretive Communities* (Cambridge, Mass.: Harvard University Press, 1980), 43.
68 See generally K. Kress, 'Legal Indeterminacy', *California Law Review*, 77 (1989), 283–337.
69 M. Tushnet, 'Following the Rules Laid Down: A Critique of Interpretivism and Neutral Principles', *Harvard Law Review*, 96 (1982), particularly 824–7.
70 M. Tushnet, 'An Essay on Rights', *Texas Law Review*, 62 (1984), 1363–403, quotation at 1382. For the essay on deconstruction see M. Tushnet, 'Critical Legal Studies and Constitutional Law: An Essay · on Deconstruction', *Stanford Law Review*, 36 (1984), 623–47.
71 White, 'Law as Language', 415.
72 J. Frug, 'Argument as Character', *Stanford Law Review*, 40 (1988), 871.
73 White, 'Law as Language', 416–17.
74 *Ibid.*, 419.
75 *Ibid.*, 425–6.
76 *Ibid.*, 420, and again making much the same point at 433.
77 *Ibid.*, 419.
78 *Ibid.*, 434–6.
79 *Ibid.*, 437.
80 White, *Justice as Translation*, xiii.
81 *Ibid.*, chapter 1, particularly 12–21.
82 *Ibid.*, 100.
83 This is the central theme of chapters 2 and, in particular, 3. The position that White reaches with regard to externalised language is reminiscent of that defined by Peter Gabel as 'reified' language. See P. Gabel, 'Reification in Legal Reasoning', in S. Spitzer, ed., *Research in Law and Sociology*, 3 (1980) 25–38, and 'The Phenomenology of Rights-Consciousness', *Texas Law Review*, 62 (1984), 1564–98.
84 White, *Justice as Translation*, 19–20.
85 White uses a quotation of Dewey's as the trigger for his chapter 4: 'Democracy begins in conversation'. See *ibid.*, 91.
86 See *ibid.*, chapter 10, particularly 215–17 and 223–4. The quotation is at 217–18.
87 *Ibid.*, particularly chapter 11.
88 Richard Weisberg, 'Text Into Theory', 946–76.
89 *Ibid.*, 976–8.
90 See Weisberg, 'Coming of Age Some More', particularly 123–4, and 'Family Feud', 76–7.
91 See *Poethics*, chapter 3.
92 See Posner, 'A Relation Reargued', 1361–75. Quotation at 1374.

93 Posner, *Law and Literature*, 245. For the repeated unsuitability of literary theory as a technique applicable to the interpretation of legal texts, see 254–63.

94 See Posner, 'A Relation Reargued', 383, and *Law and Literature*, 372.

95 The comparison that Posner makes is between Holmes and Mark Antony in Julius Caesar. Following his analysis of Holmes, Posner then compares his rhetoric with that of a number of leading US judges. See *Law and Literature*, 281–96.

96 Posner, *ibid.*, 302.

97 The educative ambition of CLS was eloquently suggested by Peter Gabel in 'Roll Over Beethoven', 26.

98 See Dunlop, 'Literature Studies', 63.

99 *Ibid.*, 63–109. For Said's comments on over-intellectualising see *The World, the Text and the Critic* (London: Vintage, 1983), 1–53 and 140–57.

100 N. Cook, 'Shakespeare Comes to the Law School Classroom', *Denver University Law Review*, 68 (1988), 387–411.

101 Bonsignore, 'In Parables', 191–210.

102 Cook, 'Shakespeare Comes to the Law School Classroom', 411.

103 J. Getman, 'Voices', *Texas Law Review*, 66 (1988), 577–88.

104 Gabel and Kennedy, 'Roll Over Beethoven', 26.

105 Getman, 'Voices', 579–82.

106 *Ibid.*, 580.

107 Getman particularly uses the example of *The Adventures of Huckleberry Finn*, a popular text and well-used by law and literature scholars. See 'Voices', 587–8.

108 *Ibid.*, 588.

109 E. Perry Hodges, 'Writing in a Different Voice', *Texas Law Review*, 66 (1988), 633.

110 *Ibid.*, 638.

111 *Ibid.*, 639.

112 See White, *Justice as Translation*, 19.

113 Cook, 'Shakespeare Comes to the Law School Classroom', 410–11.

2 THE TEXT, THE AUTHOR AND THE USE OF LITERATURE
IN LEGAL STUDIES

1 R. Barthes, *The Rustle of Language* (Oxford: Blackwell, 1986), 54.

2 *Ibid.*, 55.

3 *Ibid.*, 49–55.

4 U. Eco, *Reflections on the Name of the Rose* (London: Secker and Warburg, 1985), 1–2.

5 Barthes, *Language*, 61–2.

6 See S. Fish, 'Fiss v Fish', in *Doing What Comes Naturally: Change, Rhetoric, and the Practice of Theory in Literary and Legal Studies* (Oxford University

Press, 1990), 120–40, and O. Fiss, 'Objectivity and Interpretation', *Stanford Law Review*, 34 (1982), 739–63.

7 M. Foucault, 'What is an Author?', in J. Harari, ed., *Textual Strategies: Perspectives in Post-Structuralist Criticism* (Ithaca: Cornell University Press, 1979), 142–3.

8 *Ibid.*, 146–7.

9 *Ibid.*, 147 and 158.

10 *Ibid.*, 159–60.

11 T. Eagleton, *Literary Criticism: An Introduction* (Oxford: Blackwell, 1983), 74–5, 118–21.

12 Published as U. Eco, *Interpretation and Overinterpretation* (Cambridge University Press, 1992), at 48–50 and 62–9.

13 U. Eco, *The Role of the Reader* (London: Hutchinson, 1981), 175–99.

14 Eco, *Interpretation and Overinterpretation*, 48–50 and 62–9.

15 E. Said, *The World, the Text, and the Critic* (London: Vintage, 1984), 140–7.

16 *Ibid.*, 2–33.

17 H.G. Gadamer, *Truth and Method* (London: Sheed and Ward, 1975).

18 H.G. Gadamer, 'The Universality of the Hermeneutic Problem', in *Philosophical Hermeneutics* (Berkeley: University of California Press, 1977), 13.

19 Gadamer, *Truth and Method*, 302.

20 *Ibid.*, 305.

21 E. Hirsch, *Validity in Interpretation* (New Haven: Yale University Press, 1967).

22 See P. Ricoeur, 'On Interpretation', in A. Montefiore, ed., *Philosophy in France Today* (Cambridge University Press, 1983), 175–96. See also Peter Goodrich's comments in *Languages of Law: from Logics of Memory to Nomadic Masks* (London: Weidenfeld, 1990), particularly chapters 2 and 7.

23 See volume 6 of the *Jewish Law Annual*.

24 M. Maimonides, *The Guide to the Perplexed*, trans. M. Friedlaender (London: Dover, 1956), 23–7.

25 R. West, 'Communities, Texts, and Law: Reflections on the Law and Literature Movement', *Yale Journal of Law and the Humanities*, 1 (1988), 132–40.

26 Richard Weisberg, *The Failure of the Word: The Lawyer as Protagonist in Modern Fiction* (New Haven: Yale University Press, 1984), 114–29.

27 J.P. Sartre, *What is Literature?* (London: Methuen, 1967), 123–220.

28 Eagleton, *Literary Criticism*, 17–53 and 194–217.

29 Said, *World*, 11–14 and 20–5.

30 R. Rorty, *Contingency, Irony, and Solidarity* (Cambridge University Press, 1989), xvi.

31 *Ibid.*, 3–21, 28–9 and 36–42.

32 *Ibid.*, 47–61.

33 *Ibid.*, 60–1.

34 *Ibid.*, 189–97.
35 *Objectivity, Relativism, and Truth: Philosophical Papers Volume 1* (Cambridge University Press, 1991), 84–91.

3 CASES IN THE LAWS OF READING

1 For a discussion of Heidegger's turn towards language, see P. Lacoue-Labarthe, *Heidegger, Art and Politics* (Oxford: Blackwell, 1990). For a selection of Heidegger's later writings on language, see M. Heidegger, *Poetry, Language, Thought* (New York: Harper and Row, 1971).
2 Heidegger reached this conclusion following his 'dialogue' with Kant. For a commentary, see F. Schalow, *The Renewal of the Heidegger–Kant Dialogue* (Albany: SUNY, 1992).
3 See H.G. Gadamer, *Truth and Method* (London: Sheed and Ward, 1975), 294. For a discussion of Gadamer's thesis in a particularly jurisprudential perspective, see B. Sherman, 'Hermeneutics in Law', *Modern Law Review*, 51 (1988), 386–402; W. Eskridge, 'Gadamer/Statutory Interpretation', *Columbia Law Review*, 90 (1990), 609–81; and S. Feldman, 'The New Metaphysics: The Interpretive Turn in Jurisprudence', *Iowa Law Review*, 76 (1991), 661–99.
4 There is no obviously accessible Derrida text. The best introductions to Derrida are C. Norris, *Derrida* (London: Fontana, 1987), and G. Bennington, *Jacques Derrida* (University of Chicago Press, 1993). For a piece of Derridean jurisprudence, see his 'Force of Law: "The Mystical Foundation of Authority"', *Cardozo Law Review*, 11 (1990), 921–1045. The best introductory commentary, however, remains J. Balkin, 'Deconstructive Practice and Legal Theory', *Yale Law Journal*, 96 (1987), 743–86.
5 See D. Michelfelder and R. Palmer, eds., *Dialogue and Deconstruction: The Gadamer–Derrida Encounter* (Albany: SUNY, 1989).
6 Gadamer, 'Text and Understanding', in *Dialogue and Deconstruction*, 32 and 35–6.
7 J. Derrida, 'Three Questions to Hans-Georg Gadamer', in *Dialogue and Deconstruction*, 52–4.
8 Gadamer, 'Reply to Jacques Derrida', in *Dialogue and Deconstruction*, 55–7.
9 O. Fiss, 'Objectivity and Interpretation', *Stanford Law Review*, 34 (1982), 739–63.
10 *Ibid.*, 739.
11 *Ibid.*, 744.
12 *Ibid.*, 744, 750–5 and 761–3.
13 For Fish's version of their differences, see his 'With the Compliments of the Author: Reflections on Austin and Derrida' in his *Doing What Comes Naturally: Change, Rhetoric, and the Practice of Theory in Literary and Legal Studies* (Oxford University Press, 1989), 37–67.

14 Fish, *Is There a Text in this Class? The Authority of Interpretive Communities* (Cambridge, Mass.: Harvard University Press, 1980), 276–7 and 355.

15 See particularly Fish, 'Introduction: Going Down the Anti-Formalist Road', and 'Change', in *Doing What Comes Naturally*, at 1–33 and 141–60.

16 See his 'Fish v Fiss', in *Doing What Comes Naturally*, at 126.

17 *Ibid.*, 1328.

18 *Ibid.*, 1334 and 1345–6.

19 R. Dworkin, 'Law as Interpretation', *Texas Law Review*, 60 (1982), 527.

20 *Ibid.*, 530–40 and 546–8.

21 *Ibid.*, 540–6.

22 R. Dworkin, *Law's Empire* (Cambridge, Mass.: Belknap, 1986), particularly chapters 2, 6, 7 and 11.

23 *Ibid.*, 400 and 410.

24 For Fish's various critiques of Dworkin's work, see his 'Working on the Chain Gang', 'Wrong Again', and 'Still Wrong After All These Years', in *Doing What Comes Naturally*, at 87–102, 103–19 and 356–71 respectively.

25 K. Kress, 'Legal Indeterminacy', *California Law Review*, 97 (1989), 283–337.

26 M. Moore, 'The Interpretive Turn in Modern Theory: A Turn for the Worse?', *Stanford Law Review*, 41 (1989), 871–957.

27 See M. Tushnet, 'Following the Rules Laid Down: A Critique of Interpretivism and Neutral Principles', *Harvard Law Review*, 96 (1982), 781–827.

28 R. West, 'Adjudication is Not Interpretation', in her *Narrative, Authority, and Law* (Ann Arbor: University of Michigan Press, 1993), 93–4.

29 *Ibid.*, 96, 107 and 174–5.

30 See J. Frug, 'Argument as Character', *Stanford Law Review*, 40 (1988), 869–927, and P. Goodrich, *Reading the Law: A Critical Introduction to Legal Method and Techniques* (Oxford: Blackwell, 1986), *Languages of Law: From Logics of Memory to Nomadic Masks* (London: Weidenfeld, 1990), and 'Critical Legal Studies in England: Prospective Histories', *Oxford Journal of Legal Studies*, 12 (1992), 195–236. For a commentary on the importance of textualism in critical legal scholarship, see G. Peller, 'The Metaphysics of American Law', *California Law Review*, 73 (1985), 1152–290.

31 A. Hutchinson, 'In Training', in *Dwelling on the Threshold: Critical Essays in Modern Legal Thought* (Toronto: Carswell, 1988), 13–14.

32 A. Hutchinson, 'The Three "Rs": Reading/Rorty/Radically', *Harvard Law Review*, 103 (1989), 555–85.

33 Hutchinson, 'Doing Interpretive Numbers', in *Dwelling on the Threshold*, 145–62.

34 See A. Hutchinson, 'Of Kings and Dirty Rascals: The Struggle for Democracy', *Queens Law Journal*, 17 (1984), 273–92.

35 A. Hutchinson, 'From Cultural Construction to Historical Deconstruction', *Yale Law Journal*, 94 (1984), 226–7.
36 Hutchinson, *Dwelling on the Threshold*, 127.
37 J. White, 'Law as Language: Reading Law and Reading Literature', *Texas Law Review*, 60 (1982), 415.
38 *Ibid.*, 434–6.
39 J. White, *When Words Lose Their Meaning: Constitutions and Reconstitutions of Language, Character, and Community* (University of Chicago Press, 1984), 276–80. For an interesting review of the book, and a particular investigation of it as an advocation of reader-response theory, see W. Page, 'The Place of Law and Literature', *Vanderbilt Law Review*, 39 (1986), 408–15.
40 J. White, *Justice as Translation: An Essay in Cultural and Legal Criticism* (University of Chicago Press, 1990), 13–16.
41 *Ibid.*, 11 and 246–69.
42 See West, 'Disciplines, Subjectivity, and Law', in *Narrative*, particularly 283–90.
43 See Richard Weisberg, 'Text Into Theory: A Literary Approach to the Constitution', *Georgia Law Review*, 20 (1986), 946–8, and 'Coming of Age Some More: "Law and Literature" Beyond the Cradle', *Nova Law Review*, 13 (1988), 121–4.
44 Richard Weisberg, *Poethics: And Other Strategies of Law and Literature* (New York: Columbia University Press, 1992), 249–50. See generally 224–50.
45 *Ibid.*, 168–75.
46 *Ibid.*, 248 and 305.
47 D. Cornell, 'Toward a Modern/Postmodern Reconstruction of Ethics', *University of Pennsylvania Law Review*, 133 (1985), 378.
48 Cornell, 'Institutionalization of Meaning, Recollective Imagination and the Potential for Transformative Legal Interpretation', *University of Pennsylvania Law Review*, 136 (1988), 1204.
49 Cornell, 'The Good, the Right, and the Possibility of Legal Interpretation', in her *The Philosophy of the Limit* (London: Routledge, 1992), 113 and 115.
50 Cornell, 'The Relevance of Time to the Relationship between the Philosophy of the Limit and Systems Theory: The Call to Judicial Responsibility', in *The Philosophy of the Limit*, 147.

4 SHAKESPEARE REVISITED

1 Too numerous even to attempt to provide a list. Simply by way of example, there have already been studies of the law as recorded in Chaucer's *Canterbury Tales* and in *Piers Plowman*. See J. Hornsby, *Chaucer and the Law* (London: Pilgrim Books, 1988), and M. Stokes, *Justice*

and Mercy in Piers Plowman (London: Croom Helm, 1984). Similarly, Jane Austen's novels have been read as a supplement for the study of eighteenth-century contract and trust law. See G. Treitel, 'Jane Austen and the Law', *Law Quarterly Review*, 100 (1984), 549–86; E. Hildebrand, 'Jane Austen and the Law', *Persuasions*, 4 (1982), 34–41; L. Redmond, 'Land, Law and Love', *Persuasions*, 11 (1989), 46–52.

2 The most popular 'jurisprudential' comedy has been *The Merchant of Venice*. It has been one of Richard Weisberg's most popular texts. See *Poethics: And Other Strategies of Law and Literature* (New York: Columbia University Press, 1992), 94–104. See also the recent collection of essays in volume 5 of the *Cardozo Studies in Law and Literature*.

3 See T. Watkin, 'Hamlet and the Law of Homicide', *Law Quarterly Review*, 100 (1984), 282–310; T. Meron, *Henry's Wars and Shakespeare's Laws* (Oxford: Clarendon, 1993); and D. Hamilton, *Shakespeare and the Politics of Protestant England* (Louisville: University of Kentucky Press, 1992).

4 See J. Lander, *The Limitations of English Monarchy in the Later Middle Ages* (University of Toronto Press, 1989), 4–5, suggesting that there was an 'unenthusiastic acceptance' of the 'inevitability' of monarchy. See also J. Kenyon, *The Stuart Constitution* (Cambridge University Press, 1966), at 7, noting Sir Arthur Haselrigg's observation in 1659 that back in 1642 no one had seriously contemplated an alternative to monarchy.

5 For a recent and authoritative restatement of this thesis, see J. Burns, *Lordship, Kingship and Empire* (Oxford: Clarendon, 1992).

6 See Lander, *Limitations*, particularly 41–55. See also G. Elton, *Policy and Police: The Enforcement of the Reformation in the Age of Thomas Cromwell* (Cambridge University Press, 1972), 45–54, and again in his *The Tudor Constitution* (Cambridge University Press, 1982), chapter 1. For a recent reassessment of Lander's thesis, see G. Harriss, 'Political Society and the Growth of Government in Late Medieval England', *Past and Present*, 138 (1993), 28–57.

7 For a general discussion of the intermittently unsettled nature of late Elizabethan England see W. MacCaffrey, *Elizabeth I: War and Politics 1588–1603* (Princeton University Press, 1992).

8 See MacCaffrey, *Elizabeth I*, 453–536, and S. Adams, 'Eliza Enthroned?: The Court and Politics', in C. Haigh, ed., *The Reign of Elizabeth I* (Athens: University of Georgia Press, 1987), 55–77. See also J. Hurstfield, 'The Politics of Corruption in Shakespeare's England', *Shakespeare Survey*, 28 (1975), 15–28.

9 See C. Morris, *Political Thought In England: From Tyndale to Hooker* (Oxford University Press, 1953), particularly chapters 2 and 6–9. For a more recent commentary see D. Kelley, 'Elizabethan Political Thought', in J. Pocock, ed., *The Varieties of British Political Thought 1500–1800* (Cambridge University Press, 1993), 58–64. See also Hamilton, *Politics of Protestant England*, particularly 1–29.

10 For an interesting exploration of popular dissent and its economic perspective during the 1590s, see J. Walter, 'A "Rising of the People?" The Oxfordshire Rising of 1596', *Past and Present*, 107 (1985), 90–143.

11 For a discussion of the 'cult' of Elizabeth, see J. King, 'Queen Elizabeth I: Representations of the Virgin Queen', *Renaissance Quarterly*, 34 (1990), 30–74. See also D. Woolf, 'The Power of the Past: History, Ritual and Political Authority in Tudor England', in P. Fideler and T. Mayer, eds., *Political Thought and the Tudor Commonwealth* (London: Routledge, 1992), 19–49, and S. Orgel, 'Making Greatness Familiar', in S. Greenblatt, ed., *The Power of Forms in the English Renaissance* (Norman: University of Oklahoma Press, 1982), 41–8.

12 See Lander, *Limitations*, 4–5 and 50–1, and Burns, *Lordship*, at 7, citing Carlyle's famous postulation of the fifteenth century as an intellectual dark age.

13 See J. Somerville, *Politics and Ideology in England 1603–1640* (London: Longman, 1986), and G. Burgess, *The Politics of the Ancient Constitution* (London: Macmillan, 1992).

14 For the definitive discussion of the Ancient Constitution see J. Pocock, *The Ancient Constitution and the Feudal Law* (Cambridge University Press, 1957). For a broadly sympathetic recent revision, see Burgess, *Politics*. See also D. Kelley, 'Elizabethan Political Thought', and L. Peck, 'Kingship, Counsel and Law in Early Stuart Britain', in J. Pocock, ed., *Varieties*, at 47–79 and 80–115 respectively for discussions of Pocock's thesis.

15 This central distinction lies at the heart of Fortescue's two important works, *The Governance of England* (Oxford: Clarendon, 1885) and *De Laudibus Legum Angliae*, ed. S. Chrimes (Cambridge University Press, 1942).

16 For a commentary on the debate regarding Fortescue, see R. Hinton, 'English Constitutional Theories from Sir John Fortescue to Sir John Eliot', *English Historical Review*, 75 (1960), 410–17. For more recent commentaries on Fortescue and the Ancient Constitution, which have tended to reaffirm the original portrayal of Fortescue, see Burns, *Lordship*, 59–70; J. Blythe, *Ideal Government and the Mixed Constitution in the Middle Ages* (Princeton University Press, 1992), 260–5; Somerville, *Politics and Ideology*, 88–90.

17 Although the theory of mixed monarchy as such might be associated particularly with the English constitution, the idea of a monarchy well counselled was common across Europe, even if rarely employed, and enjoyed a very considerable pedigree amongst theories of conciliar government. See Burns, *Lordship*, chapters 1 and 3, Blythe, *Mixed Constitution*, chapters 13 and 14, and also J. Guy, 'The Henrician Age', in Pocock, ed., *Varieties*, particularly 13–22.

18 See Morris, *Political Thought*, 23–47.

19 See Blythe, *Mixed Constitution*, 273–7, and Hinton, 'English Constitutional Theories', 419–21.
20 See Burgess, *Politics*, 11–18.
21 Tuck also suggests that *Richard II* can be best understood as an articulation of the emerging English humanism. See R. Tuck, *Philosophy and Government 1572–1651* (Cambridge University Press, 1993), 104–19, 146–53 and 202–78.
22 See David Wooton's Introduction to his *Divine Right and Democracy*, (Harmondsworth: Penguin, 1986), 51–5. For a discussion of resistance theories such as Buchanan's, see Kelley, 'Elizabethan Political Thought', in Pocock, ed., *Varieties*, 58–61.
23 This thesis is most stridently suggested by Morris, *Political Thought*, 172–98. See also Burgess, *Politics*, 28–9, in support.
24 For a vigorous attack upon absolutism and incipient tyranny see Thomas Starkey's *Dialogue between Cardinal Pole and Thomas Lupset*; see Blythe, *Mixed Constitution*, 273–4.
25 Burns, *Lordship*, 156–7.
26 See Elton, *The Tudor Constitution*, 12–13, and also 'Parliament', in Haigh, ed., *The Reign of Elizabeth I*, 79–100.
27 Hinton, 'English Constitutional Theories', 424–5.
28 For a discussion of James's treatise see Kenyon, *The Stuart Constitution*, 7–8 and 12–14; Wooton, *Divine Right and Democracy*, 28–30 and 99–107; Peck, 'Kingship, Counsel and Law in Early Stuart Britain', in Pocock, ed., *Varieties*, 84–7.
29 R. Filmer, *Partriarcha and Other Writings*, J. Somerville, ed. (Cambridge University Press, 1991), and T. Hobbes, *Leviathan* (Harmondsworth: Penguin, 1985).
30 Somerville, *Politics and Ideology*, 9–56.
31 Perhaps the most significant of which was 'An Homily against Disobedience and Wylful Rebellion', published in 1570. See Wooton, *Divine Right and Democracy*, 94–8.
32 See H. Kelly, *Divine Providence in the England of Shakespeare's Histories* (Cambridge, Mass.: Harvard University Press, 1970), for a discussion of the various theories of providence around in the sixteenth century.
33 See Elton, *Tudor Constitution*, 17–18, and Wooton, *Divine Right and Democracy*, 26.
34 Burgess, *Politics*, chapters 6 and 7. See also Somerville, *Politics and Ideology*, chapters 4–6.
35 H. Kantorowicz, *The King's Two Bodies: A Study in Medieval Political Theology* (Princeton University Press, 1957). The crisis in the reception of this thesis by the end of the sixteenth century, he intimates in chapter 2, provided the catalyst for Shakespeare's *Richard II*.
36 For a general discussion of this retreat, see D. Burden 'Shakespeare's History Plays: 1952–1983', *Shakespeare Survey*, 38 (1985), 1–18.

37 E. Tillyard, *Shakespeare's History Plays* (London: Peregrine, 1962), particularly chapters 1 and 2.

38 See G. Holderness, *Shakespeare Recycled: The Making of Historical Drama* (London: Harvester Wheatsheaf, 1992), 21–9.

39 See M. Reese, *The Cease of Majesty* (London: Edward Arnold, 1961), 20–41 and 91–2; M. Prior, *The Drama of Power* (Chicago: Northwestern University Press, 1973), particularly chapters 1 and 2; R. Burckhardt, 'Obedience and Rebellion in Shakespeare's Early History Plays', *English Studies*, 55 (1974), 108–17, articulating the orthodox Tillyard thesis.

40 See, for example, M. Parker, *The Slave of Life* (London: Chatto and Windus, 1955), particularly chapters 1 and 2, and V. Kiernan, *Shakespeare: Poet and Citizen* (London: Verso, 1993), 3–17.

41 For a general discussion of which see P. Rackin, *Stages of History: Shakespeare's English Chronicles* (London: Routledge, 1991), 40–6. See also Holderness, *Shakespeare Recycled*, 21–40, and L. Barroll, 'A New History for Shakespeare and His Time', *Shakespeare Quarterly*, 39 (1988), 441–64.

42 For example, in one of the most influential of these studies, Ornstein persuasively suggests that the Tudor myth which Tillyard suggests that Shakespeare consistently articulates is in fact a particularly political 'Yorkist myth'. See R. Ornstein, *A Kingdom for a Stage* (Cambridge, Mass.: Harvard University Press, 1972), 1–32.

43 There are innumerable such historicist and cultural materialist studies. See, for example, Ornstein, *Kingdom for a Stage*, and more recently, Holderness, *Shakespeare Recycled*; R. Wells, *Shakespeare, Politics and the State* (London: Macmillan, 1986), particularly chapters 1–8; S. Greenblatt, *Shakespearean Negotiations: The Circulation of Social Energy in Renaissance England* (Berkeley: University of California Press, 1988), 1–20; and J. Dollimore, 'Introduction: Shakespeare, Cultural Materialism and the New Historicism', in J. Dollimore and A. Sinfield, eds., *Political Shakespeare: New Essays in Cultural Materialism* (Manchester University Press, 1985), 2–17.

44 Kiernan, *Poet and Citizen*, particularly 1–17. See also D. Kastan, '"To Set a Form upon that Indigest": Shakespeare's Fictions of History', *Comparative Drama*, 17 (1983), 1–15, and W. Carroll, 'Language, Politics, and Poverty in Shakespearian Drama', *Shakespeare Survey*, 44 (1991), 17–24.

45 See G. Melchiori, 'The Corridors of History: Shakespeare the Remaker', in E. Honigmann, ed., *British Academy Shakespeare Lectures, 1980–1989* (Oxford University Press, 1993), 165–83.

46 See L. Knights, 'Shakespeare's Politics: with Some Reflections on the Nature of Tradition', *Proceedings of the British Academy*, 43 (1957), 115–32.

47 For a general accessible account of Richard's reign, see P. Sacchio,

Shakespeare's English Kings: History, Chronicle and Drama (Oxford University Press, 1977), 157–86, stressing how much of the Shakespearean Richard is without foundation. For more substantive revisionist accounts of Richard, see C. Ross, *Richard III* (London: Methuen, 1981) and A. Sutton, '"A Curious Searcher for our Weal Public": Richard III, Piety, Chivalry and the Concept of the "Good Prince'", in P. Hammond, ed., *Richard III: Loyalty, Lordship and Law* (London: Alan Sutton, 1986), 58–90.

48 For an interesting discussion of More's *The History of Richard III*, see R. Warnicke, 'More's *Richard III* and the Mystery Plays', *Historical Journal*, 35 (1992), 761–78. See also Hammond's introduction to the Arden Shakespeare *Richard III* (London: Routledge, 1981), 97–119.

49 See Tillyard, *History Plays*, 205–18. For a review of this thesis, see W. McNeir, 'The Masks of Richard the Third', *Studies in English Literature*, 11 (1971), 168–86.

50 See A. Rossiter, 'The Structure of *Richard the Third*', *Durham University Journal*, 31 (1938), 44–75, for the suggestion that the structure and themes of *Richard III* must be approached from *Henry VI* part 3.

51 The plainest of all Shakespeare's tyrants. See Prior, *Drama of Power*, 131–2.

52 See L. Champion, *Perspective in Shakespeare's English Histories* (Athens: University of Georgia Press, 1980), 54–69; J. Candido, 'Thomas More, the Tudor Chronicles, and Shakespeare's Altered Richard', *English Studies*, 2 (1987), 137–41; E. Pearlman, 'The Invention of Richard of Gloucester', *Shakespeare Quarterly*, 43 (1992), 410–29.

53 As, for example, used by Marlowe in *Barabas*. See Hammond, ed., *Richard III*, 74–119. For a discussion of Richard as 'Vice', see Pearlman, 'Invention', 421–2. It has been suggested that in portraying such an unambiguously evil tyrant, Shakespeare was in fact merely redescribing a common caricature. See Prior, *Drama of Power*, 283–4 and 288–95. See also Reese, *Cease of Majesty*, at 98 and 208–10, suggesting that Shakespeare's portrayal of Richard is the only 'vulgarisation' of a type in the histories, and that the character has 'less of Cesare Borgia than of Captain Hook.'

54 *Henry VI Part 3*, Arden Shakespeare (London: Routledge, 1969), A. Cairncross, ed., 3.2.124–95 [hereafter *HVI*].

55 *Ibid.*, 4.7.58–9.

56 *Ibid.*, 5.6.68.

57 *Richard III*, Arden Shakespeare (London: Routledge, 1981), 1.1.1–41 [hereafter *RIII*]. See also Kelly, *Divine Providence*, 277, and G. Day, '"Determined to prove a villain": Theatricality in *Richard III*', *Critical Survey*, 3 (1991), 149–56.

58 According to Kiernan, the 'first real master' of the 'technique of politics' in Shakespeare's plays: see *Poet and Citizen*, 90–1.

59 *RIII*, 4.2.61.
60 *Ibid.*, 1.3.318–19 and 334–8.
61 See Kelly, *Divine Providence*, 282.
62 *RIII*, 1.2.70.
63 *Ibid.*, 1.4.174–81 and 184–9.
64 *Ibid.*, 1.3.216–33.
65 *Ibid.*, 5.2.14–6 and 156–7.
66 See A. French, 'The World of *Richard III*', *Shakespeare Studies*, 4 (1968), 31–2, discussing the bare portrayal of Richmond.
67 *RIII*, 5.3.109.
68 See also Kelly, *Divine Providence*, 295 and Prior, *Drama of Power*, 34–5 and 43.
69 See Reese, *Cease of Majesty*, 212; Ornstein, *Kingdom for a Stage*, 81. See also P. Sahel, 'Some Versions of Coup d'état, Rebellion and Revolution', *Shakespeare Survey*, 44 (1991), 26–8, and Burckhardt, 'Obedience and Rebellion', 116.
70 For a discussion of the idea that Shakespeare wrote *Richard III* as a particular response to 'tyranny' in late sixteenth-century government, see M. Hotine, '*Richard III* and *Macbeth* – Studies in Tudor Tyranny?', *Notes and Queries*, 236 (1991), 480–6.
71 See W. Carroll, 'Desacralization and Succession in *Richard III*', *Deutsche Shakespeare-Gesellschaft West Jahrbuch* (1991), 82–96, stressing Richard's concern with legal formality and legitimacy.
72 For Shakespeare's problem here, see Prior, *Drama of Power*, 121–3 and 134–8. The problem is exacerbated, Prior suggests, because Richard's claim to lineal legitimacy is at least as strong as Richmond's. See also A. Gurr, '*Richard III* and the Democratic Process', *Essays in Criticism*, 24 (1974), 39–47.
73 *RIII*, 5.3.124.
74 *Ibid.*, 5.3.236–71.
75 *Ibid.*, 5.3.315–42.
76 *Ibid.*, 5.5.18–21 and 29–34.
77 *Ibid.*, 4.4.377–87. For the suggestion that Richard's greatest failure was his failure to establish his legitimacy, see Carroll, 'Desacralization', 82–96.
78 For the suggestion that Richard's wooing of the crowd in fact shows his greater awareness of the importance of popular support in times of civil disturbance, see Gurr, 'Democratic Process', 39–47.
79 *RIII*, 3.7.46–50 and 60–3.
80 *Ibid.*, 5.2.1–16.
81 *Ibid.*, 3.7.1–3, 24–43 and 200.
82 *Ibid.*, 3.6.1–14.
83 For the significance of Richard's rhetorical capabilities as part of his overall deceitful character, and the suggestion that such an ability is

always a mask of danger, see Pearlman, 'Invention', 414, and R. Berry, '*Richard III*: Bonding the Audience', in J. Gray, ed., *Mirror up to Shakespeare* (University of Toronto Press, 1984), 114–27.

84 McNeir, 'Masks', 181–2.

85 *RIII*, 4.2. See also Ornstein's observations in *Kingdom for a Stage*, 75.

86 Reese, *Cease of Majesty*, 128–9.

87 Prior suggests that Shakespeare moves from a providentialist postition in *Richard III* to a more sceptical humanism in the second tetralogy. He also suggests that the fate of the two princes reveals Shakespeare's own doubts with regard to providential justice. See *Drama of Power*, 8 and 51–3.

88 For the contemporary popularity of *Richard III*, see Champion, *Perspective*, 68 and Ornstein, *Kingdom for a Stage*, 62. For the idea that *Richard III* was simply not disturbing enough and demanded of Shakespeare a thematic revision in subsequent plays, see French, 'World of *Richard III*', 38.

89 See Ornstein, *Kingdom for a Stage*, 83 and 101; H. Richmond, *Shakespeare's Historical Plays* (New York: Random House, 1967), 96; J. Simmons, 'Shakespeare's *King John* and its Source: Coherence, Pattern, and Vision', *Tulane Studies in English*, 17 (1969), 53–72; E. Grennan, 'Shakespeare's Satirical History: A Reading of *King John*', *Shakespeare Studies*, 11 (1978), 21. The famous exception here is Honigmann who, in his Introduction to the Arden edition of *John*, suggests a very early dating of the play, to around 1591, and would thus have it preceding both *Richard* plays. See E. Honigmann, ed., 'Introduction', *King John*, Arden Shakespeare (London: Routledge, 1967), xliii–xliv [hereafter *J*].

90 See Reese, *Cease of Majesty*, 263; Rackin, *Stages of History*, 66; Grennan, 'Satirical History', 23; and Champion, *Perspective*. For the neglect of *John*, see E. Waith, '*King John* and the Drama of History', *Shakespeare Quarterly*, 29 (1978), 192–211.

91 See D. Womersley, 'The Politics of Shakespeare's *King John*', *Review of English Studies*, 40 (1989), 497–8.

92 For the origins, and the various Johns, see Simmons, 'Coherence, Pattern, and Vision', 53–72; J. Elliot, 'Shakespeare and the Double Image of King John', *Shakespeare Studies*, 1 (1965), 56–72; C. Levin, 'The Historical Evolution of the Death of John in Three Renaissance Plays', *Journal of the Rocky Mountain Medieval and Renaissance Association*, 3 (1982), 85–106.

93 See Simmons, 'Coherence, Pattern, and Vision', 53–72; Elliot, 'Double Image', 72–81; Grennan, 'Satirical History', 29.

94 It has been suggested that Shakespeare was describing a character closer to the 'real' Machiavelli than the stage Machiavel. See Elliot, 'Double Image', 76–7.

95 *J*, 1.2.94–8.

96 *Ibid.*, 3.2.16–21.
97 For the importance of Shakespeare's presentation of John as an anti-Catholic figure, see R. Battenhouse, 'King John: Shakespeare's Perspective and Others', *Notre Dame English Journal*, 14 (1982), 191–215, and Rackin, *Stages of History*, 11.
98 *J*, 3.1.73–4.
99 *Ibid.*, 3.1.89–110.
100 *Ibid.*, 3.1.105–16, 150–79 and 235–8.
101 *Ibid.*, 4.2.40–105.
102 See B. Traister, 'The King's One Body: Unceremonial Kingship in *King John*', in D. Curren-Aquino, ed., *King John: New Perspectives* (Newark: University of Delaware, 1989), 91–8.
103 *J*, 4.2.208–14.
104 *Ibid.*, 5.1.1–4 and 43–61.
105 *Ibid.*, 5.3.3–4 and 14, and 5.7.35–43.
106 According to Manheim, the Bastard, as the transitional figure between the two tetralogies, emerges as the most important figure in Shakespeare's histories. See his 'The Four Voices of the Bastard', in Curren-Aquino, ed., *New Perspectives*, 126–35. See also Kastan, 'Fictions of History', 11–15, and J. van de Water, 'The Bastard in *King John*', *Shakespeare Quarterly*, 11 (1960), 137–46 and Womersley, 'Politics', 499–515.
107 See Tillyard, *History Plays*, 239; Champion, *Perspectives*, 99–100; Grennan, 'Satirical History', 30–1. For the thesis that the Bastard preshadows Henry, see Reese, *Cease of Majesty*, 285.
108 Levin, 'Historical Evolution', 105.
109 *J*, 1.1.182–219.
110 *Ibid.*, 4.2.141–52 and 4.3.140–59.
111 Thus, according to Levin, making a preliminary critique of the 'king's two bodies' thesis: See 'Historical Evolution', 105. See also Van de Water, 'Bastard', 142–5, and Tillyard, *History Plays*, 226.
112 *J*, 5.1.65–76.
113 *Ibid.*, 5.2.127–58.
114 *Ibid.*, 5.7.110–18.
115 *Ibid.*, 5.7.100–5. See J. Calderwood, 'Commodity and Honour in *King John*', *University of Toronto Quarterly*, 29 (1960), 341–56, and Simmons, 'Coherence, Pattern, and Vision', 68–9. See also Van de Water, 'Bastard', 144, and Battenhouse, 'King John', 204, for the Bastard's role as the ideal subject.
116 Womersley, 'Politics', 501–15.
117 See Richmond, *Political Plays*, 102–3 and 108, suggesting that both characters can thus be seen as developments of Richard III.
118 *J*, 2.1.373–96.
119 *Ibid.*, 3.2.16–26.

120 *Ibid.*, 2.1.167–90. For a discussion of Constance's role in debunking providence, see Grennan, 'Satirical History', 32–3.
121 *Ibid.*, 3.1.34–7.
122 *Ibid.*, 2.2.52.
123 See L. Champion, '"Answere to this Perillous Time": Ideological Ambivalence in *The Raigne of King Edward III* and the English Chronicle Plays', *English Studies*, 69 (1988), 128. For the suggestion that the Bastard shares Hubert's conversion, see Battenhouse, 'King John', 208.
124 See Tillyard, *History Plays*, 227.
125 The crucial theme, according to Champion, for example, in *Perspective*, 103, and Rackin in *Stages of History*, 186.
126 *J*, 1.1.5.
127 *Ibid.*, 1.1.39–40. See also Richmond, *Political Plays*, 110–11, emphasising John's own appreciation of his situation.
128 See Sacchio, *Shakespeare's English Kings*, 190–1.
129 *J*, 1.1.116–252.
130 *Ibid.*, 2.1.85–8.
131 *Ibid.*, 1.2.89–109 and 112–17.
132 *Ibid.*, 1.2.118.
133 *Ibid.*, 2.1.97–8.
134 *Ibid.*, 2.1.236–66 and 273.
135 See Richard's similar question in *RIII*, 4.4.469–73. See also Richmond's commentary in *Political Plays*, 99. It is also less certain than it was in the *Troublesome Raigne*, where John's usurpation was much more clearly condemned. See Simmons, 'Coherence, Pattern, and Vision', 59–60.
136 See Champion, *Perspectives*, 105, and Hamilton, *Politics of Protestant England*, 56–7.
137 See Simmons, 'Coherence, Pattern, and Vision', 66–7.
138 The strongest line here is taken by Hamilton, in *Politics of Protestant England*, 30–58. According to Hamilton, Shakespeare was not merely attacking absolutism in general, but more precisely the absolutist pretensions of the ecclesiastical courts in late Elizabethan England. In jurisprudential terms, she adds, Shakespeare was aligning himself with the arguments of the common lawyers.
139 *J.*, 2.1.281–2. See also V. Vaughan, '*King John*: A Study in Subversion and Containment', in Curren-Aquino, ed., *King John*, 68–9.
140 *J*, 2.1.368–72.
141 *Ibid.*, 2.1.373–96.
142 *Ibid.*, 5.2.8–39. See also Simmons, 'Coherence, Pattern, and Vision', 66–7, stressing the extent to which Shakespeare has created a dilemma which was less evident in the *Troublesome Raigne*.
143 See Elliot, 'Double Image', 81, and Battenhouse, 'King John', 206–7.

144 See Womersley, 'Politics', 514–15. According to Tillyard, it is the Bastard who appreciates the fact that although John is both a bad person and a bad king, he is not a tyrant, and so there is no question of rebellion. See *History Plays*, 231. See also Battenhouse, 'King John', 203.

145 See Champion, 'Ideological Ambivalence', 128; Simmons, 'Coherence, Pattern, and Vision', 67–8; Burckhardt, 'Obedience and Rebellion', 112–13; Hamilton, *Politics of Protestant England*, 49–58.

146 See Manheim, 'Four Voices', 126–35, discussing the idea that the Bastard can thus be seen as the most subversive character in the histories, and also as the crucial transitional character between the two tetralogies. See also Grennan, 'Satirical History', 34–5; Kastan, 'Fictions of History', 11–5, and Vaughan, 'Subversion and Containment', in Curren-Aquino, ed. *King John*, 62–75.

147 See Hamilton, *Politics of Protestant England*, 42–9. This conclusion is also reached by Simmons in 'Coherence, Pattern, and Vision', 71.

148 Ornstein sees similarities with Lear. See *Kingdom for a Stage*, 108. See also J. Elliott, 'History and Tragedy in *Richard II*', *Studies in English Literature*, 8 (1968), 253–71; Champion, *Perspective*, 70–1 and 90–1; Prior, *Drama of Power*, 156–82.

149 See Ure's comments in his Introduction to *Richard II*, Arden Shakespeare (London: Routledge, 1966), xxx–xlix [hereafter *RII*], J. Theilmann, 'Stubbs, Shakespeare, and Recent Historians of Richard II', *Albion*, 8 (1976), 107–24; S. Schoenbaum, '*Richard II* and the Realities of Power', *Shakespeare Survey*, 28 (1975), 1–6; Elliott, 'History and Tragedy', at 257–60.

150 See Tillyard, *History Plays*, 250–1, and Reese, *Cease of Majesty*, 116–19.

151 See Prior, *Drama of Power*, 141–2, suggesting that Richard emerges as the 'ideal protagonist' for such a venture.

152 See Prior, *Drama of Power*, 141–3, and J. Gohn, '*Richard II*: Shakespeare's Legal Brief on the Royal Prerogative and the Succession to the Throne', *Georgetown Law Journal*, 70 (1982), 955–9.

153 See A. Tuck, *Richard II and the English Nobility* (London: Edward Arnold, 1973) and B. Bevan, *King Richard II* (London: Rubicon Press, 1990).

154 See Richmond, *Political Plays*, 124, and G. Lanier, 'From Windsor to London: The Destruction of Monarchial Authority in *Richard II*', *Selected Papers from the West Virginia Shakespeare and Renaissance Association*, 13 (1988), 1.

155 *RII*, 1.2.196–205.

156 See Kantorowicz, *King's Two Bodies*, 24–41, suggesting that Richard is the classic portrayal of such a monarch.

157 See Tillyard, *History Plays*, 258–61, and P. Philias, 'The Medieval in Richard II', *Shakespeare Quarterly*, 12 (1961), 305–10.

158 See D. Bornstein, 'Trial by Combat and Official Irresponsibility in *Richard II*', *Shakespeare Studies*, 8 (1975), 131–41, and M. Ranald, 'The Degradation of *Richard II*: An Inquiry into the Ritual Backgrounds', *English Literary Renaissance*, 7 (1977), 170–83. See also Ure, Introduction, *Richard II*, xliv, suggesting the combat's legality but unorthodoxy, and Champion, *Perspective*, 77–8, discussing its prerogative justification.

159 See Gohn, 'Legal Brief', 959–65; Hamilton; 'State of Law', 15; Bornstein, 'Trial by Combat', 131–41.

160 *RII*, 1.3.216–24, 236–46 and 275–94.

161 His failure to heed good counsel is a critical failing, as Northumberland observes. See *RII*, 2.1.238–45. Bolingbroke subsequently refers to Richard's unsuitable counsel as the 'caterpillars of the commonwealth', in 2.3, at 165, and admonishes them in 3.1, at 1–30. See also P. Gaudet, 'The "Parasitical" Counselors in Shakespeare's *Richard II*: A Problem in Dramatic Interpretation', *Shakespeare Quarterly*, 33 (1982), 142–54.

162 *RII*, 3.4.29–71.

163 *Ibid.*, 1.4.42–52 and 59–64, and 2.1.17–30 and 190–210.

164 *Ibid.*, 2.1.91–114. For a discussion of the 'farming' of the realm, see D. Hamilton, 'The State of Law in *Richard II*', *Shakespeare Quarterly*, 34 (1983), 5–17.

165 *RII*, 2.1.155. See also the Captain's comments in 2.4.7–17, suggesting that Richard in abandoning the country has left it to run wild.

166 *Ibid.*, 3.2.54–7 and 60–2. For a commentary on Richard's invocation of providence, and its rather unconvincing portrayal, see Prior, *Drama of Power*, 60–2.

167 *Ibid.*, 3.2.83, 129–34 and 144–77.

168 *Ibid.*, 3.2.177.

169 *Ibid.*, 3.2.178–85.

170 *Ibid.*, 3.3.77–8.

171 *Ibid.*, 3.3.172–4.

172 See Elliott, 'History and Tragedy', 264–5, and Richmond, *Political Plays*, 123 and 133–6.

173 *RII*, 1.4.24–36.

174 *Ibid.*, 2.2.112–35.

175 *Ibid.*, 3.3.35–61. For a discussion of Bolingbroke's rather shadowy appearances, and the almost secretive portrayal of his ambition, see B. Stirling, 'Bolingbroke's "Decision"', *Shakespeare Quarterly*, 2 (1951), 27–34.

176 *RII*, 3.3.209. Richard acknowledges that his earthly realm is lost and, in his physical descent from the battlements of Flint castle, identifies himself with Phaeton. See *ibid.*, 3.3.178–9. For a discussion of this analogy, see S. Heninger, 'The Sun-King Analogy in *Richard II*', *Shakespeare Quarterly*, 11 (1960), 319–27, and R. Merrix, 'The

Phaeton Allusion in *Richard II*: The Search for Identity', *English Literary Renaissance*, 17 (1987), 277–87.

177 See Lanier, 'From Windsor to London', 3, and Stirling, 'Bolingbroke's "Decision"', 30–4.

178 *RII*, 4.1.114–49.

179 *Ibid.*, 4.1.173. His assumption of the crown is most immediately a response to York. See *ibid.*, 4.1.107–13.

180 Lanier, 'From Windsor to London', 5–7.

181 *RII* 4.1.232–6.

182 *Ibid.*, 4.1.191–3.

183 *Ibid.*, 4.1.276–91. See Kantorowicz, *King's Two Bodies*, at 39, suggesting that the mirror scene represents the final dissolution of the 'two bodies thesis'.

184 *RII*, 4.1.250–2.

185 See Kantorowicz, *King's Two Bodies*, 24–41.

186 *RII*, 4.1, 201–22.

187 *Ibid.*, 5.1.7–21, 5.3.129 and 135–43, and 5.6.2–29. See Champion, *Perspective*, 83–4 and 87–90.

188 *RII*, 5.6.39.

189 *Ibid.*, 5.6.49–50.

190 *Ibid.*, 5.5.31–8. See Richmond, *Political Plays*, at 137, suggesting that the the degree of self–understanding which Richard accesses in his final soliloquay is exceptional, even in comparison with Shakespeare's later tragedies.

191 *RII*, 5.5.102–12. See P. Jensen, 'Beggars and Kings: Cowardice and Courage in Shakespeare's *Richard II*', *Interpretation*, 18 (1990), 137–8, suggesting that, in fact, this presents Richard at his most majestic.

192 *RII.*, 3.2.27–8.

193 *Ibid.*, 4.1.114–49.

194 *Ibid.*, 4.1.321–34. This theme was to reach its epitome in Shakespeare's Wolsey in *Henry VIII*.

195 For Shakespeare's development of the two characters, see Ornstein, *Kingdom for a Stage*, 123, and Elliott, 'History and Tragedy', 266–7.

196 *RII*, 1.2.37–41.

197 *Ibid.*, 1.4.40–3, 57–60 and 65–6. For an interesting use of Gaunt's speech, by Coke in a 1606 judgement, see M. Schwarz, 'Sir Edward Coke and "This Scept'red Isle": A Case of Borrowing', *Notes and Queries*, 233 (1988), 54–6.

198 *RII.*, 2.1.73–87. For a discussion of the symbolism of England's decline as 'paradise', see C. MacKenzie, 'Paradise and Paradise Lost in *Richard II*', *Shakespeare Quarterly*, 37 (1986), 318–39.

199 For Northumberland's comments, see *RII*, 2.1.238–45, 262–6 and 285–98.

200 *Ibid.*, 2.2.109–14.
201 *Ibid.*, 2.3.139–41.
202 For an appreciation of York's role, see Elliott, 'History and Tragedy', 268–9, and M. Kelly, 'The Function of York in *Richard II*', *Southern Humanities Review*, 6 (1972), 257–67.
203 *RII*, 2.3.139–46.
204 *Ibid.*, 4.1.107–12.
205 *Ibid.*, 5.2.23–40 and 72–110.
206 Ure expresses doubts with regard to the authenticity of the entire episode. See his Introduction to *Richard II*, at lxii. For a revisionist discussion of Lambarde's account, see Barroll, 'New History', 442–54, and A. Kinney, 'Essex and Shakespeare versus Hayward', *Shakespeare Quarterly*, 44 (1993), 464–6.
207 If they did feel that a play was at all subversive they were quick to act. Two years earlier, Sir John Hayward's book on Henry IV had been quickly suppressed, and Hayward himself imprisoned. See Barroll, 'New History', 446–54.
208 For a discussion, see Barroll, 'New History', 448–9; C. Greer, 'The Deposition Scene of *Richard II*', *Notes and Queries*, 197 (1952), 492–3, and 'More about the Deposition Scene of *Richard II*', *Notes and Queries*, 198 (1953), 49–50; J. Clare, 'The Censorship of the Deposition Scene in *Richard II*', *Review of English Studies*, 41 (1990), 89–94.
209 See D. Kastan, 'Proud Majesty Made a Subject: Shakespeare and the Spectacle of Rule', *Shakespeare Quarterly*, 37 (1986), 468–73, suggesting that it was the fact that the ceremony of kingship was being revealed as merely a piece of theatre which was potentially subversive, but that the authorities in late Elizabethan England were, if anything, keen to support the enactment of such ceremony.
210 See Gohn, 'Legal Brief', 953–5, and A. Potter, 'Shakespeare as Conjuror: Manipulation of Audience Response in *Richard II*', *Communique*, 6 (1981), 1–9.
211 See Richmond, *Political Plays*, 139–40, and Kiernan, *Poet and Citizen*, 37–8 and 77–81.
212 For a convincing argument that Richard's invocation of divine right is consistently compromised by Shakespeare, see Kelly, *Divine Providence*, 208–9. See also Holderness, *Shakespeare Recycled*, at 8–9, suggesting that *Richard II* signals Shakespeare's conversion to humanism. For the implication that *Richard II* is more subversive, at least in fact that it suggests a degeneracy of kingship itself, see Lanier, 'From Windsor to London', 1–8, and Ranald, 'Degradation', 170–96.
213 For a strong suggestion that this is so, see Hamilton, 'State of Law', 5–17; Kiernan, *Poet and Citizen*, 77–81 and 114; P. Brockbank, *Brockbank on Shakespeare* (Oxford: Blackwell, 1989), 104–21; Reese, *Cease of Majesty*, 128–41; L. Cowan, 'God Will Save the King: Shakespeare's *Richard II*', in J. Alvis and T. West, eds., *Shakespeare as a Political Thinker* (Durham:

Carolina Academic, 1981), 63–9, all stressing the anti-absolutist message of the play. For the suggestion that *Richard II* signals Shakespeare's disillusion with providentialism and absolutism, see Holderness, *Shakespeare Recycled*, 8–9 and 51–71. The alternative is articulated by Gohn in 'Legal Brief' at 971–2, suggesting that the deposition scene is a 'vindication' of absolutism, and that Bolingbroke merely becomes an alternative absolutist monarch ruling by divine right.

5 CHILDREN'S LITERATURE AND LEGAL IDEOLOGY

1 W. Auden, 'Today's "wonder-world" needs Alice', in R. Phillips, ed., *Aspects of Alice* (Harmondsworth: Penguin, 1974), 7.
2 See P. Hunt, *Criticism, Theory and Children's Literature* (Oxford: Blackwell, 1991), 5–6.
3 For a very early statement stressing the importance of differentness, see Elizabeth Rigby, 'Children's Books', *The Quarterly Review*, 74 (1844), 1–3 and 16–26, in P. Hunt, ed., *Children's Literature* (London: Routledge, 1990), 19–22. See also Hunt, *Criticism*, 20–1 and 39.
4 Hunt, *Criticism*, 21.
5 *Ibid.*, 60.
6 See Hunt, *Children's Literature*, 81–6.
7 N. Tucker, *Suitable for Children? Controversies in Children's Literature* (Brighton: Sussex University Press, 1976), 18–19.
8 Hunt, *Criticism*, 104.
9 See Chambers in Hunt, ed., *Literature for Children: Contemporary Criticism* (London: Routledge, 1992), 66–77.
10 Hunt, *Criticism*, 44–64.
11 Taken to an extreme this pragmatic approach leads to children's literature being determined as children's literature if it appears as such on a publisher's list. See John Rowe Townsend, 'Standards of Criticism for Children's Literature', *Top of the News*, 1971, in Hunt, ed., *Children's Literature*, 57–61.
12 See Paul, 'Intimations of Imitations', in Hunt, ed., *Literature for Children*, 66–77. For the use of Iser see Chambers, 'The Reader in the Book', in Hunt, ed., *ibid.*, 91–114. See also Hunt, *Criticism*, 9 and 66, 105–17.
13 See, for example, Umberto Eco, *Interpretation and Overinterpretation* (Cambridge University Press, 1992).
14 Their essays and observations are collected in Hunt, *Children's Literature*, 24–32.
15 P. Hollindale, 'Ideology and the Children's Book', in Hunt, ed., *Literature for Children*, 24–5.
16 Hunt, *Criticism*, 109.
17 Hunt, ed., *Literature for Children*, 18.
18 L. Paul, 'Enigma Variations: What Feminist Theory Knows About Children's Literature', *Signal*, 54 (1987), 186–201.

19 Hollindale, 'Ideology and the Children's Book', 19–40.
20 Hunt, *Criticism*, 151–4.
21 See *ibid.*, 81–96, Paul, 'Enigma Variations', 198–201, and Townsend, 'Standards of Criticism', 69–71.
22 M. Myers, 'Missed Opportunities and Critical Malpractice: New Historicism and Children's Literature', *Children's Literature Association Quarterly*, 13 (1988), 42.
23 Watkins, 'Cultural Studies, New Historicism and Children's Literature', in Hunt, ed., *Literature for Children*, 183.
24 In Eagleton, *Literary Criticism: An Introduction* (Oxford: Blackwell, 1983), 151–93.
25 *Ibid.*, 176–9.
26 R. Unger, *Passion: An Essay on Personality* (New York: Free Press, 1984), 3–89, and 275–300.
27 Most importantly, his *The Child and the Book: A Psychological and Literary Exploration* (Cambridge University Press, 1981).
28 See J. Piaget, *The Moral Judgment of the Child* (London: Routledge and Kegan Paul, 1932), ix.
29 *Ibid.*, 1–2 and 16–17.
30 Tucker, *The Child and the Book*, 4.
31 Piaget, *Moral Judgment*, 18 and 32–8.
32 *Ibid.*, 41–56.
33 *Ibid.*, 250–75.
34 *Ibid.*, 38–41, 270–94 and 314.
35 *Ibid.*, 98–9. See also 23 and 45.
36 *Ibid.*, 106–7.
37 *Ibid.*, 56–69.
38 *Ibid.*, 104–94.
39 J. Adelson, 'The Political Imagination of the Young Adolescent', *Daedalus*, 100 (1971), 1013–50.
40 Piaget, *Moral Judgment*, 195–6. For the difficulties in determining fact and fantasy, see Hunt, *Literature for Children*, 41–3.
41 See S. Gilead, 'Magic Abjured: Closure in Children's Fantasy Fiction', in Hunt, ed., *Literature for Children*, 80–109, a suspicion shared by Tucker: *The Child and the Book*, 183–5.
42 Tucker, *The Child and the Book*, 5–17.
43 *Ibid.*, 46–65.
44 *Ibid.*, 67–94.
45 *Ibid.*, 98–132.
46 *Ibid.*, 136 and 144–87. Another 'classic' type of this text for teenage children is *Anne Frank's Diary*.
47 Green, 'The Golden Age of Children's Books', in Hunt, ed., *Children's Literature*, 47.
48 Tucker, *The Child and the Book*, 58–60. See also Margaret Lane's observations in *The Tale of Beatrix Potter* (Harmondsworth: Penguin, 1985), 116–18.

49 For a commentary on the construction of Potter's tales, see Tucker, *The Child and the Book*, 57–66.
50 See Tucker's observations in *ibid.*, 62.
51 *The Tale of Peter Rabbit* is included in *The Complete Tales of Beatrix Potter* (London: Warne, 1989), 11–20.
52 *Ibid.*, 55–68.
53 *Ibid.*, 133–8.
54 *Ibid.*, 199–208.
55 *Ibid.*, 175–96.
56 *Ibid.*, 71–84.
57 *Ibid.*, 211–22.
58 See Lancelyn Green's comments in 'The Golden Age of Children's Books', in Hunt, ed., *Children's Literature*, 40–1, and Tucker's in *The Child and the Book*, 19.
59 See Tucker, *The Child and the Book*, 10 and 98.
60 For a recent essay on Carroll's use of 'framing' and dreams, and the extent to which he was perhaps writing for an audience of two or just one, see Gilead, 'Magic Abjured', in Hunt, ed., *Literature for Children*, 80–109. See also Martin Gardner's comments in his 'Introduction' to *The Annotated Alice* (Harmondsworth: Penguin, 1970), 8–10. The obvious evidence from the actual *Alice* text is Carroll's final tease, at the end of *Looking Glass*, 'Life, what is it but a dream?', at 345.
61 K. Blake, *Play, Games and Sport: The Literary Works of Lewis Carroll* (Ithaca: Cornell University Press, 1974), 128–31.
62 *Annotated Alice*, 143–62.
63 Blake, *Play, Games and Sport*, 15.
64 *Annotated Alice*, 143–4.
65 A verse of Father William's nonsense runs:
> 'In my youth,' said his father, 'I took to the law,
> and argued each case with my wife;
> And the muscular strength, which it gave to my jaw,
> Has lasted the rest of my life.'

See *ibid.*, 71.
66 See M. Gardner, *The Annotated Snark* (Harmondsworth: Penguin, 1974), 83–8.
67 *Annotated Alice*, 51.
68 Gardner, *Snark*, 83–4.
69 *Annotated Alice*, 148–50.
70 *Ibid.*, 269.
71 S. Islam, *Kipling's 'Law'* (London: Macmillan, 1975). See also Tucker's concurring view in *The Child and the Book*, 160.
72 The particular virtue of Islam, according to Kipling, was that it was always accompanied by 'a comprehensible civilisation' The same was not always true of Christianity, although the influence of the Judaeo-Christian is evident in the repeated use of biblical quotations throughout

Kipling's works. According to Islam, it was the nature of contingent truths in Buddhism which appealed to Kipling. See Islam, *ibid.*, 25–47.

73 Islam, *ibid.*, 48–85. See particularly 67–8 for evidence of Kipling's fear of lawlessness.

74 *Ibid.*, 7–8.

75 *Ibid.*, 86–120.

76 M. Seymour-Smith, *Rudyard Kipling* (London: Macmillan, 1990), 101–20 and 244–54.

77 Islam, *Kipling's Law*, 122–3.

78 R. Kipling, *The Jungle Books* (Harmondsworth: Penguin, 1989), 173–88.

79 In a strictly Thomist determination Tha's 'Law' is a divine law revealed and then rationalised as natural law.

80 *Jungle Books*, 189–91.

81 *Ibid.*, 36–42.

82 *Ibid.*, 94–5.

83 *Ibid.*, 49–53.

84 *Ibid.*, 341–3.

85 *Ibid.*, 117–31, and 256.

86 *Ibid.*, 55–78, and 298–321.

87 *Ibid.*, 55–60 and 73–8.

88 J. White, *The Legal Imagination* (Boston: Little, Brown and Company, 1973), 19–25.

89 R. West, 'Communities, Texts and Law: Reflections on the Law and Literature Movement', *Yale Journal of Law and the Humanities*, 1 (1988), 132–40.

90 M. Twain, *The Adventures of Huckleberry Finn* (Harmondsworth: Penguin, 1985), 66–7.

91 *Ibid.*, 71–3.

92 *Ibid.*, 74.

93 Nor of course to Huck's father. See *ibid.*, 77–8.

94 *Ibid.*, 78.

95 *Ibid.*, 103–4, 123–5, 205–7, 227–40 and 249–53.

96 *Ibid.*, 145–9, 281–7 and 319.

97 *Ibid.*, 266–8 and 302.

98 The controversial final passages, when Huck rejoins Tom Sawyer and play an elaborate game in trying to release Jim from his 'captivity', have remained controversial. See Peter Coveney's comments on the controversy in his Introduction to *Huckleberry Finn*, 37.

99 See the observations of Mark Kinkead-Weekes and Ian Gregor in *William Golding: A Critical Study* (London: Faber, 1967), 18–19.

100 For a commentary on the descent symbolism in the *Lord of the Flies*, see Kinkead-Weekes and Gregor, *Golding*, 27.

101 W. Golding, *Lord of the Flies* (London: Faber, 1954), 17 and 36, and Kinkead-Weekes and Gregor, *Golding*, 56–9.

102 *Lord of the Flies*, 20–5, 29–32, 36, 46–7, and 60–5.

103 See Kinkead-Weekes and Gregor, *Golding*, 26.
104 *Lord of the Flies*, 67.
105 *Ibid.*, 77–8.
106 *Ibid.*, 99–100.
107 *Ibid.*, 154–5, 165, 176, 198 and 209.
108 *Ibid.*, 188–9, 150–4, 176 and 191–223.
109 *Ibid.*, 17, 23–4 and 36.
110 *Ibid.*, 200 and 223. See also Kinkead-Weekes and Gregor, *Golding*, 64.
111 See his Introduction to *Gulliver's Travels* (Harmondsworth: Penguin, 1985), 9; also D. Nokes, *Jonathan Swift: A Hypocrite Reversed* (Oxford University Press, 1985), 317.
112 Nokes, *ibid.*, 317.
113 See L. Bellamy, *Gulliver's Travels* (London: Harvester Wheatsheaf, 1992). Perhaps the most impressive handling of the political symbolism is still to be found in W. Speck, *Swift* (London: Evans, 1969), 100–34.
114 See 'Introduction', *Gulliver's Travels*, 18.
115 Bellamy, *Gulliver's Travels*, 8–9, 19–25 and 110–18.
116 J. Traugott, 'The Yahoo in the Doll's House: *Gulliver's Travels* the Children's Classic', in C. Rawson and J. Mezciems, eds., *English Satire and the Satiric Tradition* (Oxford University Press, 1984), 127–50.
117 Nokes, *Swift*, 319.
118 J. White, *When Words Lose Their Meaning: Constitutions and Reconstitutions of Language, Character and Community* (University of Chicago Press, 1990), 133–4.
119 *Gulliver's Travels*, 297.
120 *Ibid.*, 103–8. The satire of Gulliver's 'trial' may have been intended as a more precise satire of Bishop Atterbury's trial, famously conducted with an almost total lack of evidence, and thus as a satire of the use of the legal process for political means.
121 *Gulliver's Travels*, 89. For this challenging interpretation presented by Arthur Case, see Bellamy, *Gulliver's Travels*, 47–9.
122 It has been commonly asserted that rather than advocating a progressive republicanism, Swift is in fact suggesting a return to the balanced polity of the Ancient Constitution. For the ridicule of the Emperor of Lilliput, see *Travels*, 62, and 65–7. For commentaries on Swift's conservatism, see Speck, *Swift*, 15 and 111–12, and perhaps most interestingly George Orwell's essay 'Politics v Literature: An Examination of *Gulliver's Travels*' in *The Penguin Essays of George Orwell* (Harmondsworth: Penguin, 1968), 376–93.
123 *Gulliver's Travels*, 79 and 84–6.
124 *Ibid.*, 94–7. See also Speck, *Swift*, 117.
125 The second book, like the fourth, is a satire of philosophy, rather than of politics. Most particularly it is a satire of formalist Aristotelian philosophy which, like law, present its own specialised language. See *Gulliver's Travels*, 143 and 176–7.

126 *Ibid.*, 214–17.
127 Perhaps to his own delight, the position of Swift's own sympathies remains an unresolved issue. For discussions of Swift's position in the contemporary Hobbes–Locke debate, see Nokes, *Swift*, 325–8, and Speck, *Swift*, 127–30.
128 *Gulliver's Travels*, 296–8.
129 *Ibid.*, 306.
130 See Speck, *Swift*, 114, and Foot, 'Introduction', 28–9.

6 LAW, LITERATURE AND FEMINISM

1 M. Atwood, *The Handmaid's Tale* (London: Virago, 1987), 67.
2 M. Eagleton, ed., *Feminist Literary Criticism* (London: Longman, 1991), 1–21.
3 See T. Moi, *Sexual/Textual Politics* (London: Routledge, 1985), and C. Kaplan, *Sea Changes: Culture and Feminism* (London: Verso, 1986).
4 K. Millett, *Sexual Politics* (London: Virago, 1977).
5 See Kaplan's 'Radical Feminism and Literature: Rethinking Millett's *Sexual Politics*', in *Sea Changes*, 15–30.
6 Kaplan's use of psychoanalysis, particularly that of Jacques Lacan, pervades the essays in *Sea Changes*.
7 The most accessible introduction to Kristeva's semiotics can be found in T. Moi, ed., *A Kristeva Reader* (Oxford: Blackwell, 1986).
8 Moi, *Sexual/Textual Politics*, 31–40.
9 *Ibid.*, 97.
10 *Ibid.*, 66–7 and 102–4.
11 *Ibid.*, 150–73.
12 R. Barthes, *The Rustle of Language* (Oxford: Blackwell, 1986).
13 Most recently Showalter, 'The Feminist Critical Revolution', in E. Showalter, ed., *The New Feminist Criticism: Essays on Women, Literature and Theory* (London: Virago, 1986), 3–17.
14 See her *A Literature of Their Own: British Women Novelists from Bronte to Lessing* (Princeton University Press, 1978) for an emphasis on the need to isolate and identify the nature of a specifically feminist literature.
15 M. Jehlen, 'Archimedes and the Paradox of Feminist Criticism', *Signs*, 6 (1981), 575–601.
16 See A. Kolodny, 'Some Notes on Defining a "Feminist Literary Criticism"', *Critical Inquiry*, 2 (1975), 75–92.
17 See A. Kolodny, 'A Map for Misreading: Or Gender and the Interpretation of Literary Texts' and 'Dancing Through the Minefield: Some Observations on the Theory, Practice and Politics of a Feminist Literary Criticism', reprinted in Showalter, *Feminist Criticism*, at 46–62 and 144–67 respectively.
18 See R. Coward, 'This Novel Changes Women's Lives: Are Women's

Novels Feminist Novels?', and L. Robinson, 'Treason Our Text: Feminist Challenges to the Literary Canon', both in Showalter, *Feminist Criticism*, at 105–21 and 225–39 respectively.

19 For an interesting discussion on the relationship between feminist literary criticism and left politics, and the paradoxical difficulties which Anglo-Americans, who cherish a female identity, can encounter by aligning so closely with political movements, see J. Goode, 'Feminism, Class and Literary Criticism', in K. Campbell, ed., *Critical Feminism: Argument in the Disciplines* (Buckingham: Open University Press, 1992), 123–55.

20 G. Spivak, 'French Feminism in an International Frame', in M. Eagleton, ed., *Feminist Literary Criticism*, 102.

21 Kaplan, 'The Feminist Politics of Literary Theory' in *Sea Changes*, 57–66.

22 A. Leclerc, 'Woman's Word', in D. Cameron, ed., The *Feminist Critique of Language: A Reader* (London: Routledge, 1990), 79.

23 Observations in 'Women's Exile. Interview with Luce Irigaray', in Cameron, ed., *Feminist Critique of Language*, 80–96.

24 Leclerc, 'Woman's Word', in Cameron, ed., *Feminist Critique*, 74–9.

25 Kaplan, 'Pandora's Box: Subjectivity, Class and Sexuality in Socialist Feminist Criticism', in *Sea Changes*, 147–76.

26 Clement in dialogue with Hélène Cixous, in *The Newly Born Women* (Manchester University Press, 1985), 136–60.

27 For various commentaries on the law in Jane Austen's novels, see E. Hildebrand, 'Jane Austen and the Law', *Persuasions*, 4 (1982), 34–41; L. Redmond, 'Land, Law and Love', *Persuasions*, 4 (1989), 46–52; G. Treitel, 'Jane Austen and the Law', *Law Quarterly Review*, 100 (1984), 549–86.

28 S. Mann, 'The Universe and the Library: A Critique of James Boyd White as Writer and Reader', *Stanford Law Review*, 41 (1989), 959–1009.

29 E. Hartigan, 'From Righteousness to Beauty: Reflections on *Poethics* and *Justice as Translation*', *Tulane Law Review*, 67 (1992), 455–83, particularly at 460 where she specifically distances herself from Mann's analysis of White.

30 C. Sanger, 'Seasoned to the Use', *Michigan Law Review*, 87 (1989), 1338–65.

31 J. Koffler, 'Forged Alliance: Law and Literature', *Columbia Law Review*, 89 (1989), 1375–93.

32 Mann, 'White', 981.

33 J. Schroeder, 'Feminism Historicized: Medieval Misogynist Stereotypes in Contemporary Feminist Jurisprudence', *Iowa Law Review*, 75 (1990), 1135–217.

34 MacKinnon's most substantial contribution to feminist legal theory remains her *Towards a Feminist Theory of State* (Cambridge, Mass.:

Harvard University Press, 1989). For a commentary on MacKinnon's work and its political aspect, see E. Jackson, 'Catherine MacKinnon and Feminist Jurisprudence: A Critical Appraisal', *Journal of Law and Society*, 19 (1992), 195–213. For a more general commentary on critical legal feminism and its associations with CLS, see D. Rhode, 'Feminist Critical Theories', *Stanford Law Review*, 42 (1990), 617–38.

35 See West's 'Communities, Texts, and Law: Reflections on the Law and Literature Movement', *Yale Journal of Law and the Humanities*, 1 (1988), 129–56, and more recently her *Narrative, Authority, and Law* (Ann Arbor: University of Michigan Press, 1993).

36 See L. Brown and C. Gilligan, *Meeting at the Crossroads: Women's Psychology and Girls' Development* (Cambridge, Mass.: Harvard University Press, 1992).

37 See her 'Jurisprudence and Gender', *University of Chicago Law Review*, 55 (1988), 1–72, and 'Jurisprudence as Narrative: An Aesthetic Analysis of Modern Legal Theory', *New York University Law Review*, 60 (1985), 145–211.

38 West, 'Communities', particularly 146–56. She reached essentially the same conclusion in 'Jurisprudence and Gender', 71.

39 C. Heilbrun and J. Resnik, 'Convergences: Law, Literature, and Feminism', *Yale Law Journal*, 99 (1990), 1913–53.

40 W. Goetz, 'The Felicity and Infelicity of Marriage in *Jude the Obscure*', *Nineteenth Century Fiction*, 38 (1983–4), 189–213.

41 See L. Hirshman, 'Brontë, Bloom, and Bork: An Essay on the Moral Education of Judges', *University of Pennsylvania Law Review*, 137 (1988), 177–231. For a comment on Hirshman's essay, see J. Honnold, 'Hirshman, Brontë, and Hawthorne on Law, Abortion and Society: Brava and Addendum', *University of Pennsylvania Law Review*, 137 (1989), 1247–50.

42 Heilbrun and Resnick, 'Convergences', 1921 and 1927.

43 See MacKinnon, *Feminist Theory of State*, 172–83.

44 *Ibid.*, 180–2.

45 This is covered particularly in her *Feminism Unmodified* (Cambridge, Mass.: Harvard University Press, 1987), 80–2.

46 In West's words, such approaches are 'disappointingly unidimensional' and 'unsatisfying'. See her 'Jurisprudence and Gender', particularly 28–35, 42–50 and 64–6.

47 See P. Williams, 'Alchemical Notes: Reconstructed Ideals from Deconstructed Rights', *Harvard Civil Rights–Civil Liberties Law Review*, 22 (1987), 401–34.

48 S. Estrich, 'Rape', *Yale Law Journal*, 95 (1986), 1087–184, and *Real Rape* (Cambridge, Mass.: Harvard University Press, 1987).

49 Estrich, 'Rape', particularly 1105–121.

50 *Ibid.*, 1121–32. The Michigan Reform Statute is noteworthy in its abandonment of consent as a factor, and its substitution of sole

reliance on force. The Statute has met with something of a mixed response. Whilst Estrich is wary of its decision to abandon rather than redefine, Martha Chamallas is prepared to hail it as a major step forward. See M. Chamallas, 'Consent, Equality, and the Legal Control of Sexual Conduct', 61 *Southern California Law Review* 1988, 796–800.

51 Estrich, 'Rape', 1147–57 and 1179–82.
52 Estrich, *Real Rape*, 102.
53 Schroeder, 'Feminism Historicized', 1149.
54 See *ibid.*, 1170 and 1177–8. See also Cameron, ed., *Feminist Critique*, emphasising at 16–18 the enduring effects of the language of rape.
55 C. Smart, 'Law's Power, the Sexed Body, and Feminist Discourse', *Journal of Law and Society*, 17 (1990), particularly 203–8. It is the failure to fully comprehend the power of discourse which, according to Smart, flaws MacKinnon's rape thesis.
56 See Schroeder, 'Feminism Historicized', 1189, 1201 and 1215–17, suggesting that the linguistic basis provides the most important hope of all, 'the hope of translation'.
57 See Hirshman, 'Brontë, Bloom and Bork', 224–30.
58 Atwood, *The Handmaid's Tale*, 185–6.
59 *Ibid.*, 104–5.
60 *Ibid.*, 106.
61 *Ibid.*, 83.
62 *Ibid.*, 67.
63 *Ibid.*, 47–8.
64 *Ibid.*, 170.
65 *Ibid.*, 39.
66 *Ibid.*, 59.
67 *Ibid.*, 81–2.
68 *Ibid.*, 98.
69 *Ibid.*, 91.
70 *Ibid.*, 290–2.
71 *Ibid.*, 70–1.
72 *Ibid.*, 66–7.
73 *Ibid.*, 124.
74 *Ibid.*, 128.
75 *Ibid.*, 166–7 and 266–7.
76 A. Dworkin, *Mercy* (London: Arrow, 1990).
77 *Ibid.*, 20–8.
78 *Ibid.*, 331.
79 *Ibid.*, 10–2, 132–3, 274–86 and 329–30.
80 *Ibid.*, 214–8.
81 *Ibid.*, 149–51.
82 *Ibid.*, 224–6.
83 *Ibid.*, 30 and 32.
84 *Ibid.*, 46, 60, 68, 113 and 163.

85 *Ibid.*, 230, and also 163 and 175.

86 *Ibid.*, 232. The idea that the existential relationship between any two parties was one of friend and enemy was perhaps most famously asserted by the German existential jurist, Carl Schmitt in *Political Theology, The Crisis of Parliamentary Democracy* and a number of other texts.

87 See Dworkin, *ibid.*, 2, invoking Sartre as authority for the notion of responsibility.

88 *Ibid.*, 334–9.

89 E. Danica, *Don't* (London: Women's Press, 1988).

90 A. Walker, *The Color Purple* (London: Women's Press, 1983), particularly 3–4, 7, 34, 59, 83–4, 96–7, 107 and 221.

91 J. Voznesenskaya, *The Women's Decameron* (London: Minerva, 1986), 150–82.

92 See Goode, 'Feminism, Class and Literary Criticism', and also S. Heath, 'Male Feminism', in M. Eagleton, ed., *Feminist Literary Criticism*, 193–225.

93 C. Sanger, 'Seasoned to the Use', 1338–65.

94 R. Patterson, *Degree of Guilt* (London: Hutchinson, 1993).

95 See T. Eagleton, *The Rape of Clarissa* (Oxford: Blackwell, 1982), particularly 2–6, 47–50, 54–6, 61–3, 76–88 and 101.

96 Choderlos de Laclos, *Les Liaisons Dangereuses* (London: Ark, 1970), particularly 263–7 for the alternative accounts of the rape of Cecile. See also 203–6, 262, 316, 335–8 and 372 for the language of sexuality.

97 M. Richler, *St. Urbain's Horseman* (London: Vintage, 1971), particularly 427–51.

7 LAW AND JUSTICE IN THE MODERN NOVEL: THE CONCEPT
OF RESPONSIBILITY

1 Richard Weisberg, *The Failure of the Word: The Lawyer as Protagonist in Modern Fiction* (New Haven: Yale University Press, 1984), 114–29.

2 A. Camus, *The Outsider* (London: Penguin, 1983), 119.

3 Weisberg, *Failure*, 116–22.

4 E. Simon, 'Palais de Justice and Poetic Justice in Camus's *The Stranger*', *Cardozo Studies in Law and Literature*, 3 (1990), 111–25.

5 A. Camus, *The Myth of Sisyphus* (London: Penguin, 1975), 86–95 and 111.

6 M. Blanchot, 'La Lecture de Kafka', *La Part du Feu* (Paris: Gallimard, 1949), 9–19, and J. Derrida, 'Before the Law', in D. Attridge, ed., *Acts of Literature* (London: Routledge, 1992), 181–211.

7 Camus, *Myth*, 120–3, and E. Fromm, *Man for Himself* (London: Routledge, 1960), 141–72.

8 M. Heidegger, 'The Self-Assertion of the German University', *Review of Metaphysics*, 38 (1985), 476.

9 M. Heidegger, 'Facts and Thoughts', *Review of Metaphysics*, 38 (1985), 481–502.

10 The recent Heidegger controversy was rekindled by Victor Farias's *Heidegger and Nazism* (Philadelphia: University of Pennsylvania Press, 1989). Volume 15 of *Critical Inquiry* (1989) presents a series of essays discussing the controversy, including Habermas's 'Work and *Weltanschauung*: The Heidegger Controversy from a German Perspective'. A number of other works written in response to Farias include Phillippe Lacoue-Labarthe's *Heidegger, Art and Politics* (Oxford: Blackwell, 1990) and L. Ferry and A. Renaut's *Heidegger and Modernity* (University of Chicago Press, 1990). A collection of the 'controversy' literature can be found in Richard Wolin, ed., *The Heidegger Controversy* (New York: Columbia University Press, 1991). For Derrida's essay on the *Rektorat*, see *Of Spirit: Heidegger and the Question* (University of Chicago Press, 1987).

11 M. Heidegger, 'On the Essence of Truth', in D. Krell, ed., *Basic Writings* (New York: Harper and Row, 1978), 127–9.

12 M. Heidegger, *Being and Time* (Oxford: Blackwell, 1962), 38 and 279–89.

13 Derrida, *Of Spirit*, 5, 14 and 31.

14 D. Dahlstrom, 'Heidegger's Kantian Turn: Notes on His Commentary on the *Kritik der Reinen Vernunft*', *Review of Metaphysics*, 45 (1991), 329–61.

15 Heidegger, 'Self-Assertion', 470–6.

16 In Farias, *Heidegger and Nazism*, 131–3.

17 Heidegger, 'Facts and Thoughts', 199.

18 P. Lacoue-Labarthe, 'Neither Accident Nor Mistake', *Critical Inquiry*, 15 (1989), 481–4.

19 M. Blanchot, 'Thinking the Apocalypse: A Letter from Maurice Blanchot to Elizabeth David', *Critical Inquiry*, 15 (1989), 475–80.

20 See M. Foucault, *The History of Sexuality*, 3 vols. (London: Penguin, 1979–88).

21 D. Hoy, 'A History of Consciousness: from Kant and Hegel to Derrida and Foucault', *History of the Human Sciences*, 4 (1991), 261–81.

22 Derrida, 'Before the Law', 190.

23 See M. Foucault, 'Maurice Blanchot: The Thought from the Outside', in *Foucault/Blanchot* (New York: Zone, 1987), 55–8. This later essay tends to run against the gist of Foucault's earlier writings in the uses of fiction.

24 H. Marcuse, *Eros and Civilization* (Boston: Beacon, 1955), xiv–xxiii, 3–51, 89–102 and 140–98.

25 H. Marcuse, *One-Dimensional Man* (Boston: Beacon, 1964), 236–41.

26 H. Arendt, *The Life of the Mind* (New York: Harcourt Brace Jovanovich, 1971), 22–78 and 248–325, and *The Human Condition* (University of Chicago Press, 1958), 19–216.

27 R. Unger, *Knowledge and Politics* (New York: Free Press, 1975), 174–90 and 221–2.

28 R. Unger, *Passion: An Essay on Personality* (New York: Free Press, 1984), 15–42, 72–7 and 275–300.

29 P. Gabel and D. Kennedy, 'Roll Over Beethoven', *Stanford Law Review*, 36 (1984), 36–42.
30 P. Gabel, 'The Phenomenology of Rights-Consciousness', *Texas Law Review* , 62 (1984), 1593.
31 A. Hutchinson, 'The Three "Rs": Reading/Rorty/Radically', *Harvard Law Review*, 103 (1989), 367–9.
32 J. Singer, 'The Player and the Cards: Nihilism and Legal Theory', *Yale Law Journal*, 94 (1984), 1–70.

8 IVAN KLIMA'S *JUDGE ON TRIAL*

1 G. Steiner, *In Bluebeard's Castle* (London: Faber, 1971), particularly 47–8 and 61.
2 For the importance of the Holocaust in progressive as well as literary legal studies, see Richard Weisberg, *Poethics: and Other Strategies of Law and Literature* (New York: Columbia University Press, 1992), 127–87.
3 This is, of course, only one argument. Converts to law and literature see relative values in both 'real' and metaphorical presentations of the legal situation. See Weisberg, *Poethics*, x–xi. Interestingly, those cooler in their attitude towards the use of literary texts, such as Posner, insist that only those narratives that can convey a 'sense of reality' and present a 'real' situation can be of some limited use in legal discourse. See Posner's *Law and Literature: A Misunderstood Relation* (Cambridge, Masss.: Harvard University Press, 1988), particularly 1–21.
4 I. Klima, *Judge on Trial* (London: Vintage, 1991), 32–69.
5 *Ibid.*, 32.
6 *Ibid.*, 36.
7 *Ibid.*, 38.
8 *Ibid.*, 69.
9 *Ibid.*, 162.
10 *Ibid.*, 163.
11 *Ibid.*,72.
12 *Ibid.*, 173–4.
13 *Ibid.*, 175–7.
14 *Ibid.*, 212–14.
15 *Ibid.*, 219–20.
16 *Ibid.*, 233–5.
17 *Ibid.*, 271–2.
18 *Ibid.*, 277. He makes specific note of the abstraction of Kant's *Critique of Pure Reason*. His similar dismissal of Dostoevsky's *Crime and Punishment*, 'which someone had apparently classified as a legal work', carries its own irony.
19 Klima, *Judge on Trial*, 278.
20 *Ibid.*, 280.
21 John Rawls has represented the most influential neo-Kantian school of 'constructivists' in legal scholarship. His most famous presentation

was in *A Theory of Justice* (Oxford University Press, 1971). But perhaps his most accessible work is 'Kantian Constructivism in Moral Theory', *Journal of Philosophy*, 77 (1980), 515–72.

22 *Judge on Trial*, 281–3.
23 *Ibid.*, 286–9.
24 *Ibid.*, 343.
25 *Ibid.*, 392–411.
26 *Ibid.*, 445–9.
27 *Ibid.*, 456–63.
28 *Ibid.*, 191.
29 *Ibid.*, 190–3.
30 *Ibid.*, 184–6.
31 *Ibid.*, 258.
32 *Ibid.*, 317.
33 *Ibid.*, 450 and 460.
34 *Ibid.*, 478–9.
35 Richard Weisberg, *Poethics*, 46.
36 H. Hart, 'Positivism and the Separation of Law and Morals', *Harvard Law Review*, 71 (1958), 593–629 and L. Fuller, 'Positivism and Fidelity to Law – A Reply to Professor Hart', *Harvard Law Review*, 71 (1958), 630–72.
37 See E. Wolf, 'Revolution or Evolution in Gustav Radbruch's Legal Philosophy', *Natural Law Forum*, 3 (1958), 1–22; and I. Ward, 'Radbruch's *Rechtsphilosophie*: Law, Morality and Form', *Archiv fuer Rechts- und Sozialphilosophie*, 78 (1992), 332–54.
38 See D. Dahlstrom, 'Heidegger's Kantian Turn: Notes on His Commentary on the *Kritik der Reinen Vernunft*', *Review of Metaphyics*, 45 (1991), 329–59.
39 See I. Kant, *The Metaphysics of Morals*, trans. M. Gregor (Cambridge University Press, 1991), particularly 35–67 and 181–213.
40 *Judge on Trial*, 498.
41 *Ibid.*, 508–9.
42 See A. Camus, *The Myth of Sisyphus* (Harmondsworth: Penguin, 1975), 111.
43 *Judge on Trial*, 535–6.
44 It is not surprising that the central themes of *Judge on Trial*, overcoming the alienation of the individual, the centrality of the Holocaust as a metaphor for such alienation, the realisation of the power of freedom and of self-assertion, and the intrusiveness of a legal system that seeks to exclude, are repeated in Klima's other novels, most particularly perhaps in *My First Loves* and *Love and Garbage*.

9 UMBERTO ECO'S *THE NAME OF THE ROSE*

1 See T. Colletti, *Naming the Rose: Eco, Medieval Signs, and Modern Theory* (Ithaca: Cornell University Press, 1988), 31. The interdisciplinary

potentialities of the novel were explored in volume 14 of the journal *SubStance*.

2 See J. Marenbon, *Later Medieval Philosophy* (London: Routledge, 1991), 9.

3 See Marenbon, *Medieval Philosophy*, 7–26, who provides an excellent and accessible introduction to medieval intellectualism.

4 *Ibid.*, 35–49.

5 J. Roberts, *A Philosophical Introduction to Theology* (London: SCM, 1991), 78.

6 See Marenbon, *Medieval Philosophy*, 14–16 and 54–5.

7 *Ibid.*, 58–74 and 106–8, and Roberts, *Theology*, 106–7.

8 See Marenbon, *Medieval Philosophy*, 170–88.

9 U. Eco, *Art and Beauty in the Middle Ages* (New Haven: Yale University Press, 1986), 88–9.

10 Eco, *The Name of the Rose* (London: Minerva, 1992), 48–52.

11 See Roberts, *Theology*, 95–104.

12 *Ibid.*, 109.

13 Aristotle, *Ethics* (Harmondsworth: Penguin, 1976), 1094b 12–28, at 64–5.

14 See Marenbon, *Medieval Philosophy*, 74–8 and 116–30, and F. Copplestone, *Aquinas* (Harmondsworth: Penguin, 1955), 63–9.

15 For the centrality of jurisprudence and questions of justice in Aquinas' philosophy of theology, and the resolution of the problem of speculative knowledge, see Marenbon, *Medieval Philosophy*, 116–17.

16 See the collection of essays on Aquinas and Maimonides in volume 6 of the *Jewish Law Annual*. See also Marvin Fox's influential essay 'Maimonides and Aquinas on Natural Law', *Dine Israel*, 3 (1972), v–xxxvi.

17 Particularly in Part 2. See Maimonides, *The Guide to the Perplexed*, trans. M. Friedlaender (London: Dover, 1956), 145–250. See also S. Schwarzschild, 'Moral Radicalism and "Middlingness" in the Ethics of Maimonides', *Studies in Medieval Culture*, 11 (1978), 65–94.

18 See I. Twersky, *Introduction to the Code of Maimonides* (New Haven: Yale University Press, 1980), 457.

19 Maimonides, *Guide*, Book 2 chapter 40, at 232–4.

20 *Ibid.*, Book 3 chapter 29, 317–20.

21 Maimonides returns to this theme in the closing paragraphs of the final chapter of the *Guide*, at 396–7.

22 See Aquinas, *Summa Theologiae*, T. McDermott, ed. (London: Methuen, 1991), 83–149.

23 *Ibid.*, particularly 152–63.

24 See Copplestone, *Aquinas*, 199–242, emphasising at 206–7 the centrality of a normative ethics in the natural political orders of both Aquinas and Aristotle.

25 See E. Damich, 'The Essence of Law According to Thomas Aquinas', *American Journal of Jurisprudence*, 30 (1985), 79–96.

26 For Aquinas's most explicit statements on the nature of government,

see his *Treatise on Princely Government*, in *Aquinas: Selected Political Writings*, ed. A. D'Entreves (Oxford: Blackwell, 1987), 2–42, and also D'Entreves's own comments in the 'Introduction', at xv–xxxiii. See also *Summa*, Questions 92 and 96, at 283–4 and 290–2. For the 'congruence' of the individual and common good, see Plato, *Republic* (Harmondsworth: Penguin, 1974), Book 5, 196–224.

27 Aquinas, *Summa*, 280–1.
28 *Ibid.*, 281–94.
29 See Copplestone, *Aquinas*, 243–64.
30 Eco, *Rose*, 28.
31 *Ibid.*, 29–31.
32 *Ibid.*, 57–63.
33 *Ibid.*, 86–8.
34 *Ibid.*, 35–8.
35 *Ibid.*, 24–5.
36 *Ibid.*, 86–7.
37 *Ibid.*, 40–5.
38 *Ibid.*, 46–7.
39 Eco, *Art and Beauty*, 114.
40 Eco, *Rose*, 78–80.
41 *Ibid.*, 95–7.
42 *Ibid.*, 105–6.
43 *Ibid.*, 120.
44 *Ibid.*, 176.
45 *Ibid.*, 165–6 and 172.
46 *Ibid.*, 111. For Eco's observations on Aquinas' position, see *Art and Beauty*, 63.
47 Eco, *Rose*, 130–2.
48 *Ibid.*, 142–3.
49 *Ibid.*, 146–53.
50 *Ibid.*, 196.
51 *Ibid.*, 214–15.
52 *Ibid.*, 206–7.
53 *Ibid.*
54 *Ibid.*, 184–5. For Eco's comments on the movement of centres of learning, see *Art and Beauty*, 94–119.
55 Eco, *Rose*, 201–3.
56 *Ibid.*, 192.
57 *Ibid.*, 245–8.
58 *Ibid.*, 279.
59 *Ibid.*, 281–4.
60 *Ibid.*, 312–15 and 320–1.
61 *Ibid.*, 294–8.
62 *Ibid.*, 261–2.
63 *Ibid.*, 304–6.

64 *Ibid.*, 328–32.
65 *Ibid.*, 284–6.
66 *Ibid.*, 314–17.
67 *Ibid.*, 336–7.
68 *Ibid.*, 341.
69 *Ibid.*, 341–7.
70 *Ibid.*, 352–6.
71 *Ibid.*
72 *Ibid.*, 64.
73 *Ibid.*, 370–3.
74 *Ibid.*, 374–6.
75 *Ibid.*, 378 and 381.
76 According to Adso, '[w]hat Bernard wanted was clear. Without the slightest interest in knowing who had killed the other monks, he wanted to show that Remegio somehow shared the ideas propounded by the Emperor's theologians.' See *ibid.*, 381–2.
77 *Ibid.*, 382–5.
78 *Ibid.*, 385–6.
79 *Ibid.*, 386–8.
80 *Ibid.*, 389–90.
81 William thus strenuously advises Ubertino against going to dispute his case at Avignon. But, as Adso observes, Ubertino did not heed William's warnings, and thus paid the predicted penalty. *Ibid.*, 391–2.
82 *Ibid.*, 396.
83 *Ibid.*, 396 and 399–400.
84 Indeed, the accounts of Days Six and Seven are noticeably shorter in themselves.
85 *Ibid.*, 423–5.
86 *Ibid.*, 444–8.
87 *Ibid.*, 470–1.
88 *Ibid.*, 471–3.
89 For Plato's attempts to accommodate the essentially contradictory demands of state and individual, see his *Republic*, part 5.
90 Eco, *Rose*, 374–5.
91 *Ibid.*, 484–9.
92 *Ibid.*, 491.
93 *Ibid.*, 492.
94 U. Eco, *Reflections on the Name of the Rose* (London: Secker and Warburg, 1985).
95 Eco, *ibid.*, 1–7.
96 *Ibid.*, 13–14 and 23.
97 *Ibid.*, 34 and 47–53. See also Colletti's comments in *Naming the Rose*, 12–38.
98 Eco, *Reflections*, 20.

99 This is Colletti's opinion. See *Naming the Rose*, 12–13 and 34–8. Eco himself does not see Adso as being educated towards some previously unattainable knowledge. But then Eco might be wrong.

100 Eco, *Reflections*, 66–7 and 74–5, commenting at 75, 'I wanted to write a historical novel.'

101 Colletti, *Naming the Rose*, 20–3.

102 *Ibid.*, 12–13, 20–6 and 34–8. See also W. Stephens, 'Ec[h]o in Fabula', *Diacritics*, 13 (1983), 51–64.

103 Eco, *Art and Beauty*, 2–10.

104 See particularly *ibid.*, 17–26 and 52–64. See also Eco's restatement of Aquinas' role in 'Two Models of Interpretation' in his *The Limits of Interpretation* (Bloomington: Indiana University Press, 1990), 14–6.

105 Eco, *Art and Beauty*, 78–9 and 106–10.

106 Eco, *Reflections*, 26. See also Colletti's comments in *Naming the Rose* at 26, suggesting the semiotics of the novel as presented by Eco are themselves essentially Ockhamite.

107 Eco, *Art and Beauty*, 87–114.

108 U. Eco, *Semiotics and the Philosophy of Language* (London: Macmillan, 1984), 147–63.

109 Eco, *Art and Beauty*, 118–19.

110 Eco, *Interpretation*, 78.

111 Eco, *Reflections*, 54.

112 *Ibid.*, 81.

113 U. Eco, *Foucault's Pendulum* (Picador: London, 1990), 95.

114 *Ibid.*, 459.

115 *Ibid.*, 640–1.

116 A. Camus, *The Myth of Sisyphus* (Harmondsworth: Penguin, 1975), 111.

117 See Richard Weisberg's 'ressentiment' thesis, which is contructed around the literature of Camus and Dostoevsky in particular, in *The Failure of the Word: The Lawyer as Protagonist in Modern Fiction*, (New Haven: Yale University Press, 1984).

118 Eco, *Rose*, 198.

119 *Ibid.*, 14 and 18.

120 *Ibid.*, 501.

Bibliography

Adams, S., 'Eliza Enthroned?: The Court and Politics', in C. Haigh ed., *The Reign of Elizabeth I* (Athens: University of Georgia Press, 1987), 55–77.

Adelson, J., 'The Political Imagination of the Young Adolescent', *Daedalus*, 100 (1971), 1013–50.

Aquinas, St Thomas, *Aquinas: Selected Political Writings*, ed., A. D'Entreves (Oxford: Blackwell, 1987).

Summa Theologiae, ed.T. McDermott (London: Methuen, 1991).

Arendt, H., *The Human Condition* (University of Chicago Press, 1958).

The Life of the Mind (New York: Harcourt Brace Jovanovich, 1971).

Aristotle, *Rhetoric* (Cambridge University Press, 1909).

Ethics (Harmondsworth: Penguin, 1976).

Atwood, M., *The Handmaid's Tale* (London: Virago, 1987).

Bacon F., *The Advancement of Learning*, J. Johnston, ed. (Oxford University Press, 1974).

The Essays, ed. J. Pitcher (Harmondsworth: Penguin, 1985).

Balkin, J., 'Deconstructive Practice and Legal Theory', *Yale Law Journal*, 96 (1987), 743–86.

'The Promise of Legal Semiotics', *Texas Law Review*, 69 (1991), 1831–52.

Barroll, L., 'A New History for Shakespeare and His Time', *Shakespeare Quarterly*, 39 (1988), 441–64.

Barthes, R., *The Rustle of Language* (Oxford: Blackwell, 1986).

Battenhouse, R., 'King John: Shakespeare's Perspectives and Others', *Notre Dame English Journal*, 14 (1982), 191–215.

Bellamy, L., *Gulliver's Travels* (London: Harvester Wheatsheaf, 1992).

Bennington, G., *Jacques Derrida* (University of Chicago Press, 1993).

Berry, R., '*Richard III*: Bonding the Audience', in J. Gray, ed., *Mirror up to Shakespeare* (University of Toronto Press, 1984), 114–27.

Bevan, B., *King Richard II* (London: Rubicon Press, 1990).

Blake, K., *Play, Games and Sport: The Literary Works of Lewis Carroll* (Ithaca: Cornell University Press, 1974).

Blanchot, M., *La Part du Feu* (Paris: Gallimard, 1949).

'Thinking the Apocalypse: A Letter from Maurice Blanchot to Elizabeth David', *Critical Inquiry*, 15 (1989), 475–80.

Blythe, J., *Ideal Government and the Mixed Constitution in the Middle Ages* (Princeton University Press, 1992).

Bonsignore, J., 'In Parables: Teaching Through Parables', *Legal Studies Forum*, 12 (1988), 191–210.

Bornstein, D., 'Trial by Combat and Official Irresponsibility in *Richard II*', *Shakespeare Studies*, 8 (1975), 131–41.

Brockbank, P., *Brockbank on Shakespeare* (Oxford: Blackwell, 1989).

Brown, L. and Gilligan, C., *Meeting at the Crossroads: Women's Psychology and Girl's Development* (Cambridge, Mass.: Harvard University Press).

Burckhardt, R., 'Obedience and Rebellion in Shakespeare's Early History Plays', *English Studies*, 55 (1974), 108–17.

Burden, D., 'Shakespeare's History Plays: 1952–1983', *Shakespeare Survey*, 38 (1985), 1–18.

Burgess, G., *The Politics of the Ancient Constitution* (London: Macmillan, 1992).

Burns, J., *Lordship, Kingship, and Empire* (Oxford: Clarendon, 1992).

Calderwood, J., 'Commodity and Honour in *King John*', *University of Toronto Quarterly*, 29 (1960), 341–56.

Cameron, D. ed., *The Feminist Critique of Language: A Reader* (Routledge, 1990).

Camus, A., *The Myth of Sisyphus* (Harmondsworth: Penguin, 1975).

The Outsider (Harmondsworth: Penguin, 1983).

Candido, J., 'Thomas More, the Tudor Chronicles, and Shakespeare's Altered Richard', *English Studies*, 2 (1987), 137–41.

Cardozo Studies in Law and Literature, volume 5.

Carroll, W., 'Language, Politics and Poverty in Shakespearian Drama', *Shakespeare Survey*, 44 (1991), 17–24.

'Desacralization and Succession in *Richard III*', *Deutsche Shakespeare-Gesellschaft West Jahrbuch* 1991, 82–96.

Chamallas, M., 'Consent, Equality, and the Legal Control of Sexual Conduct', *Southern California Law Review*, 61 (1988), 777–862.

Chambers, A., 'The Reader in the Book', in A. Hunt, ed., *Children's Literature* (London: Routledge, 1990), 91–114.

Champion, L., *Perspective in Shakespeare's English Histories* (Athens: University of Georgia, 1980).

'"Answere to this Perilous Time": Ideological Ambivalence in *The Raigne of King Edward III* and the English Chronicle Plays', *English Studies*, 69 (1988), 117–129.

Cixous, H. and Clement C., *The Newly Born Woman* (Manchester University Press, 1985).

Clare, J., 'The Censorship of the Deposition Scene in *Richard II*', *Review of English Studies*, 41 (1990), 89–94.

Colletti, T., *Naming the Rose: Eco, Medieval Signs, and Modern Theory* (Ithaca: Cornell University Press, 1988).

Cook, N., 'Shakespeare Comes to the Law School Classroom', *Denver University Law Review*, 68 (1988), 387–411.

Copplestone, F., *Aquinas* (Harmondsworth: Penguin, 1955).
Cornell, D., 'Toward a Modern/Postmodern Reconstruction of Ethics', *University of Pennsylvania Law Review*, 133 (1985), 291–380.
'Institutionalization of Meaning, Recollective Imagination and the Potential for Transformative Legal Interpretation', *University of Pennsylvania Law Review*, 136 (1988), 1135–229.
The Philosophy of the Limit, (London: Routledge, 1992).
Coveney, P., Introduction to M. Twain, *Huckleberry Finn* (Harmondsworth: Penguin, 1985).
Cowan, L., 'God Will Save the King: Shakespeare's *Richard II*', in J. Alvis and T. West, eds., *Shakespeare as a Political Thinker* (Durham: Carolina Academic, 1981), 63–81.
Coward, R., 'This Novel Changes Women's Lives: Are Women's Novels Feminst Novels?' in E. Showalter, ed., *The New Feminist Criticism: Essays on Women, Literature and Theory* (London: Virago, 1986), 225–39.
Curren-Aquino, D., ed., *King John: New Perspectives* (Newark: University of Delaware Press, 1989).
Dahlstrom, D., 'Heidegger's Kantian Turn: Notes on his Commentary on the *Kritik der Reinen Vernunft*', *Review of Metaphysics*, 45 (1991), 329–61.
Damich, E., 'The Essence of Law According to Thomas Aquinas', *American Journal of Jurisprudence*, 30 (1985), 79–96.
Danica, E., *Don't* (London: Women's Press, 1988).
Day, G., '"Determined to prove a villain": Theatricality in *Richard III*', *Critical Survey*, 3 (1991), 149–56.
Delgado, R. and Stefancic J., 'Norms and Narratives: Can Judges Avoid Serious Moral Error?', *Texas Law Review*, 69 (1991), 1929–83.
Derrida, J., *Of Spirit: Heidegger and the Question* (University of Chicago Press, 1987)
'Force of Law: The Mystical Foundation of Authority', *Cardozo Law Review*, 11 (1990), 921–1045.
'Before the Law', in D. Attridge, ed., *Acts of Literature* (London: Routledge, 1992).
Dollimore, J. and Sinfield, A., eds., *Political Shakespeare: New Essays in Cultural Materialism* (Manchester University Press, 1985).
Dunlop, C., 'Literature Studies in Law Schools', *Cardozo Studies in Law and Literature*, 3 (1991), 63–110.
Dworkin, A., *Mercy* (London: Arrow, 1990).
Dworkin, R., 'Law as Interpretation', *Texas Law Review*, 60 (1982), 527–50.
Law's Empire (Cambridge, Mass.: Belknap, 1986).
Eagleton, M., ed., *Feminist Literary Criticism* (London: Longman, 1991).
Eagleton, T., *The Rape of Clarissa* (Oxford: Blackwell, 1982).
Literary Criticism: An Introduction (Oxford: Blackwell, 1983).
Eco, U., *The Role of the Reader* (London: Hutchinson, 1981).
Semiotics and the Philosophy of Language (London: Macmillan, 1984).

Reflections on the Name of the Rose (London: Secker and Warburg, 1985).
Art and Beauty in the Middle Ages (Newhaven: Yale University, 1986).
The Limits of Interpretation (Bloomington: Indiana University, 1990).
Foucault's Pendulum, (Picador: London, 1990).
Interpretation and Overinterpretation (Cambridge University Press, 1992).
The Name of the Rose, (London: Minerva, 1992).
Elliot, J., 'Shakespeare and the Double Image of *King John*', *Shakespeare Studies*, 1 (1965), 56–72.
  'History and Tragedy in *Richard II*', *Studies in English Literature*, 8 (1968), 253–71.
Elton, G., *Policy and Police: The Enforcement of the Reformation in the Age of Thomas Cromwell* (Cambridge University Press, 1972).
  The Tudor Constitution (Cambridge University Press, 1982).
  'Parliament', in Haigh, ed., *The Reign of Elizabeth I* (Athens: University of Georgia Press, 1987), 79–100.
Englard, H., 'Research in Jewish Law: Its Nature and Function', *Mishpatim*, 7 (1975–6), 34–65.
Eskridge, W., 'Gadamer/Statutory Interpretation', *Columbia Law Review*, 90 (1990), 609–81.
Estrich, S., 'Rape', *Yale Law Journal*, 95 (1986), 1087–184.
  Real Rape (Cambridge Mass.: Harvard University Press, 1987).
Farias, V., *Heidegger and Nazism* (Philadelphia: University of Pennsylvania Press, 1989).
Feldman, S., 'The New Metaphysics: The Interpretive Turn in Jurisprudence', *Iowa Law Review*, 76 (1991), 661–99.
Ferry, L. and Renaut, A. *Heidegger and Modernity* (University of Chicago Press, 1990).
Filmer, R., *Patriarcha and Other Writings*, ed. J. Somerville (Cambridge University Press, 1991).
Fish, S., *Is There a Text in this Class?: The Authority of Interpretive Communities* (Cambridge Mass.: Harvard University Press, 1980).
  Doing What Comes Naturally: Change, Rhetoric, and the Practice of Theory in Literary and Legal Studies (Oxford University Press, 1989).
Fiss, O., 'Objectivity and Interpretation', *Stanford Law Review*, 34 (1982), 739–63.
Foot, M., Introduction to J. Swift, *Gulliver's Travels* (Harmondsworth: Penguin, 1985).
Fortescue, J., *The Governance of England* (Oxford: Clarendon, 1885.)
  De Laudibus Legum Angliae (Cambridge University Press, 1942).
Foucault, M., *The History of Sexuality*, 3 vols. (London: Penguin, 1979–88).
  'What is an Author?', in J. Harari, ed., *Textual Strategies: Perspectives in Post-Structuralist Criticism* (Ithaca: Cornell University Press, 1979), 141–60.
  'Maurice Blanchot: The Thought from the Outside', in *Foucault/Blanchot* (New York: Zone, 1987).

Fox, M., 'Maimonides and Aquinas on Natural Law', *Dine Israel*, 3 (1972), v–xxxvi.

French, A., 'The World of *Richard III*', *Shakespeare Studies*, 4 (1968), 25–39.

Fromm, E., *Man for Himself* (London: Routledge, 1960).

Frug, J., 'Argument as Character', *Stanford Law Review*, 40 (1988), 867–927.

Fuller, L., 'Positivism and Fidelity to Law – A Reply to Professor Hart', *Harvard Law Review*, 71 (1958), 630–72.

Gabel, P., 'Reification in Legal Reasoning', *Research in Law and Sociology*, 3 (1980), 25–38.

  'The Phenomenology of Rights-Consciousness', *Texas Law Review*, 62 (1984), 1564–98.

  and Kennedy, D., 'Roll Over Beethoven', *Stanford Law Review*, 36 (1984), 1–52.

Gadamer, H.-G., *Truth and Method* (London: Sheed and Ward, 1975).
  Philosophical Hermeneutics (Berkeley: University of California, 1977).

Gardner, M., ed., *The Annotated Alice* (Harmondsworth: Penguin, 1970).
  The Annotated Snark (Harmondworth: Penguin, 1974).

Gaudet, P., 'The "Parasitical" Counselors in Shakespeare's *Richard II*: A Problem in Dramatic Interpretation', *Shakespeare Quarterly*, 33 (1982), 142–54.

Getman, J., 'Voices', *Texas Law Review*, 66 (1988), 577–88.

Gilead, S., 'Magic Abjured: Closure in Children's Fantasy Fiction', in P. Hunt, ed., *Literature for Children: Contemporary Criticism* (London: Routledge, 1992), 80–109.

Goetz, W., 'The Felicity and Infelicity of Marriage in *Jude the Obscure*', *Nineteenth Century Fiction*, 38 (1983–4), 189–213.

Gohn, J., '*Richard II*: Shakespeare's Legal Brief on the Royal Prerogative and the Succession to the Throne', *Georgetown Law Journal*, 70 (1982), 953–73.

Golding, W., *Lord of the Flies* (London: Faber, 1954).

Goode, J., 'Feminism, Class and Literary Criticism', in K. Campbell, ed., *Critical Feminism: Argument in the Disciplines* (Buckingham: Open University Press, 1992), 123–55.

Goodrich P., *Reading the Law: A Critical Introduction to Legal Method and Techniques* (Oxford: Blackwell, 1986).
  Languages of Law: From Logics of Memory to Nomadic Masks (London: Weidenfeld, 1990).
  'Critical Legal Studies in England: Prospective Histories', *Oxford Journal of Legal Studies*, 12 (1992), 195–236.

Green, R., 'The Golden Age of Children's Literature', in P. Hunt, ed., *Children's Literature* (London: Routledge, 1990), 36–48.

Greenblatt, S., *Shakespearean Negotiations: The Circulation of Social Energy in Renaissance England* (Berkeley: University of California Press, 1988).

Greer, C., 'The Deposition Scene of *Richard II*', *Notes and Queries*, 196 (1952), 492–3.

'More about the Deposition Scene of *Richard II*', *Notes and Queries*, 198 (1953), 49-50.

Grennan, E., 'Shakespeare's Satirical History: A Reading of *King John*', *Shakespeare Studies*, 11 (1978), 21-37.

Gurr, A., '*Richard III* and the Democratic Process', *Essays in Criticism*, 24 (1974), 39-47.

Guy, J., 'The Henrician Age', in J. Pocock, ed., *The Varieties of British Political Thought 1500-1800* (Cambridge University Press, 1993).

Habermas, J., 'Work and *Weltanschauung*: The Heidegger Controversy from a German Perspective', *Critical Inquiry*, 15 (1989), 431-56.

Hamilton, D., 'The State of Law in *Richard II*', *Shakespeare Quarterly*, 34 (1983), 5-17.

Shakespeare and the Politics of Protestant England (Louisville: University of Kentucky, 1992).

Harriss, G., 'Political Society and the Growth of Government in Late Medieval England', *Past and Present*, 138 (1993), 28-57.

Hart, H., 'Positivism and the Separation of Law and Morals', *Harvard Law Review*, 71 (1958), 593-629.

Hartigan, E., 'From Righteousness to Beauty: Reflections on *Poethics* and *Justice as Translation*' *Tulane Law Review*, 67 (1992), 455-83.

Heath, S., 'Male Feminism', in M. Eagleton, ed., *Feminist Literary Criticism* (London: Longman, 1989).

Heidegger, M., *Being and Time* (Oxford: Blackwell, 1962).

Poetry, Language, Thought (New York, Harper and Row, 1971).

'On the Essence of Truth', in D. Krell, ed., *Basic Writings* (New York: Harper and Row, 1978).

'The Self-Assertion of the German University', *Review of Metaphysics*, 38 (1985), 467-480.

'Facts and Thoughts', *Review of Metaphysics*, 38 (1985), 481-502.

Heilbrun, C. and Resnik, J., 'Convergences: Law, Literature, and Feminism', *Yale Law Journal*, 99 (1990), 1913-53.

Heninger, S., 'The Sun-King Analogy in *Richard II*', *Shakespeare Quarterly*, 11 (1960), 319-27.

Hildebrand, E., 'Jane Austen and the Law', *Persuasions*, 4 (1982), 34-41.

Hinton, R., 'English Constitutional Theories from Sir John Fortescue to Sir John Eliot', *English Historical Review*, 75 (1960), 410-25.

Hirsch, E., *Validity in Interpretation* (New Haven: Yale University Press, 1967).

Hirshman, L., 'Brontë, Bloom, and Bork: An Essay on the Moral Education of Judges', *University of Pennsylvania Law Review*, 137 (1988), 177-231.

Hobbes, T., *Leviathan* (Harmondsworth: Penguin, 1985),

Hodges, E. Perry, 'Writing in a Different Voice', *Texas Law Review*, 66 (1988), 629-40.

Holderness G., *Shakespeare Recycled: The Making of Historical Drama* (London: Harvester Wheatsheaf, 1992).

Hollindale, P., 'Ideology and the Children's Book', in P. Hunt, ed., *Literature for Children: Contemporary Criticism* (London: Routledge, 1992), 19–40.

Honnold, J., 'Hirshman, Brontë, and Hawthorne on Law, Abortion and Society: Brava and Addendum', *University of Pennyslvania Law Review*, 137 (1989), 1247–250.

Hornsby J., *Chaucer and the Law* (London: Pilgrim, 1988).

Hotine, M., '*Richard III* and *Macbeth* – Studies in Tudor Tyranny?', *Notes and Queries*, 236 (1991), 480–6.

Hoxie, F., 'Towards a "New" North American Legal History', *American Journal of Legal History*, 30 (1986), 351–7.

Hoy, D., 'Interpreting the Law: Hermeneutical and Poststructuralist Perspectives', *Southern California Law Review*, 58 (1985), 135–76.

'A History of Consciousness: from Kant and Hegel to Derrida and Foucault', *History of the Human Sciences*, 4 (1991), 261–81.

Hunt, P., ed., *Children's Literature* (London: Routledge, 1990).

Criticism, Theory and Children's Literature (Oxford: Blackwell, 1991).

ed., *Literature for Children: Contemporary Criticism* (London: Routledge, 1992).

Hurstfield, J., 'The Politics of Corruption in Shakespeare's England', *Shakespeare Survey*, 28 (1975), 15–28.

Hutchinson, A., 'Of Kings and Dirty Rascals: The Struggle for Democracy', *Queens Law Journal*, 17 (1984), 273–92.

'From Cultural Construction to Historical Deconstruction', *Yale Law Journal*, 94 (1984), 209–37.

Dwelling on the Threshold (Toronto: Carswell, 1988).

'The Three "Rs": Reading/Rorty/Radically', *Harvard Law Review*, 103 (1989), 555–85.

Irigaray, L., 'Women's Exile. Interview with Luce Irigaray', in D. Cameron, ed., *The Feminist Critique of Language: A Reader* (London: Routledge, 1990), 80–96.

Islam, S., *Kipling's 'Law'* (London: Macmillan, 1975).

Ives, E., 'Shakespeare and History: Divergences and Agreements', *Shakespeare Survey*, 38 (1985), 19–35.

Jackson, E., 'Catherine MacKinnon and Feminist Jurisprudence: A Critical Appraisal', *Journal of Law and Society*, 19 (1992), 195–213.

Jehlen, M., 'Archimedes and the Paradox of Feminist Criticism', *Signs*, 6 (1981), 575–601.

Jensen, P., 'Beggars and Kings: Cowardice and Courage in Shakespeare's *Richard II*', *Interpretation*, 18 (1990), 111–43.

Jewish Law Annual volume 6.

Kant, I., *The Metaphysics of Morals* trans. M. Gregor (Cambridge University Press, 1991).

Kantorowicz, H., *The King's Two Bodies: A Study in Medieval Political Theology* (Princeton University Press, 1957).

Kaplan, C., *Sea Changes: Culture and Feminism* (London: Verso, 1986).

Kastan, D., '"To Set a Form upon that Indigest": Shakespeare's Fictions of History', *Comparative Drama*, 17 (1983), 1–15.

'Proud Majesty Made a Subject: Shakespeare and the Spectacle of Rule', *Shakespeare Quarterly*, 37 (1986), 459–75.

Kelley, D., 'Elizabethan Political Thought', in J. Pocock, ed., *The Varieties of British Political Thought 1500–1800* (Cambridge University Press, 1993).

Kelly, H., *Divine Providence in the England of Shakespeare's Histories* (Cambridge, Mass.: Harvard University Press, 1970).

Kelly, M., 'The Function of York in *Richard II*', *Southern Humanities Review*, 6 (1972), 257–67.

Kenyon, J., *The Stuart Constitution* (Cambridge University Press, 1966).

Kiernan, V., *Shakespeare: Poet and Citizen* (London: Verso, 1993).

King, J., 'Queen Elizabeth I: Representations of the Virgin Queen', *Renaissance Quarterly*, 43 (1990), 30–74.

Kinkead–Weekes, M. and Gregor, I., *William Golding: A Critical Study* (London: Faber, 1967).

Kinney, A., 'Essex and Shakespeare versus Hayward', *Shakespeare Quarterly*, 44 (1993), 464–6.

Kipling, R., *The Jungle Books* (Harmondsworth: Penguin, 1989).

Klima, I., *Judge on Trial* (London: Vintage, 1991).

Knights, L., 'Shakespeare's Politics: with Some Reflections on the Nature of Tradition', *Proceedings of the British Academy*, 43 (1957), 115–32.

Koffler, J., 'Forged Alliance: Law and Literature', *Columbia Law Review*, 89 (1989), 1375–93.

Kolodny, A., 'Some Notes on Defining a "Feminist Literary Criticism"', *Critical Inquiry*, 2 (1975), 75–92.

'A Map for Misreading: Or Gender and the Interpretation of Literary Texts', in E. Showalter, ed., *The New Feminist Criticism: Essays on Women, Literature and Theory* (London: Virago, 1986), 46–62.

'Dancing Through the Minefield: Some Observations on Theory, Practice and Politics of a Feminist Literary Criticism' in E. Showalter ed., *The New Feminist Criticism: Essays on Women, Literature and Theory* (London: Virago, 1986), 144–67.

Kress, K., 'Legal Indeterminacy', *California Law Review*, 77 (1989), 283–337.

Laclos, C. de, *Les Liaisons dangereuses* (London: Ark, 1970).

Lacoue-Labarthe, P., 'Neither Accident Nor Mistake', *Critical Inquiry*, 15 (1989), 481–4.

Heidegger, Art, and Politics (Oxford: Blackwell, 1990).

Lander, J., *The Limitations of English Monarchy in the Later Middle Ages* (University of Toronto Press, 1989).

Lane, M., *The Tale of Beatrix Potter* (Harmondsworth: Penguin, 1985).

Lanier, G., 'From Windsor to London: The Destruction of Monarchial Authority in *Richard II*', *Selected Papers from the West Virginia Shakespeare and Renaissance Association*, 13 (1988), 1–8.

Leaman, O., *An Introduction to Medieval Islamic Philosophy* (Cambridge University Press, 1985).

Leclerc, A., 'Woman's Word', in D. Cameron, ed., *The Feminist Critique of Language: A Reader* (London: Routledge, 1990), 74–89.

Levin, C., 'The Historical Evolution of the Death of John in Three Renaissance Plays', *Journal of the Rocky Mountain Medieval and Renaissance Association*, 3 (1982), 85–106.

Llewellyn, K. and Hoebel, F., *The Cheyenne Way* (Norman: University of Oklahoma Press, 1941).

MacCaffrey, W., *Elizabeth I: War and Politics 1588–1603* (Princeton University Press, 1992).

MacKenzie, C., 'Paradise and Paradise Lost in *Richard II*', *Shakespeare Quarterly*, 37 (1986), 318–39.

MacKinnon, C., *Feminism Unmodified* (Cambridge, Mass.: Harvard University Press, 1987).

Towards a Feminist Theory of State (Cambridge, Mass.: Harvard University Press, 1989).

McNeir, W., 'The Masks of Richard the Third', *Studies in English Literature*, 11 (1971), 168–86.

Maimonides, M., *The Guide to the Perplexed*, trans. M. Friedlaender (London: Dover, 1956).

Manheim, M., 'The Four Voices of the Bastard', in D. Curren-Aquino, ed., *King John: New Perspectives* (Newark: University of Delaware Press, 1989), 126–35.

Mann, S., 'The Universe and the Library: A Critique of James Boyd White as Writer and Reader', *Stanford Law Review*, 41 (1989), 959–1009.

Marcuse, H., *Eros and Civilization* (Boston: Beacon, 1955).

One-Dimensional Man (Boston: Beacon, 1964).

Marenbon, J., *Later Medieval Philosophy* (London: Routledge, 1991).

Melchiori, G., 'The Corridors of History: Shakespeare the Remaker', in E. Honigmann, ed., *British Academy Shakespeare Lectures, 1980–1989* (Oxford University Press, 1993), 165–83.

Meron, T., *Henry's Wars and Shakespeare's Laws* (Oxford: Clarendon, 1993).

Merrix, R., 'The Phaeton Illusion in *Richard II*: The Search for Identity', *English Literary Renaissance*, 17 (1987), 277–87.

Michelfelder, D. and Palmer, R., eds., *Dialogue and Deconstruction: The Gadamer–Derrida Encounter* (Albany: SUNY, 1989).

Millett, K., *Sexual Politics* (London: Virago, 1977).

Moi, T., *Sexual/Textual Politics* (London: Routledge, 1985).

ed., *A Kristeva Reader* (Oxford: Blackwell, 1986).

Moore, M., 'The Interpretive Turn in Modern Theory: A Turn for the Worse?', *Stanford Law Review*, 41 (1989), 871–957.

Morris, C., *Political Thought in England: From Tyndale to Hooker* (Oxford University Press, 1953).

Myers, M., 'Missed Opportunities and Critical Malpractice: New Historicism and Children's Literature', *Children's Literature Association Quarterly*, 13 (1988), 41–3.

Nokes, D., *Jonathan Swift: A Hypocrite Reversed* (Oxford University Press, 1985).

Norris, C., *Derrida* (London: Fontana, 1987).

Orgel, S., 'Making Greatness Familiar', in S. Greenblatt, ed., *The Power of Forms in the English Renaissance* (Norman: University of Oklahoma Press, 1982), 41–8.

Ornstein, R., *A Kingdom for a Stage* (Cambridge, Mass.: Harvard University Press, 1972).

Orwell, G., 'Politics v Literature: An Examination of *Gulliver's Travels*', in *The Penguin Essays of George Orwell* (Harmondsworth: Penguin, 1968).

Page, W., 'The Place of Law and Literature', *Vanderbilt Law Review*, 39 (1986), 408–15.

Parker, M., *The Slave of Life* (London: Chatto and Windus, 1955).

Patterson, R., *Degree of Guilt* (London: Hutchinson, 1993).

Paul, L., 'Enigma Variations: What Feminist Theory Knows About Children's Literature', *Signal*, 45 (1987), 186–201.

Pearlman, E., 'The Invention of Richard of Gloucester', *Shakespeare Quarterly*, 45 (1992), 410–29.

Peck, L., 'Kingship, Counsel and Law in early Stuart Britain', in J. Pocock, ed., *The Varieties of British Political Thought 1500–1800* (Cambridge University Press, 1993), 80–115.

Peller, G., 'The Metaphysics of American Law', *California Law Review*, 73 (1985), 1152–290.

Philias, P., 'The Medieval in *Richard II*', *Shakespeare Quarterly*, 12 (1961), 305–10.

Phillips, R., *Aspects of Alice* (Harmondsworth: Penguin, 1974).

Piaget, J., *The Moral Judgement of the Child* (London: Routledge Kegan Paul, 1932).

Plato, *Republic* (Harmondsworth: Penguin, 1974).

Pocock, J., *The Ancient Constitution and the Feudal Law* (Cambridge University Press, 1957).

ed., *The Varieties of British Political Thought 1500–1800* (Cambridge University Press, 1993)

Posner, R., 'The Ethical Significance of Free Choice: A Reply to Professor West', *Harvard Law Review*, 99 (1985), 1431–48.

'Law and Literature: A Relation Reargued', *Virginia Law Review*, 72 (1986), 1351–92.

Law and Literature: A Misunderstood Relation (Cambridge, Mass.: Harvard University Press, 1988).

Potter, A., 'Shakespeare as Conjuror: Manipulation of Audience Response in *Richard II*', *Communique*, 6 (1981), 1–9.

Potter, B., *The Complete Tales of Beatrix Potter* (London: Warne, 1989).

Prior, M., *The Drama of Power* (Chicago: Northwestern University Press, 1973).

Rackin, P., 'The Role of the Audience in Shakespeare's *Richard II*', *Shakespeare Quarterly*, 36 (1985), 273–81.

Stages of History: Shakespeare's English Chronicles (London: Routledge, 1991).

Ranald, M., 'The Degradation of *Richard II*: An Inquiry into the Ritual Backgrounds', *English Literary Renaissance*, 7 (1977), 170–96.

Rawls, J., *A Theory of Justice* (Oxford University Press, 1971).

'Kantian Constructivism in Moral Theory', *Journal of Philosophy*, 77 (1980), 515–72.

Redmond, L., 'Land, Law, and Love', *Persuasions*, 11 (1989), 46–52.

Reese, M., *The Cease of Majesty* (London: Edward Arnold, 1961).

Richler, M., *St. Urbain's Horseman* (London: Vintage, 1971).

Richmond, H., *Shakespeare's Political Plays* (New York: Random House, 1967).

Ricoeur, P., *The Rule of Metaphor* (London: Routledge and Kegan Paul, 1978).

Hermeneutics and the Human Sciences (Cambridge University Press, 1981).

'On Interpretation', in A. Montefiore ed., *Philosophy in France Today* (Cambridge University Press, 1983), 175–96.

Rigby, E., 'Children's Books', in P. Hunt, ed., *Children's Literature* (London: Routledge, 1990).

Roberts, J., *A Philosophical Introduction to Theology* (London: SCM, 1991).

Robinson, L., 'Treason Our Text: Feminist Challenges to the Literary Canon' in E. Showalter, ed., *The New Feminist Criticism: Essays on Women, Literature and Theory* (London: Virago, 1986), 105–21.

Rohde, D., 'Feminist Critical Theories', *Stanford Law Review*, 42 (1990), 617–38.

Rorty, R., *Contingency, Irony, and Solidarity* (Cambridge University Press, 1989).

Objectivity, Relativism and Truth: Philosophical Papers Volume 1 (Cambridge University Press, 1991).

Essays on Heidegger and Others: Philosophical Papers Volume 2 (Cambridge University Press, 1991).

Ross, C., *Richard III* (London: Methuen, 1981).

Rossiter, A., 'The Structure of *Richard the Third*', *Durham University Journal*, 31 (1938), 44–75.

Sacchio, P., *Shakespeare's English Kings: History, Chronicle and Drama* (Oxford University Press, 1977).

Sahel, P., 'Some Versions of Coup d'état, Rebellion and Revolution', *Shakespeare Survey*, 44 (1991), 25–32.

Said, E., *The World, the Text, and the Critic* (London: Vintage, 1983).

Sanger, C., 'Seasoned to the Use', *Michigan Law Review*, 87 (1989), 1338–65.

Sartre, J.-P., *What is Literature?* (London: Methuen, 1967).

Schalow, F., *The Renewal of the Heidegger-Kant Dialogue* (Albany: SUNY, 1992).

Schoenbaum, S., '*Richard II* and the Realities of Power', *Shakespeare Survey*, 28 (1975), 1–13.

Schroeder, J., 'Feminism Historicized: Medieval Misogynist Stereotypes in Contemporary Feminist Jurisprudence', *Iowa Law Review*, 75 (1990), 1135–217.

Schwarz, M., 'Sir Edward Coke and "This Scept'red Isle": A Case of Borrowing', *Notes and Queries*, 233 (1988), 54–6.

Schwarzschild, S., 'Moral Radicalism and "Middlingness" in the Ethics of Maimonides', *Studies in Medieval Culture*, 11 (1978), 65–94.

Seymour-Smith, M., *Rudyard Kipling* (London: Macmillan, 1990).

Shakespeare, W., *Richard II*, ed. P. Ure (London: Routledge, 1966).

King John, ed. E. Honigmann (London: Routledge, 1967).

Henry VI part 3, ed. A. Cairncross (London: Routledge, 1969).

Richard III, ed. A. Hammond (London: Routledge, 1981).

Sherman, B., 'Hermeneutics in Law', *Modern Law Review*, 51 (1988), 386–402.

Showalter, E., *A Literature of Their Own: British Women Novelists from Bronte to Lessing* (Princeton University Press, 1978).

ed., *The New Feminist Criticism* (London: Virago, 1986)

Simmons, J., 'Shakespeare's *King John* and its Source: Coherence, Pattern, and Vision', *Tulane Studies in English*, 17 (1969), 53–72.

Simon, E., 'Palais de Justice and Poetic Justice in Camus's *The Stranger*', *Cardozo Studies in Law and Literature*, 3 (1990), 111–25.

Singer, J., 'The Player and the Cards: Nihilism and Legal Theory', *Yale Law Journal*, 94 (1984), 1–70.

Smart, C., 'Law's Power, the Sexed Body, and Feminist Discourse', *Journal of Law and Society*, 17 (1990), 194–210.

Smith, J., 'The Coming Renaissance in Law and Literature', *Journal of Legal Education*, 30 (1979), 13–26.

Somerville, J., *Politics and Ideology in England 1603–1640* (London: Longman, 1986).

Speck, W., *Swift* (London: Evans, 1969).

Spivak, G., 'French Feminism in an International Frame', in Eagleton, M., ed., *Feminist Literary Criticism* (London: Longman, 1991), 83–109.

Steiner, G., *In Bluebeard's Castle* (London: Faber, 1971).

Stevens, W., 'Ec[h]o in Fabula', *Diacritics*, 13 (1983), 51–64.

Stirling, B., 'Bolingbroke's "Decision"', *Shakespeare Quarterly*, 2 (1951), 27–34.

Stokes, M., *Justice and Mercy in Piers Plowman* (London: Croom Helm, 1984).

Sutton, A., '"A Curious Searcher for our Weal Public": Richard III, Piety, Chivalry and the Concept of the "Good Prince"', in P. Hammond ed., *Richard III: Loyalty, Lordship and Law* (London: Alan Sutton, 1986), 58–90.

Swift, J., *Gulliver's Travels* (Harmondsworth: Penguin, 1985).

Theilmann, J., 'Stubbs, Shakespeare, and Recent Historians of Richard II', *Albion*, 8 (1976), 107–24.

Thomas, B., 'Reflections on the Law and Literature Revival', *Critical Inquiry*, 17 (1991), 510–37.

Tillyard, E., *Shakespeare's History Plays* (London: Peregrine, 1962).

Townsend, J., 'Standards of Criticism for Children's Literature', in P. Hunt, ed., *Children's Literature* (London: Routledge, 1990), 57–70.

Traister, B., 'The King's One Body: Unceremonial Kingship in *King John*' in D. Curren-Aquino, ed., *King John: New Perspectives* (Newark: University of Delaware Press, 1989), 91–98.

Traugott, J., 'The Yahoo in the Doll's House: *Gulliver's Travels* the Children's Classic', in C. Rawson and J. Mezciems, eds., *English Satire and the Satiric Tradition* (Oxford University Press, 1984), 127–50.

Treitel, G., 'Jane Austen and the Law', *Law Quarterly Review* 100 (1984), 549–86.

Tuck, A., *Richard II and the English Nobility* (London: Edward Arnold, 1973).

Tuck, R., *Philosophy and Government 1572–1651* (Cambridge University Press, 1993).

Tucker, N., *Suitable for Children? Controversies in Children's Literature* (Brighton: Sussex University Press, 1976).

   The Child and the Book: A Psychological and Literary Exploration (Cambridge University Press, 1981).

Tushnet, M., 'Following the Rules Laid Down: A Critique of Interpretivism and Neutral Principles', *Harvard Law Review*, 86 (1982), 781–827.

   'Critical Legal Studies and Constitutional Law: An Essay in Deconstruction', *Stanford Law Review*, 36 (1984), 632–47.

   'An Essay on Rights', *Texas Law Review*, 62 (1984), 1363–403.

Twain, M., *The Adventures of Huckleberry Finn* (Harmondsworth: Penguin, 1985).

Twersky, I., *Introduction to the Code of Maimonides* (New Haven: Yale University Press, 1980).

Unger, R., *Knowledge and Politics* (New York: Free Press, 1975).

   Passion: An Essay on Personality (New York: Free Press, 1984).

Van de Water, J., 'The Bastard in *King John*', *Shakespeare Quarterly*, 11 (1960), 137–46.

Vaughan, V., '*King John*: A Study in Subversion and Containment', in D. Curren-Aquino, ed., *King John: New Perspectives* (Newark: University of Delaware Press, 1989), 62–75.

Voznesenskaya, J., *The Women's Decameron* (London: Minerva, 1986).

Waith, E., '*King John* and the Drama of History', *Shakespeare Quarterly*, 29 (1978), 192–211.

Walker, A., *The Color Purple* (London: Women's Press, 1983).

Walter, J., 'A "Rising of the People"? The Oxfordshire Rising of 1596', *Past and Present*, 107 (1985), 90–143.

Ward, I., 'Radbruch's *Rechtsphilosophie*: Law, Morality and Form', *Archiv fuer Rechts- und Sozialphilosophie*, 78 (1992), 332–54.

'Natural Law and Reason in the Philosophies of Maimonides and St Thomas Aquinas', *Durham University Journal*, 86 (1994), 21–32.

Warnicke, R., 'More's *Richard III* and the Mystery Plays', *Historical Journal*, 35 (1992), 761–78.

Watkin, T., 'Hamlet and the Law of Homicide', *Law Quarterly Review*, 100 (1984), 283–310.

Watkins, A., 'Cultural Studies, New Historicism and Children's Literature', in P. Hunt, ed., *Literature for Children: Contemporary Critcism* (London: Routledge, 1992), 173–95.

Weinrib, E., 'Legal Formalism: On the Immanent Rationality of Law', *Yale Law Journal*, 97 (1988), 949–1016.

Weisberg, Richard, *The Failure of the Word: The Lawyer as Protagonist in Modern Fiction* (New Haven: Yale University Press, 1984).

'Text into Theory: A Literary Approach to the Constitution', *Georgia Law Review*, 20 (1986), 946–79.

'Coming of Age Some More: "Law and Literature" Beyond the Cradle', *Nova Law Review*, 13 (1988), 107–24.

'Family Feud: A Response to Robert Weisberg on Law and Literature', *Yale Journal of Law and the Humanities*, 1 (1988), 69–77.

Poethics: and Other Strategies of Law and Literature, (New York: Columbia University Press, 1992)

Weisberg, Robert, 'The Law–Literature Enterprise', *Yale Journal of Law and the Humanities*, 1 (1988), 1–67.

Wells, R., *Shakespeare, Politics and the State* (London: Macmillan, 1986).

West, R., 'Authority, Autonomy and Choice: The Role of Consent in the Moral and Political Visions of Franz Kafka and Richard Posner', *Harvard Law Review*, 99 (1985), 384–428.

'Submission, Choice, and Ethics: A Rejoinder to Judge Posner', *Harvard Law Review*, 99 (1985), 1449–56.

'Jurisprudence as Narrative: An Aesthetic Analysis of Modern Legal Theory', *New York University Law Review*, 60 (1985), 145–211.

'Jurisprudence and Gender', *University of Chicago Law Review*, 55 (1988), 1072.

'Communities, Texts, and Law: Reflections on the Law and Literature Movement', *Yale Journal of Law and the Humanities*, 1 (1988), 129–56.

Narrative, Authority, and Law (Ann Arbor: University of Michigan Press, 1993).

White, J., *The Legal Imagination* (Boston: Little, Brown and Co., 1973).

'Law as Language: Reading Law and Reading Literature', *Texas Law Review*, 60 (1982), 415–45.

When Words Lose Their Meaning: Constitutions and Reconstitutions of Language, Character and Community (University of Chicago Press, 1984).

Heracles' Bow: Essays on the Rhetoric and Poetics of Law (Madison: University of Wisconsin Press, 1985).

Justice as Translation: An Essay in Cultural and Legal Criticism (University of Chicago Press, 1990).

Williams, P., 'Alchemical Notes: Reconstructing Ideals from Deconstructed Rights', *Harvard Civil Rights–Civil Liberties Review*, 22 (1987), 401–37.

Wolf, E., 'Revolution or Evolution in Gustav Radbruch's Legal Philosophy', *Natural Law Forum*, 3 (1958), 1–22.

Wolin, R., *The Heidegger Controversy* (New York: Columbia University Press, 1991).

Womersley, D., 'The Politics of Shakespeare's *King John*', *Review of English Studies*, 40 (1989), 497–515.

Woolf, D., 'The Power of the Past: History, Ritual and Political Authority in Tudor England', in P. Fideler and T. Mayer, eds., *Political Thought and the Tudor Commonwealth* (London: Routledge, 1992).

Wooton, D., *Divine Right and Democracy* (Harmondsworth: Penguin, 1986).

Worden, B., 'Shakespeare and Politics', *Shakespeare Survey*, 44 (1991), 1–15.

Index

LaVergne, TN USA
18 January 2010
170381LV00001B/133/A